Writing  Comedy Movie

Writing the Comedy Movie

Marc Blake

Bloomsbury Academic
An imprint of Bloomsbury Publishing Inc

B L O O M S B U R Y
LONDON · OXFORD · NEW YORK · NEW DELHI · SYDNEY

Bloomsbury Academic

An imprint of Bloomsbury Publishing Inc

1385 Broadway	50 Bedford Square
New York	London
NY 10018	WC1B 3DP
USA	UK

www.bloomsbury.com

BLOOMSBURY and the Diana logo are trademarks of Bloomsbury Publishing Plc

First published 2016

© Marc Blake, 2016

All rights reserved. No part of this publication may be reproduced or transmitted in any form or by any means, electronic or mechanical, including photocopying, recording, or any information storage or retrieval system, without prior permission in writing from the publishers.

No responsibility for loss caused to any individual or organization acting on or refraining from action as a result of the material in this publication can be accepted by Bloomsbury or the author.

Library of Congress Cataloging-in-Publication Data

Blake, Marc.

Writing the comedy movie / Marc Blake.

pages cm

Summary: "A practical guide to creating the comedy movie, referencing its subgenres, history, and tropes.

Includes bibliographical references and index.

ISBN 978-1-62892-595-1 (paperback)– ISBN 978-1-5013-1634-0 (hardback) 1. Comedy films--Authorship. 2. I. Title.

PN1996.B57 2015

808.2′523–dc23

2015018853

ISBN:	HB:	9781501316340
	PB:	9781628925951
	ePub:	9781628925937
	ePDF:	9781628925920

Typeset by Fakenham Prepress Solutions, Fakenham, Norfolk NR21 8NN
Printed and bound in the United States of America

This book is dedicated to three people who left the party early. **Rod Hall**, agent extraordinaire, whose advice has helped to this day; to **Matt Cogger** who loved life and laughter in equal measure; and to **Malcolm Hardee**, mentor, madcap and all round charlatan.

We loved you all and remember you still.

Contents

Introduction

There's a lot to be said for making people laugh. Did you know that's all some people have? It isn't much, but it's better than nothing in this cockeyed caravan.

JOHN SULLIVAN, *SULLIVAN'S TRAVELS*: (STURGES 1941)

Accelerated technology has changed our approach to watching movies. The first run at the local mall or independent cinema is part of a bigger strategy to include online and DVD releases. Couples no longer trawl the video store arguing over date night movies. Streaming has removed the necessity of a physical object. Movies compete with, or are a narrative part of, Games and Gaming. Viewing habits are fractured, discordant. You can pause a movie and return to it anytime on your tablet device. There is the binge watching of box sets and a limited attention span. There is *YouTube,* the world's instant TV station, which can make a star out of anyone or their family pet. The number of hits achieved online has replaced the overnights. Production values and picture quality are subservient to the messages delivered from teenage bedrooms.

This is nothing new, only in its form. The rise of television in the 1950s caused serious problems for the studio system, which was once more brought to the brink of collapse as it had been in the 1930s. Today, the focus is on Fantasy, motion capture, CG and blockbusting superhero franchises. The carnival tent is back and the snake oil hucksters are vying to pull us in. We watch while commuting, in vehicles, on cellphones, on tablet or on giant plasma HD screens. We download. We stream. Your local Blockbuster is a derelict wreck or a coffee franchise.

Digitalization has its advantages in terms of picture quality and being able to skip or swipe to any part of what you are watching. 'Rewind' and 'Chapters' are losing their meaning. We expect instant download and groan at the buffering symbol. Increasingly, we watch for free or as part of a TV cable channel bundle. We consume at an unprecedented rate and with highly developed critical faculties. At home, we are on our smartphones as we watch, texting and tweeting our commentary.

What does this mean for the producer of movies? A massive market yes, but greatly increased competition. To launch a new movie you will need a star or a high-concept idea. Where once we had *Twins* and *Groundhog Day*, we now have *The 40-Year-Old Virgin* and *Bridesmaids*. We have Indy, gross-out and stoner comedies. We have anti-romcoms and bromances. A new movie must sell on its logline, poster image and on its précis on onscreen listings. Before a word appears on screen the comedy writer must decide –

- Is this an intrinsically funny notion?
- Can this logline or pitch be easily understood by anyone?
- Would a ten year old get it right away?

This applies to a high percentage of the buying market and the power of pitch cannot be ignored. Whilst there are some territories and individuals who are able to fund quirky Independent pictures, they are few and far between. Comedy craves an audience and this book is dedicated to its commercial aspect.

As a writer, selling in the mainstream demands edge. Keith Giglio notes in *Writing the Comedy Blockbuster* (2012) that you can't be a 'soft' writer. This does not mean being offensive *per se*, but R and Unrated movies are sold on this aspect (e.g. the *American Pie* franchise). Areas that would never have been covered in comedy are now up for grabs: The anti-romcom *Obvious Child* (Robespierre 2014) stars Jenny Slate – a stand-up comedian who makes light of having an abortion. Gross-out, a subgenre that began with The Marx Brothers' comedy *Duck Soup* (MacCarey 1933), was popularized in the 1970s with *Animal House* and *Porky's* and which re-emerged in the 1990s with the Farrelly Brothers comedies, continues to push abject boundaries. However, few film ideas are new. With over a century of cinema to pluck from, remakes and retreads are a reliable way of exploiting a pre-existing brand, be they from Hollywood, Britain, France or elsewhere. The more comedies movies you watch, the more you learn about staging, characterization, plotting and how the comedy works.

Writing this book has given me the opportunity to revisit some classics and to catch up on the latest examples of each subgenre. I have tried to select best practice examples of each, both old and new, in order to illustrate the tropes so as the comedy writer may approach his or her next project both informed and prepared. This is NOT a How To Write Comedy book – there are plenty of those out there – but a survey of current trends, an analysis of what comedy is, and does, and how it has succeeded both in the past and presently. Hopefully, it will act as a useful resource for the writer, informing them about the structure, pace and rhythm of comedy, and be a reminder of why they got into it in the first place.

Two notes. In order to comply with W. C. Fields' dictum, I will talk little about animals and children. Whilst there are many successful comedies that are centred around them, the novice screenwriter is more likely to get a sale with a script that does not feature either, as their inclusion will automatically increase the budget for their care, caging and/or tutoring. Animated anthropomorphism is much more common and will feature in 'Animation'. Second, in the 'Comedy around the World' chapter I have omitted some nations with a thriving comic tradition or production base only for reasons of space. In no way am I suggesting there are countries that are simply not funny, although there are, and they know who they are.

Marc Blake. July 2015

Chapter 1

Writing The Comedy Script

a fool toward enlightenment

*What prompts us to action is desire; and desire has three forms –
appetite, passion, wish.*

ARISTOTLE, MAGNA MORALIA

The twenty-first-century comedy writer is no longer restricted by international boundaries and, with easily available software, he or she can submit industry-standard work from anywhere in the world and place it on websites such as *Ink Tip* or *Blacklist*. On these, the writer is required to register his work with the East or West Coast American Writers Guild or equivalent in their country. This is for copyright purposes and to protect the work. Professional readers and producers will then view it if the logline and synopsis appeals. The writer can also approach agents and production companies directly with scripts, but they operate a filter system and few get through. In order to get to the reading stage, many hurdles must be overcome.

The only visible difference between comedy and other scriptwriting is that it tends to leave a lot of white on the page: also, scene descriptions are minimal, letting the comedy flow. Just enough is needed to convey character, action and comedy. Comedy requires a *tone* and a *style*, a rhythm to it that keeps you laughing as you flick through the pages. Two vital elements are 'hilarity and heart' (Giglio 2012), in the sense that we must laugh, but the laughter must contain empathy. Many also involve idiot characters for comedy is often the fool's journey toward enlightenment. To engage us they must be human and likeable. Shakespeare wrote his fools to be laughed at, but the fool is often the smartest guy in the room.

The simple layout of comedy scripts (all that white space) does not mean you can stint in depth of characterization, complexity of plot or in any aspect of its execution, it means that less is more. An easy read is the ultimate goal and there is no need to include detailed directorial instructions of how the visual comedy ought to work or tell the actors how to (ANGRILY) say their lines. Simplicity is best.

A lot of comedy works with the juxtaposition of word and image. In *Springbreakers* (Korine 2012) when Faith makes a call home to her Grandmother, we *hear* the voiceover, but we see.

STATEMENT vs REALITY.

Faith (v/o):
It's the most beautiful trip.

The Spring Break girls are partying hard, a bunch of guys pour alcohol over their naked breasts.

Faith (cont.):
It's the most spiritual place I've ever been.

The four girls are now squatting down, urinating in the street.

This is all you need, no prose or context – simply a description of what you see. You write as though you are the camera, therefore you write what the camera sees and no more. There are subtle ways of implying the shot in your writing. 'Arthur stands wailing on Brighton Beach' suggests a medium to wide shot, whilst 'He weeps a solitary tear' can only be a close up.

It can happen off screen too. In *Adam's Rib* (Cukor 1949) much of the comedy occurred between warring married partners District Attorney Adam Bonner (Spencer Tracy) and Public Defender Amanda (Katherine Hepburn). As the camera dallied in a bedroom set, the pair headed to their respective bathrooms and the comedy came from the noises off, with their heads appearing only briefly in shot. Jay Roach's *Austin Powers* series uses the gimmick well in several sequences, often involving henchmen.

The screenplay is the blueprint for the movie. The comedy comes out of character and situation. If you have conceived of a potentially hilarious concept and peopled it with the right cast then it ought to write itself. You never need to explain the joke. The wording must be clear and simple, as must the description of visual or running gags.

In the first ten pages you will introduce the cast one by one so that we will understand who is the protagonist and whom he or she relates to in their world. We need to know who they are and what their theme is. When you introduce a character for the first time it is acceptable to put in a line of description for the major players:

David Huxtable, a buttoned up paleontologist, to whom fretting is second nature. He'd be free as a bird if his fiancé would only let him.
Howard Hawks, *Bringing Up Baby* (1938)

You have a brief opportunity for prose here. The line has to give a sense of the man and his situation, not his physical type beyond a rough idea of age. In any case, male movie stars are usually in their thirties or forties as it has taken them at least a decade or more to create a brand. Women tend to start younger, in their late teens. There are plenty of terms to describe characters (see 'Women in Comedy') but try not to sink to cliché. You may be writing about a frump, a ditz or a good time girl but the shorthand is outmoded. Find new ways to express this. Cameron Diaz in *Bad Teacher* (Kasdan 2011) looks like she could suck a golf ball through a garden hose but the IMDb script draft is less explicit.

ELIZABETH HALSEY, mid 20s, pretty and petite, walks up to the front. She sports an enormous diamond ring and dresses slightly more cosmopolitan than the other teachers.

Every line of dialogue must have a purpose and there is little room for interjection, repetition, verbal niceties and colloquialism of speech (but, surely, so, and). As in Sitcom we begin each scene *in media res* and at the last possible moment.

KNOCKED UP (Apatow 2007: IMDb Scripts)

EXT. BEN'S HOUSE – DAY

BEN STONE, 23, cute in a chunky Jewish guy sort of way, boxes one of his roommates, MARTIN. His other roommates, JAY and JASON fight with broom sticks. JONAH drinks beer on the couch spectating.

QUICK IMAGES:

We see Ben and Jay fighting. At one point they fight with gloves which are on fire, balancing on a plank over a dirty pool. Ben now has a fishbowl filled with weed smoke over his head. There is a smoking joint in his mouth, making the bowl get cloudier and cloudier. He starts coughing hysterically and takes it off.

A boom box is playing. The boys are now freestyle rapping. It is terrible but they are having a blast. Pot is being smoked. Beer is around.

The above sets out what kind of a guy Ben Stone is, immature and in stasis, but without specifically *saying* this. Instead, it shows us in montage – thus allowing the director and actors to play with the idea.

A block of dialogue ought to rarely last for more than four to five lines and even a long, heartfelt or expository monologue necessitates visual cutaways, reactions or comments to break it up. In the opening of *Wedding Crashers*, Jeremy (Vince Vaughn) makes a long speech to his bromance Buddy Jack (Owen Wilson) about 'the rules'. This is more of a comic rant or a list of dos and don'ts. These can be funny in themselves but they must be *earned*. The comedy comes from a character trait, used by Vaughn and Dan Aykroyd and harking back to Groucho Marx, that of the absurdly over-confident guy. It is something that Steve Martin and Jack Black mock well.

The comedy here comes from the sheer verbosity, truth or obscenity involved in this rococo style of speech. The mere fact of it being so unusually long and breathless puts us on tenterhooks and when we reach the end ... the combination of release and relief almost forces the laugh.

Conversely, though a line might only be a single word, it ought to have *attitude* behind it: Your 'yeah', 'okay' or 'well',[1] must convey either opposition or agreement, helping to advance character even if it hinders the desire of the protagonist. This is why sarcasm and irony are so popular in comedy.

The rhythm of dialogue can hark back to screwball or Marx Brothers' crosstalk by being fast and furious, as in *When Harry Met Sally* (Reiner 1989) or *Anchorman* (McKay 2004), using overlapping speeches, fast intercutting and cruel remarks – or it can be to the point, allowing the comedy to come across in visual reactions or cutting away to a new scene. Smart New York dialogue ought not to be spoken by every character, as that would become wearing. Each character, even if they are Upper West Side natives, ought to have their own speech rhythms, as Jerry, George, Elaine and Kramer do in *Seinfeld*. Look how Oscar opposes Felix (*The Odd Couple*), Melvin antagonizes Carol (*As Good As it Gets*) and George (Paul Rudd) and Linda (Jennifer Aniston) bicker in *Wanderlust*.

What we say and what we do are different things. Just as we are judged on our actions, comedy works by upsetting this and offering the truth. *Sideways* (Payne 2004) begins with Miles Raymond woken by Mexican workers who need him to move his car. He is hung over. On his return to his condo, he sees the clock and phones his best friend Jack, explaining that he is on his way and will be there by midday. We cut to him reading on the can. Then showering, then flossing, then getting a coffee in the car, then doing a crossword as he drives. The dissonance is amusing and tells us a lot. Once he arrives at his best friend's in-law's house we learn that he doesn't respect them, and by extension, himself. He doesn't want his friend Jack, a recidivist hound dog, to marry. He doesn't

---

[1] Watch out for 'well'. It is a word we use all the time, but ought to be struck from every screenplay.

want to lose him. It tells us so much with no need for dialogue. He's a sad sack, brilliantly played by Paul Giamatti. He *is* Charlie Brown.

Adverbs and adjectives ought to be pruned out and strong verbs are the order of the day. Prose (purple or otherwise) and metaphor are also unnecessary. Also, try to avoid similes. We do not talk in them. Clever sitcom people use them but in real life – as your movie ought to try to imitate – we never have the time to come up with the *mot juste*, instead thinking of it on the stairs (what the French call *l'esprit d'escalier*) or days afterwards, at home.

You are writing in one media that will ultimately be interpreted in another. You are aiming to present a picture in the mind of a reader, a picture of real people in a situation that is inherently comedic. That is not to say you cannot introduce drama, as most comedies have a dramatic premise at their heart:

- Two musicians witness the St Valentine's Day Massacre and flee for their lives;

- On the Wedding day the Best Man and buddies discover they have lost the groom;

- A man is trapped in his life, which repeats itself day after day.

Scenes can be as long as five pages or as short as a single line of description. If you have a long scene there had better be plenty going on, not mere banter. No dialogue is wasted. It is all driving the plot or revealing character. When you have completed the first draft of your screenplay you need to go over it ruthlessly and remove any words, lines or utterances, which do not reflect this.

A page is roughly a minute of screen time: Screwball comedies were dialogue heavy and dialogue chews up pages rapidly, but it tends to even out in the end (Pages/time). Every script I have written has come in at the same length on film.

You can either end a scene on a laugh, a cliffhanger or a plot point but you cannot end a scene 'flat'. Each scene propels us onto the next until the resolution, which will come right at the end of the story. Each scene is part of a sequence, and in comedies there are usually eight of these set pieces. The only scenes we need are those which are germane to the story, character and plot. In comedies there is the opportunity to stretch an idea to its absurd conclusion, so the writer has some leeway here, usually in the fun and games part as we enter Act Two. 4.20.16

The best comic writing often comes out of pushing the idea. In *The 40-Year-Old Virgin* or *The Invention of Lying*, true comedy comes out of taking things that bit too far, of wading through the uncomfortable into social embarrassment and way, way beyond. Writers Larry David, Albert Brooks and

SOCIAL EMBARRASSMENT

Ricky Gervais are masters of this. The characters they portray have a limited awareness of these social boundaries and so when they overstep the mark it induces the cringe factor. As they keep going, trampling convention, we cannot help but laugh at the violation. We would never say this. Do this. We might *want* to but we would be subject to censure and scorn. A comic character does not suffer remorse in the first hour of the movie. This corrective occurs only at the moment of epiphany or maturity and we are looking at the end of Act Two, as the catalyst for change.

Bill Murray in *Groundhog Day* is a great example of this. He wins Rita over and over again, a kiss seals the deal but it is not enough. He realizes, tumbling in the snow to impress her for the nth time, that he is trying to fake love and it will not do.

Comic screenplays usually come in under the 100-page mark but so long as the reader is whipping through the pages then you are doing well. If they flick or scroll to the end and see page 157 (end Act Two) then you are in trouble.

Scripts are written in 12-point Courier font, (using industry standard software such as *Final Draft* or *Celtx*) on one side of the paper only, double-spaced, with yours or your agents name and contact address on the front cover. If you are not submitting online, you will ensure that your name and contact details are prominent. The basic rule of thumb is, *make it look like a writer wrote it*.

There is no excuse for not going online and looking at how scripts are written and formatted, (www.IMDb scripts) nor is there any reason why your work ought not to be correctly spelled, formatted and delivered with a degree of acceptable grammar and syntax. This is the entry level for all script submissions – leave the illiteracy to the producer. If you have no pride in your work, then why should others?

To avoid criticism say nothing, do nothing, be nothing.

Aristotle

F**K you very much: On criticism

We are continually in a position of being judged, by our partners, family, friends and complete strangers – all of who have their own agenda. Do we care about most of this? No. We consider what to wear to a dinner, date, function or the workplace, as we consider how we must behave in those situations, but most criticism in life is simply a device for social balance.

When it comes to the criticism of cultural artefacts such as films or books, its usefulness is to direct us towards something we might appreciate or to warn us off spending money on something we won't. However, when the project is complete the creator has finished with it. He is unlikely to react by going back and re-shooting or re-writing the work in order to tailor it to the critic. The best one can do is to take note of any valid criticism so that we can improve the next time.

Where criticism has validity is during the creative process. Committees make movies and many eyes are on the work from first draft to the locked down shooting script, and even then much will change on the set (and everything in the edit). The writer must be grateful for any opinions offered up to point of sale. They represent objectivity, which you will lack if you are at the centre of it. They also represent your audience. There are those close to you who will have an agenda ('you are squandering your time/life', 'You are doing what I do not have the guts to do', 'I am not qualified to judge', 'I feel pressured by you to like it') but table readings, paying for script reads and other methods of obtaining an outside contribution are useful.

When is it done? Once you have had all the external feedback you can obtain and have worked through all notes to reach a point where you have a final 'clean' script, there comes a point where you are fed up with it. You have lived with it from conception to planning and execution to draft and redraft and you have reached the third stage of completion.

See it as a mirror of the three-act structure. Are you satisfied? Is the experience complete? Do you still have any nagging questions? Can it be funnier (it can always be funnier)? Does it 'do what it says on the can'? Is the logline and synopsis an accurate representation of your script?

If so, then perhaps you are done.

A note on perfectionism: whilst this is an ideal to which we might all aspire, it is not a practicality. As a writer you are only part of the movie, the first part, and as such your blueprint will be altered, added to and/or abused. Perfectionists seek control. This is all well and good, but ultimately this is an object for sale. Competence is what is required. The problem with creativity and *especially* screenwriting is that you will find that *everyone is a writer*. Producers or directors with opinions, notes and suggestions consider this to be writing. This is how many of them obtain screenwriting credits. There is nothing you can do about this but retain control of the 'story by' credit. It will not always be this way.

Even before a word is put on screen, the comedy screenwriter must consider budget as this will determine the sales potential of his project. Your major decision must be – am I writing this for an Independent or for Hollywood? If it is high-concept and designed for a Hollywood studio, you can allow free reign. Romcoms almost always include a wedding and these are expensive events. They are also set among the rich and in locations that reflect this from the Hamptons and Vermont to Manhattan or palatial LA homes. You can write a road movie that transports the viewer over huge distances. You might have an ensemble cast and roles that will attract big name stars as with *Meet the Fockers* (Roach 2004).

When writing the spec script you will not have any input in getting a big name to play your lead character unless you have a relationship with the star and can write directly for them. This is fraught with difficulty. You may spend considerable time writing and honing only to find your star is not available for the next three years or has fallen into rehab hell. Also, a name can overbalance a film. If you cast a well-known name above the title then they will bring a lot of baggage with them. There is a curve with comedy actresses where they move from ingénue to girl next door or sexpot to love partner (or remain as kooky best friend), and then remain there for as long as Hollywood allows.

It is clear what a Ben Stiller or a Will Ferrell movie will consist of, just as it was with W. C. Fields, Cary Grant or Charlie Chaplin. The star persona, honed over years on stage and perfected onscreen, is often the reason we choose to buy the ticket. Even in the edit, it is evident that they are only partly engaging with the other performers. The angle of the shot is often such that they are favouring the audience. Sometimes it is more overt and there is direct address to the camera, as with The Marx Brothers, Laurel and Hardy (a hangover from the Vaudeville trope of breaking the fourth wall), Bob Hope in the *Road To…* movies or his successor Woody Allen who used to ape the cowardly mensch hero.

There are clear comedy roles – the little boy lost, the Man-child, the overbearing oaf, the plastic faced gurner and the naïve idiot savant – and all have their roots in silent cinema. In most countries, there are few bankable stars that can open a picture. Hollywood has a nest of them (being the industry hub), but other territories too have their favourites. Jean DuJardin in France, Roberto Benigni in Italy, Om Puri and Paresh Rawal in India or Rowan Atkinson and Simon Pegg in the UK.

The Hollywood script must have a broad universal appeal. There may be festive occasions and locations and character dynamics that will appeal across the board. The ideal comedy movie is that of four quadrants, meaning it can be appreciated by both sexes and of all ages. *Groundhog Day*, *Home Alone*, *Trading Places*, *Ghostbusters* and *Notting Hill* are best practice examples of this.

Or there is the Independent route. In the US, most of the Independents are now adjuncts of the studios. Things have changed since the days of Kevin Smith's *Clerks* and Quentin Tarantino's *Reservoir Dogs*. The rise and fall of Independent cinema is covered exhaustively in Peter Biskind's *Down and Dirty Pictures*. In the UK, Ireland and most international territories, funding for movies is a scrappy affair, cobbled together from private individuals, corporations, film boards, government bodies and Lottery funding. Rarely do independent production companies cough up their own money so they are looking to find a script that is commercial enough to attract this sponsorship.

This precludes expensive set pieces, action adventure, road, military and sports movies, large ensemble casts (unless unknowns and shot on one or two sets). Prison and heist scenarios might work, but only if limited to a prison cell or bank vault. Think simple, such as relationship movies that can be played out in limited locations. Kevin Smith became an Indie darling with *Clerks*. There can be no car chases or custard pie fights. Make the action occur in an intimate arena. Three people are all you need for a movie. Some big hits are based on simple (read 'cheap') premises. *Meet the Parents* (Roach 2000) takes place mostly in the Byrne's family home on Long Island. If you can conceive of it as a play, as the French often do, the chances are it will work on screen.

If you do make that million-dollar sale, this fee will be distributed in parts – acceptance, re-writes,[2] final delivery, first day of principal photography, etc. – so don't go buying that Malibu condo just yet. The sale of a script can also be a long way from seeing it on screen. Projects are stunted for many reasons or go into turnaround – but for now, a small libation is in order.

Oh, you were drinking already?

OK. Finally, if you have sold one, then chances are you will sell more.

---

[2]For more on all of this and polishes, drafts and the like, read David Mamet's *Bambi vs. Godzilla*.

Chapter 2
Comedy

Analyzing humor is like dissecting a frog. Few people are interested and the frog dies of it.

E. B. WHITE

We begin regardless by cutting into the frog. French philosopher Henri Bergson stated that the comic is strictly a human phenomenon. A landscape cannot be a source of laughter and when humans make fun of animals, it is because they recognize some aspect of human behaviour in them. Man is not only a being that can laugh, but also one that is a source of laughter. It requires indifference, a detachment from sensibility and emotion. It is more difficult to laugh when one is fully aware of the seriousness of a situation, which is why we say 'too soon' if a topical comment goes awry. This indifference is often seen on screen as imperviousness to pain. Comic pain in slapstick or gross-out does not affect us as such because we have been given *permission* to ignore the boundaries.

It is difficult to laugh alone and easier to laugh collectively. One who is excluded from a group of people does not laugh with them. 'However spontaneous it seems, laughter always implies a kind of secret freemasonry, or even complicity with other laughers, real or imagined' (Bergson 1909). Comedy is also combative, as much of the focus of our humour is about establishing superiority, evaluating what is unacceptable in society and firing a broadside at its targets. In this way, comedy can either bring us together (bonding us when a perceived enemy is ridiculed) or separate (sexist, racist or homophobic humour), or act as social barometer, a taking of the National pulse, or as provocation, testing our boundaries of the notions of good and poor taste.

It can be healthy too. Whilst it is a cliché that 'humour is the best medicine' (a strong opiate or vodka-based beverage will do equally as well) there is great therapeutic value in having a good laugh. It cleanses, washing away our cares and worries, uniting us in a shared approval of how life might be lived or not. We laugh in relief when we see the comic villain vanquished or the hero get his girl. Endorphins are released. It is a physical process. We 'bust a gut' or 'roll on the floor laughing'. A joke is a side-splitter or a rib-tickler. We are invited to laugh until we cry and may even regress to infantilism, becoming as helpless with laughter as a baby laughing at its own foot.

Comedy is also a weapon. Sometimes the blade is blunt and the comedy crude, cruel or puerile. The blade can however be sharp, employing ridicule, wit and satire – the latter being the armoury of some of our greatest comic writers from Swift to Twain to *South Park*. Satire pricks pomposity and punctures the overblown, the self-serving and self-important. It is the wry grin, the dark smile and the hollow laugh. It encourages us to get *angry*; in the words of Juvenal, 'The satirical position is not to wither in despair but to take up the pen'.

The critic Basa wrote in 1999 that comedy has three social purposes, that of lubrication, sandpaper and glue. Lubrication is about ice breaking, goodwill and the ability to laugh at ourselves. It is true that some people have no sense of humour (many are in HR or government) but for most of us a drop of humour, however small, helps us to get through the day. Comedy as sandpaper conveys frankness and criticism without threat. Written comedy has been with us since the voice of the Comoedia, the satyr of one sanctioned by the state to speak against the Polis (City State) in the time of Aristophanes. It continues to be the voice of dissent. Whilst this continues to this day in the stand-up comedy tradition, on film there are those such as Michael Moore who use comic tropes (in his case within documentary) to enforce his point. British character comedian Sasha Baron-Cohen has much to say in his guises as *Borat, Brüno* and the dictator Aladeen. These act as important regulators of society and its follies. It is also social glue, in that the rhetoric of comedy relaxes, entertains and shows empathy. This is why many TV sitcoms insist on canned laughter, to encourage feelings of inclusion. In the confines of a darkened movie theatre, it is a healthy restorative. The comedian, double act or comedy ensemble purges us of an excess of bad feeling, the plot and characters amuse us and we are briefly sated.

Further, the laughter of incongruity was first suggested by Schopenhauer in *The World as Will and Idea* (Schopenhauer 1909). We are amused by random elements but too many serve to confuse. Absurdity provokes a reaction of bemusement and surprise, both essential elements of comedy. Hazlitt adds that 'man is the only animal that laughs. For he is the only animal struck by the difference between what things are and what they ought to be':[1]

---

[1]'Laughter may be defined to be the convulsive and involuntary movement, occasioned by mere surprise or contrast before it has time to reconcile its belief to contradictory appearances. We laugh at absurdity. We laugh at deformity.' – Hazlitt (*Comedy : A Critical Introduction*, Rozik 2011).

When we come to screen comedy –

Life is a tragedy when seen in close-up, but a comedy in long-shot. To truly laugh, you must be able to take your pain and play with it!

Charlie Chaplin

There is an oft-repeated story about Chaplin who was asked by another director how to shoot a sight gag with a woman and a banana skin. Chaplin said, 'first you show the woman, then the banana, then the woman and the banana, then you show her stepping over the banana and falling down an open manhole'.

Surprise is the essence of comedy. It must continually reinvent itself, minute by minute. You can build on the repetition of an idea (the 'callback') making it more ludicrous as you go ('Don't call me Shirley', *Airplane!* Zucker, Abrahams, Zucker 1980) but you cannot repeat the same joke. The art comes in making the same joke form seem new. The creativity lies in the discovery of two things that exist but have not been put together before, thus revealing the hidden connections that fuse them. It is analogic. It is right brain thinking. Arthur Koestler wrote that 'laughter is an emotion abandoned by thought.' It is a criticism and therefore not a true emotion.

The comedy screenplay must contain a great idea (often high concept), dazzling characters, wit, pathos and gags, a steamroller plot and endlessly inventive comic ideas, taking us through a series of increasingly hilarious set pieces resulting in a climax, after which order is restored, or a new order is established, and all is resolved.

And this has to come across on the page.

It has to be a funny *read*.

You don't have the actors on board. No funny faces or voices. There's no comic business, timing or magic between the cast except that which you put on the page. You are saying, in effect: here is the blueprint and *this will be funny when you come to shoot it*. This is a tough call, almost an arrogant one. Comedy is like that: it is sheer bravado when you are nothing but a schmuck. It is hubris when you are primed for a fall. It is inappropriate anger when the audience knows you are going over the top. It is comic irony because you know and yet you don't know. It is the great pratfall.

A brief comic history

Comedy goes hand in hand with film stock and the motion picture camera. From the first comedy short, *Watering the Gardener* by the Lumiere brothers (1895) to the emergent slapstick of Max Linder, Charlie Chaplin, Buster Keaton, Harry Langdon and Harold Lloyd, light entertainment for the emerging mass market was always part of its ethos.

Before sound, the title card carried information. The humour was left to the stars of the day, and increasingly so once unleashed from the fixed camera. The pratfall, the double take and the slow burn are universal concepts brought to us by silent cinema. They are all still used today, as are the editing techniques developed over a century ago. There are clear similarities between *The Great Dictator* and *The Dictator*, *Duck Soup* and *Dumb and Dumber* and *Way Out West* and *Wild, Wild West*.

The silent stars took visual comedy to its apex. Chaplin survived the transition to the spoken word as did Laurel and Hardy, but other silent stars fell away if the voice took away from the comedy instead of adding to it. Jacques Tati's creation, *Monsieur Hulot* (1950s) and his successor, *Mr Bean* (1990s–) took note of this and remained mute or as close to it as possible. Words allowed for another form of comedy, an antidote to formal drama and socialite manners involving crossed purposes and the fast rat-a-tat of chat. This became Screwball (*It Happened One Night*, *Bringing Up Baby*), which begat the romcom. The comedy of the 1930s and 1940s employed satire, farce, ridicule and wit; complex forms that went beyond being a mere string of gags hung together. There were social comedies such as *Sullivan's Travels* and great fantasy comedy dramas such as *It's A Wonderful Life* (Capra 1946), then later the cross-dressing and mistaken identity of *Some Like it Hot* (Wilder 1960)

These sophisticated comedies of manners led to a free for all in the sexual revolution of the 1960s, plus a series of star-stuffed romps (*Those Magnificent Men in Their Flying Machines*, Annakin 1965) in order to lure audiences back to the Cineplex. Auteurs appeared in the 1970s; the comic genius of Woody Allen, the parodies of Mel Brooks, coexisting with darker fare in such comedies as *Catch-22* (Nichols 1970) or *Harold and Maude* (Ashby 1971). The 1980s harked back to an imagined 1950s, with *Nine to Five* (Higgins 1980) and *Working Girl* (Nichols 1988), but the following decade produced a comeback for romantic comedy (*Four Weddings and A Funeral*, Newell 1994), fantasy (*Groundhog Day*, Ramis 1993) and parody (*Austin Powers, International Man of Mystery*, Roach 1997).

The comedy of the 2000s embraced frat boy frolics (*American Pie*, Weisz 1999), stoner antics and anti-romcomedies (*Knocked Up*, Apatow 2007) – all found wide audiences. Comedy will never go away, not while there are people, institutions and a component of behaviour that requires criticism and censure; that or fart gags.

Funny bones

In order to perform comedy you need funny bones. Whilst it is not a rare talent to perform, there are certain comedians whom you can never imagine doing anything else (Jim Carrey, Woody Allen, Eddie Izzard). They are natural clowns who, whatever they do, imbue it with comedy. Many comedy writers are also performers and it has been the accepted form since the mid-1980s that the comedian writes and creates all his or her own material – in stand-up terms at least. The comedy writer does not have to be funny in real life (many comedy writers are solipsistic beings rarely seen outside of a dressing gown or bar) but you do have to be funny in 'the room' if you are team writing for TV and, more importantly, on the page.

The comedy screenplay must demonstrate conclusively by page three that it is a funny script. Unlike in drama where you have ten pages to establish character, milieu and plot, the comedy has to hit the ground running. You may do this with its concept, a visual gag, a comic monologue, snappy dialogue or something sarcastic, sardonic, dark or obscene, but it must be there. It also needs to build. The concept must develop, as in the satire *Wag the Dog* (Levinson 1997) and the relationships must deepen, as in *I Love You, Man* (Hamburg 2009). In short, the inherently comic situation must get funnier as you go on.

One of the first things the writer must establish is our reaction to the comic character at the centre of the picture. In essence, are we laughing *at* or laughing *with* them? This distinction is easiest to see in a fish-out-of-water comedy, such as *Office Space* (Judge 1999) *or The 40-Year-Old Virgin* (Apatow 2005), in which a character with whom we identify is beset by a bunch of oddballs. Ben Stiller can play both sides of this coin. In *Meet the Fockers* he's the put-upon average Joe, but in *Zoolander* he's the idiot. In *The Hangover or Bridesmaids*, it is clear we are following the arc of groomsman Phil (Bradley Cooper) and maid of honour Annie (Kristen Wiig). The latter, whilst owing a debt to Cameron Diaz's character in *My Best Friend's Wedding* sets us up with the classic single woman looking for love. As with Meg Ryan (*Sleepless in Seattle*) or Renee Zellweger (*Bridget Jones*), they are hopeful and lost but not unlikeable or undateable – they have simply lost the knack. The man-child also appeals to the irresponsible in all of us. Indeed, Will Ferrell has made a career out of this, but the redemption and need for maturity of Billy Bob Thornton in *Bad Santa* or Jonah Hill in *The Sitter* is something we will laugh along with.

Character comedy tends to be of the opposite camp. *Brüno* is as outrageous as *Austin Powers* and then some. Jim Carrey and Eddie Murphy's creations are broad and vulgar but, despite scorn being poured on them, they will triumph in the end. The advantage of laughing *at* is that this role tends to be taken by the true comedian rather than the comic actor. These are the oddballs who swing to a different rhythm, creating a comic universe that makes its own rules and physical laws, as in a cartoon. We laugh at Homer Simpson or Peter Griffin because, although they have a nominal role as paterfamilias and breadwinner, this is merely a jumping off point for their crazed adventures. But how do we put this on paper?

A visual medium

As with action movies, comedy is visual. No matter how erudite or witty the script, it is the images that are remembered. Not to reduce the form to slapstick, but so much of the comedy is in the facial gesture, the reaction shot and the inappropriate behaviour of the protagonist or foil. When so much relies on this along with casting, timing, direction and editing, how much can the novice writer hope to convey in 100 pages of script?

In short, everything bar the pictures. The comedy writer must establish the comic world, its characters and their relation to it. Is it a performative or narrative comedy? Is it satirical? What is the tone? Does it have universality? While the relentless output of the Hollywood studios still make it the market leader, there are other countries whose films gain a wide audience: there is comedy from Working Title in Britain, Canal Plus in France and from Pedro Almodovar in Spain. Comedy break-out hits have come from Africa (*The Gods Must Be Crazy*, Uys 1980), Australia (*Muriel's Wedding*, Hogan 1994), Japan (*Tokyo Gore Police*, Nishimura 2008), Korea (*Save the Green Planet!*, Jang 2003) and Hong Kong (*Kung Fu Hustle*, Chow 2004).

These are exceptions. Much homegrown comedy contains specific cultural patterns, language, customs and other factors that make it hard to cross inter-national boundaries. At its most parochial, the US will rarely import a subtitled movie, let alone a comedy, but other audiences are equally resistant, meaning a degree of hegemony in comedy product across the world. Current stars such as Cameron Diaz, Sandra Bullock, Reece Witherspoon, Bill Murray, Ben Stiller or Jim Carrey can open a movie in any territory, but only so long as they fit into the rigid parameters of romantic comedy, knockabout caper or high concept.

For a movie to gain purchase it needs that elusive concept, that special what if? The conceit may be transient or long lasting, but no one knows the recipe for a classic. There are many examples of movies that did not do well on their first outing: *It's A Wonderful Life* took decades to become a Christmas perennial. *Withnail and I* (1987) disappeared until the 2000s, and now regularly appears in magazine polls as a favourite comedy.[2] *This is Spinal Tap* took time to become the greatest, if you will, rockumentary. Conversely, there are breakthrough hits that become culturally significant. *The Hangover* and *Bridesmaids* are examples of worldwide box office hits looking to stand the test of time. There are forgotten gems and curios. *Harold and Maude* is little known and *Sullivan's Travels* is a connoisseur's movie. *Four Lions* (Morris 2010) is one of the first comedies to address issues of homegrown fundamentalism but it struggled at the box office. Questions of transgression will be dealt with in later chapters but it takes time, sometimes, for a comedy to reach its audience.

---

[2] Russell 2003, 'How *Withnail and I* became a Cult', BBC Homepage; Jackson 2014, '"Withnail and I" Britain's best film?', *Independent*, 8 July 2014 (http://www.independent.co.uk/arts-entertainment/films/features/withnail-amp-i-britains-best-film-419228.html).

Chapter 3
Premise and Character

Every character believes the story is happening to them.

KEITH GIGLIO

On titles

Whereas drama and thrillers rely on plot and event, comedy relies on ideas. The big 'what if' is stretched to the limit in the comic screenplay whose function is to explore every facet of the question. More than other film genres, the logline needs to sell the movie. Often it is even right there in the title: *Dumb and Dumber*, *Knocked Up*, *My Big Fat Greek Wedding*, *Liar, Liar* and *School of Rock*. These are simple titles that do what it says on the can.

Although the accepted method of creating a screenplay is to develop the character and work from the inside out, it can work the other way round and the characters and situation might come from a premise. A ludicrous idea such as *Twins* (Reitman 1988) with Arnold Schwarzenegger and Danny De Vito in the title roles was enough to pull people in. *Bad Santa* (Zwigoff 2003) subverted the feel-good Christmas holiday movie, and this adjective has spawned other titles such as *Bad Teacher*, *Bad Neighbours* and *Bad Grandpa*.

Titles are important and are deceptively simple. An oxymoron is useful, as in *The Nutty Professor* (Jerry Lewis and Eddie Murphy versions) or inherent irony, as in the satire, *Thank You For Smoking*. A long title is not a good idea for reasons of space, not only on the poster and DVD but also in the advertising. Whilst *Borat: Cultural Learnings of America for Make Benefit Glorious Nation of Kazakhstan* (2006) is a spoof on lengthy communist tracts, *Who Is Harry Kellerman and Why Is He Saying Those Terrible Things About Me?* (1971) is intriguing and amusing. *Don't Be a Menace to South Central While Drinking Your Juice in the Hood* (1996) is a specific spoof on a niche subgenre. Short is best, however: four words or fewer are ideal and words that translate easily are good too.

A pun will do so long as it's good enough. *Me, Myself and Irene* is a Farrelly brothers romp and a useful title that only hints at the schizophrenia to be found within that movie ('from gentle to mental'). *Shaun of the Dead* cleverly riffs on the George Romero classic and *The Santa Clause* (Pasquin 1994) plays on an old Groucho joke (sanity clause?). In general puns tend to elicit a groan not a grin, so unless you have a really good title that plays with vowel sounds, they are best avoided. Also useful are statements, platitudes or phrases about life, love and relationships. *As Good as it Gets, It's Complicated, I Give it a Year* and *Walk of Shame* are all evocative of common experiences. Sometimes trawling a list of common phrases will spark off any number of conceptual notions.

Numbers too can provide a sort of comic rhythm. They work well overseas and on the poster – *8 Heads in a Duffel Bag, How To Lose a Guy in 10 Days, 10 Things I Hate About You, Sixteen Candles, This is 40, The 40-Year-Old Virgin, 50 First Dates* and *500 Days of Summer* were all winners. The even numbers suggests balance and the odd have a kooky offbeat touch – *3 Men and a Baby, The Seven Year Itch, Ocean's Eleven, 13 Going on Thirty*.

If your movie is to be a genre parody, your title must alert us to that fact. *The Spy Who Shagged Me* was the second in the *Austin Powers* spy spoof series and the *Epic, Teen, Disaster* and *Scary* movies all let us know what we were in for. A self-help style, How to… title has antecedents too, as in *How to Marry a Millionaire* or *How to Murder Your Wife. How To Lose a Guy in 10 Days* is a more recent addition to the canon. Names are good, so long as you have some star power to back it up. *Zoolander or Deuce Bigelow* are both intriguing titles but rely on casting to carry the conceit, but this can misfire, as with *Norbit*.

Brian of Nazareth was a Michael Palin title not favoured by the rest of the Pythons. In press meetings over *Monty Python and the Holy Grail*, they were asked repeatedly about their next film. Eric Idle quipped that it would be called *Jesus Christ: Lust for Glory*. The title ultimately became *Life of Brian*.

As with sci-fi or action movies (*Gone in 60 seconds, Fast and Furious*) comedy can riff on a single idea. It is how you present and populate it that counts. 'Can men and women ever really be friends?' is a question that *When Harry Met Sally* (Reiner 1989) sets out to answer, and goes a long way towards doing so. As long as the title grabs our interest, and better still, encapsulates a paradox, then we are on our way.

What are you writing about?

The comic premise may be a reflection of the writer's personal issues at the time of writing. It is a cliché to 'write what you know' but it is a truism that writers do tend to write out their problems and these change as we mature. In our twenties we are either still transgressing or trying to put the world to rights. We have seen that the world is not fair and does not conform to our expectation of it, so we use our writing to attempt to fix that (as Alvy Singer does so adroitly in his relationship in *Annie Hall*). This may include fantasy ideas but can also be dealing with the opposite sex and peer groups so the coming of age, teen or gross-out movie are popular options.

In our thirties we are concerned with pair bonding and success in our chosen field, broader issues that cover mainstream comedy ideas, romcoms and high-concept pieces. We begin to laugh less from the gut and more from the brain. We move into an observational period where we are trying to categorize the world. We may become politicized and begin to appreciate the bite of wit and satire. We may have begun our starter marriages, and the pranks and drunken revellery gives way to more constructed humour. We begin to appreciate character, plotting and a more honed storyline. This carries us through to middle age, where we start to ask bigger questions about faith, reality and truth. We expect more of humour than the belly laugh. We are discerning. In our forties, anger often resurfaces. Life didn't turn out as expected. We're onto the second marriage and the second bottle of wine each night. Dissatisfaction tends, in some instances, to turn us off humour, feeling that there isn't 'anything out there for the likes of me.'

Craving security, we find nostalgia tossing its pretty hair. We look back on a golden age to the comedy of our youth. Comedy is no longer about challenge but comfort – a reliable old friend whose quirks we have come to accept and love. All of this is only a general pattern, as the appreciation of comedy is not necessarily age-related. We may laugh with our gut (the belly laugh, the rib-tickler, the side-splitter) or with our heads (witticisms, double entendre, wordplay) but they are not mutually exclusive. It is good to think about what makes *you* laugh, so as to focus on what you may offer to others.

Characters in screen comedy

The lead

Comedy protagonists are driven by a blind desire. The dramatic character can step back and be aware of his situation but the comic one cannot. He lives in the here and now and has no real idea of his flaws because the point of the movie is for him to solve those problems. Even if he does have some inkling of what needs to be addressed, say, by an ally who points them out (or some degree of neurotic self-obsession, as in the films of Woody Allen), he will still be unable to address a solution.

Inspector Clouseau (*The Pink Panther* films) is obsessed with being the world's best detective. The comedy arises from the reality that he is a bumbling idiot. The members of Spinal Tap were convinced of their greatness in the face of dwindling crowds. Gracie Hart (Sandra Bullock) was a tomboy FBI agent who had lost her feminine qualities in the pursuit of justice in *Miss Congeniality* (Petrie 2000).

When the obsession is a person, this becomes romantic comedy, as in *There's Something About Mary* or *Bridget Jones*. The converse can also be true, in that the romantic leads might not be after each other, for example *When Harry Met Sally* (a tale of *two* obsessives) which concerns the impossibility of male/female platonic friendship, or *Four Weddings and A Funeral*, in which Hugh Grant is obsessed with his lack of commitment. However, due to the specific demands of genre they will end up together anyway.

There is often a lack of an inner life with comedy characters. We see limited aspects of their lives. Details will be sketched in only if relevant to the back-story: old wounds, lost loves, parenting problems and life-defining crises points are subsumed unless vital to the sub or main plot. Friends and work colleagues are reduced to ciphers and clichés – think of Oscar Madison's poker buddies in *The Odd Couple*. Complex work dynamics and interpersonal relationships are skimmed over because of the need for a clear nemesis and a storyline that contains plenty of laughs.

Their compulsion, in extremis, as with Melvin Udall (Jack Nicholson) in *As Good As It Gets* (Brooks 1997), dominates everything, and the only real conflict they undergo is in trying to deal with their obsession. When waitress Carol Connelly (Helen Hunt) leaves to be closer to her asthmatic son in Brooklyn, Melvin helps with his medical bills in order to have her serve him. It is only once he has exhausted all other options that he turns to address his misanthropy. In comedy movies, the audience doesn't want complexity unless it is a comedy of manners, such as *Carnage* (*Les Diner les Cons*) (Veber 1998) or *Bob and Ted and Carol and Alice* (Mazursky 1969). Rather like sitcom, no two characters can have the same attitude towards anything that happens and this polarization can be an ideal setting for farce.

Unlike drama, where the characters must learn vital things about themselves and change fundamentally, in comedy they merely have to acknowledge their comic flaws. Having been blind to their obsession, once they get what they want, once they achieve *realization*, the comedy is over. This does not mean that the movie is over. Often, especially in romantic comedy, the realization is that they are in love. They must now begin to pursue their goal seriously, in a dramatic context, hence 'running to the airport' scenes as the protagonist tries to explain his feelings to the love object. This can either be successful or bitter-sweet, as in *Manhattan* (Allen 1979).

In essence, the comedy protagonist creates the other characters in the story. He holds deep obsessions and the cast of characters are there to exploit this. They are extensions of his central dilemma. There cannot be too many dimensions to the character because this demands real empathy and compassion and kills the laughter. We sympathize but there must be a degree of comic distance, allowing us to appreciate the comedy from an ironic position. This holds true for most comic genres except romantic comedy, which mirrors our own experiences of love and demands that we identify closely with the protagonist(s).

The comedy hero has a comic goal. Dramatic goals are life and death to the participants, but the comic goal, although it may seem vital to the hero, is less important. It is getting laid, putting the band back together or trying NOT to fall in love. In *10,* Dudley Moore falls in love with a newlywed. The sensible person would give up and accept that the girl has gotten away. As Keith Giglio notes, 'it is an *inappropriate* goal, resulting in inappropriate behaviour and dialogue' (Giglio 2012).

There are two types of comic hero – both of whom are fools. One is the inner, one the outer, the latter being the exemplar of what Geoff King terms 'comedian-comedy'. This outer fool is an obvious comic character, as played by Steve Martin, Jim Carrey or Eddie Murphy, often an actor with a stand-up background, who throughout the movie will discover the truth about himself that will enable him to get the girl, solve the problem and obtain the elixir.

Conversely, the inner fool appears normal, as in roles played by Ben Stiller, Steve Carrell, Paul Rudd or Tina Fey, being the one who is fooling him or herself. They are the fish out of water, the one surrounded by comic mayhem, the underdog with the deep comic flaw. In *Meet the Parents* (Roach 2000), a remake of a 1992 film of the same name,[1] Gaylord Greg Focker (Stiller) is an accident-prone male nurse forced to ask his fiancée's father for her hand in marriage. He is out of his depth culturally, a Jewish character in a WASP world, a postmodern schlemiel.[2] His choice of profession too is significant. Despite nursing having been a male-dominated profession in earlier times,[3] it has come to be seen as a female choice. Alpha male and prospective father-in-law Jack

---

[1] Starring and directed by Greg Glienna. When Universal purchased the rights it was slated to star Jim Carrey, and to be directed by Steven Spielberg.
[2] Jason Biggs' character Jim Levenstein in *American Pie* is another.
[3] O'Lynn and Tranbarger 2007, *Men in Nursing: History, Challenges, and Opportunities*, p. 6.

Byrnes (Robert De Niro) takes every opportunity to emasculate and belittle him. Greg's inner fool, put under pressure, starts to act up and is soon flooding toilets, setting altars on fire and spray-painting cats. The external normality is bent out of shape by circumstance. It is Freud's Id rising to subsume the Ego.

Most comedy characters do not undergo a deep psychological change; rather there is a change of fortune; for example, moving from not being in love to being in love, from failure to success or from injustice to justice. In *Liar, Liar*, Jim Carrey loves his son, but his comic flaw of being a compulsive liar prevents him from expressing this properly. Being forced to tell the truth for twenty-four hours (on a birthday wish) leads to him reuniting with his estranged family and rising above the venal aspects of his profession as a lawyer. It is a revelation of character rather than a change because the opportunity for change was inside him all the time. Give the character richness and humanity and we will love and laugh with him.

Often too there is a basic irony to the comedy when a character is seen to get what he wants, as in Josh – Tom Hanks' character in *Big*, or Lindsay Lohan in *Freaky Friday*, but it only makes them miserable. Getting rid of the curse will bring them maturity and happiness.

In order for the character to reach his goal he must initially take steps to lead him away from it (*Tootsie*, *The Producers*) until he is as far away as possible. The comedy writer will spend much of his time trying to find more complex ways to push the character further away until, at the eureka moment, he sees that he has been led right to it.

Sometimes he is presented with his goal in the form of a person who is his diametric opposite, as in *When Harry Met Sally*. However, they are never complete opposites. In life we do not seek an opposite but someone who is close to us in temperament, class, opinion and lifestyle. Likewise in comedy the character differences are surface traits, not fundamental ones. The opposition is what keeps the lovers apart in *It Happened One Night*. Gable and Colbert are of a different class with differing needs: she's a rich girl running away from daddy; he's a smooth talking reporter after a good story. In *Sullivan's Travels*, the older film director, John Sullivan, goes on an idealistic search for realism, whereas the ingénue (Veronica Lake) is cynical, having failed to make it in Hollywood despite her awesome beauty. They are in the same business but the roles are reversed.

Character is all about making choices. A character cannot remain idle or inert. He will struggle against the inevitable change in his circumstances, but he must act to drive the plot onwards, usually for the worst. A deeper understanding of the protagonist will generate scenes. Decisions about where he lives and with whom, will inform the story. Most importantly, what does he have to lose? There are comedies that come at this from both ways – in *Trading Places*, it is simultaneous. The rich man is brought down as the fool is elevated. It is the world turned upside down.

Characters also tend to be proficient at something other than their profession. They have hobbies. Not only are the *Wedding Crashers* competent in their regular jobs as divorce mediators, but they also are accomplished liars. Alan in *The Hangover* plays cards and when needed is a card sharp and a winner. Andy Stitzer[4] paints figurines. The hobby tends to be an aspect of the older character, as most teenagers tend to drift between fads and fashions, except for gamers and comic book nerds.

Aspects of the foil

Playwright/director Francis Veber wrote that comedy is a cat and a dog in a room together, a metaphor that describes the oppositional nature inherent in comedy. Heraclitus wrote of the unity of opposites, being the existence of something that depends on the co-existence of two conditions that are opposite yet dependent on and presupposing each other within a field of tension. Put more simply, 'The road up and the road down are the same thing' (Hippolytus, *Refutations* 9.10.3).

The slanted road has opposite qualities of ascent and descent and, according to Heraclitus, everything is in constant flux, and every changing object co-instantiates at least one pair of opposites and acts as a base for change. So for Austin Powers to exist there must be a Dr Evil. For every Oscar Madison there is a Felix Unger. The foil is an intrinsic part of the comedy narrative.

The comic double act was a feature of vaudeville in the US and music hall in Britain. Its most notable successes were George Burns and Gracie Allen,[5] Abbot and Costello and Gallagher and Shean in the US, and Flanagan and Allen in the UK. The television generation produced The Smothers Brothers and Rowan and Martin (US) and Morecambe and Wise and The Two Ronnies (UK). The addition of a second person was a necessity born out of noisy venues where audiences could not hear the comedian. Having another person onstage avoided the problem of losing the joke or having to repeat it. A second person creates a dynamic, another dimension to the act. He introduces the set-up in order for the comedian to deliver the punch. The feed or straight man creates the circumstances for comedy to occur. He *makes* the context.

The foil is often a figure of derision. He is not pitied; indeed, if there is any sympathy to be had, it comes for the comic alone. The foil may get laughs but he rarely gets the girl. He is content to be a camp follower and cannot be seen to

---

[4] *The 40-Year-Old Virgin.*
[5] Burns and Allen transferred successfully to TV, as did another male/female coupling, Nichols and May. George Burns, following the death of his wife, had a long career in movies.

be the real power behind the throne. He is a container for the wild improvisation and creativity of the comedian. Although he is the connection to the real world, he does not benefit from this or from the comedian who, as Lord of Misrule, gets all the laughs. It is a thankless task in many ways, but it has its benefits. The straight man is gifted by being in the world of the comedian and is an integral part of it. Also, he has less of the pressure, for it is the comedian who must always deliver. There are many thousands of straight one-liner comics but precious few double acts. Laurel and Hardy are the role models for this and will be examined later.

Best buddies. Worst enemies

The comedian needs someone who is not an antagonist or love interest to relate to – in part this is an expository role, but it also helps to develop his or her character. Bridget Jones has a group of friends who are either as hopeless as, or more successful than she is. In *I Love You Man* (Hamberg 2009), Peter Klaven (Paul Rudd) has no buddies and, on encountering Sydney Fife (Jason Segel) discovers everything in a man that he is not – smart guy, wild thing, man-boy and dick.[6] Rudd is an introvert who needs to be brought out of his shell, as with Andy in *The 40-Year-Old Virgin* and it takes another to do that. The wild thing is the life and soul of the party but he will always get you into trouble. Zach Galifianakis' character Alan in *The Hangover* is a prime example. He is a catalyst for plot and action. If he is a mentor, he is neither a suitable nor a reliable one, as in *Due Date*. The role is similar to that of the smart guy, who is an arrogant know-it-all. Where Will Ferrell or Vince Vaughn play these roles straight, Steve Martin played them with faux irony, reducing the character to low status by the end. These characters are not as smart as they think they are and know nothing of love, which will be their undoing. They are there primarily to demonstrate to the protagonist how *not* to behave, and that untrammelled pleasure has its limitations. They may be a man-child, as with Will Ferrell (*Old School, Anchorman*). They shirk responsibility and make a virtue out of arrested development. This role would also include the stoner best friend.

Often, the female protagonist is, or has a friend who is, a snob or a princess. These rarified creatures are too good for the world. Often obscenely wealthy, these are the Heathers in *Heathers* and the Mean Girls in *Mean Girls*. They are beautiful and their lives are perfect – only they aren't. The false cliché that will come to pass is that inner beauty will always win out and that the ugly duckling

---

[6]Rudd and Segal swap their roles in *Forgetting Sarah Marshall,* where Segal plays lost and lovelorn and Rudd is an alpha male surfing instructor.

will bloom. They are portrayed as brittle, superficial and as interchangeable parts of a clique.

If they do not get their comeuppance in the teen movie, they may appear again in the workplace (*The Devil Wears Prada*, *Working Girl*) as hard-nosed career-driven harpies who will step over anyone in their Louboutins in order to get either the promotion or the man. They are deserving villains and we want to see them knocked down. If given some degree of characterization, they may at first befriend our hero, but she is a trickster and will wait for her moment to strike.

The dick or bitch is the bad guy, the shadow. In essence, they represent everything the hero is afraid of becoming. However, the hero needs allies and this is where the best friend comes in. His or her function is to question what the hero does and to ask the questions the audience is thinking. 'Why are you entering this new world? I know you well and this cannot be good'. They offer advice and support but also important aspects of criticism. They know what the character lacks, as they have objectivity, but they cannot implement the necessary changes because it has to come from within.

The parent

Comedy exists in a juvenile world, one where coincidence and contrivance is not only accepted but encouraged. For this to work there must be an authority figure present, most often a parent, school principal or policeman. These figures are rigid, humourless, weak and blinkered and their patience is surprisingly flexible considering the amount of testing it is put to.

Male parents are never sexual, for example Eugene Levy in *American Pie*. If divorced, a female parent may be seen as inappropriately flirtatious but is often a figure of ridicule (except in the case of Mrs Robinson in *The Graduate*). Likewise, the lone male parent may be living in reduced circumstances or a storage container. If they try to be 'down with the kids' they will fail, their liberal views having been misconstrued and misplaced. Robert De Niro in *Meet the Parents/Fockers* adds the threat of violence or exposure. The authoritarian, over-protective quasi-military parent is a common device placed there as a nemesis in order to create contrast for kids who are always right (Ferris Bueller). That the teenager will grow up to become just like them is never discussed, although there are plenty of comedians who once played the fool, who have now come to represent their parents' generation, as with Adam Sandler (*Grown Ups*), Steve Martin (*Parenthood*) and Seth Rogan (*Bad Neighbours*). In general, however, mum and dad are only points of reference for movies aimed at a teenage demographic.

The police are incompetent, principally as crime in movies will always be solved by intuition and not detection. Comedy encourages the maverick. It is the instinctive method that triumphs, rather than going by the book. Authority figures are hidebound by the law and cannot stray from its parameters. Likewise, school principals are simple figures of resistance to juvenile antics. That they may have once gone to school themselves is unimportant. On occasion the authority figure will in the end give in and join in the fun. This 'what the hell' factor humanizes, neutralizes and, more importantly, erases them as an effective antagonist.

Bosses are tyrannical, demanding and sexist. Your boss is not your friend because ultimately he is the one who holds the gift of employment. He has the power not only of veto but also of controlling your financial destiny. The role of bosses in comedy has changed in today's fluid economic conditions, moving from C. C. Baxter's sleaze ball Mr Sheldrake (Fred MacMurray) in *The Apartment* (Wilder 1960) to out and out bastardry with Kevin Spacey, Jennifer Aniston and Colin Farrell in *Horrible Bosses* (Gordon 2011). The boss as flawed comic tyrant has its antecedents in Chaplin's The *Great Dictator* and perhaps reached its zenith in VP Bill Lumbergh (Gary Cole) in *Office Space* (Judge 1999).

The good wife or the girl back home

Often in comedies (*Planes, Trains and Automobiles*) there are saintly creatures that represent a male vision of the feminine ideal. They are homemakers and mothers. They are sensible and patient, objects of affection and yearning, but not lust. They are nuns. They are objectified. They are the staid other half who is a projection and is therefore convenient to tuck away as the 'goal' of the story. In part this is because the comic protagonist himself exhibits many conventionally female characteristics – taking a chance, speaking your mind, conversing and communicating, having a willingness to look foolish – and this cannot be done so effectively in the company of real females. This behaviour might be displayed for a new love object or against a callous world. This woman is chimera, and is seen less frequently in comedy movies these days having been supplanted by the ...

Manic pixie dream girl

This character exists in the fevered imaginations of writer/directors as an effervescent girlish type who selflessly helps young men to pursue their own happiness (and to embrace life's mystery) with no benefit to themselves. The term was coined by film critic Nathan Rabin after observing Kirsten Dunst's character in *Elizabethtown* (2005) and is best exemplified by Natalie Portman in *Garden State* or Zooey Deschanel as Summer Finn in *500 Days of Summer* (and again in *Yes Man*).

The character, as in the good wife, has no arc and exhibits eccentric dress styles and wild personality traits. She might be traced back to Katherine Hepburn in *Bringing up Baby*, by way of Audrey Hepburn in *Breakfast at Tiffany's,* Marilyn Monroe as Sugar Cane in *Some Like it Hot* and Barbara Streisand in *What's Up Doc? Annie Hall* is NOT a manic pixie dream girl, as she has independent career ambitions. Director Marc Webb (*500 Days of Summer*) sums it up: 'Yes, Summer has elements of the manic pixie dream girl – she is an immature view of a woman. She's Tom's view of a woman. He doesn't see her complexity and the consequence for him is heartbreak. In Tom's eyes, Summer is perfection, but perfection has no depth. Summer's not a girl, she's a phase'.[7] Sadly for us men, these girls/women do not exist.

The bad girl

This diametric opposite of the good girl back home is best exemplified by Mae West (see Women in Comedy), and played out by Rosalind Russell and Carole Lombard. The bad girl is the one who speaks her mind and who treats men with the contempt we deserve. The romantic comic character is often teased and tested by the bad girl on his journey back to the good wife. The bad girl acknowledges that his heart belongs to the girl back home, but knows that with enough tempting, she may win him through his loins. She knows that all men are weak and that this is the easiest way to exploit this. If his loins give in to her then he will have betrayed the good wife, therefore nullifying his quest.

He will also have matured, therefore changing his character. This is why she can never fully succeed in her desire to corrupt, educate or mature him. In romantic comedy, second only to the character's blind obsession, she may be a force in stopping him from reaching his goal. In *Four Weddings* Hugh Grant has sex with inappropriate women, but his obsession is his flight from commitment, which allows sex to happen so long as it is never meaningful.

A more modern take on the bad girl is the R-rated woman. She is more manipulative and less stable. She may be the freaky girlfriend, the stalker, the neurotic or the obsessive. Gloria (Isla Fisher) in *Wedding Crashers* fools Jeremy Grey (Vince Vaughn) into thinking she is a virgin, then proceeds to stalk him until he falls for her deceptions, whilst her sister Claire (Rachel McAdams) plays the good girl. Jenifer Aniston, known as the go-to good girl, has expanded her

---

[7]Wiseman, Eva. 'Is there such a thing as "the one" – and what happens if you lose her?'. *Guardian*, 16 August 2009.

repertoire and switched roles, appearing as a carnal dentist in *Horrible Bosses* and as the stripper neighbour in *We're the Millers* (Thurber 2013). Often these characters are secondary or part of an echo couple – the slightly less glamorous, less successful and less sexy friends of the lead.

Frat boys and the bully

The bully is a lesser antagonist, but nonetheless represents a rite of passage for the protagonist. He is a challenge to his manhood and the group ethic. Comic characters are individualists and this is often placed against the desires of the peer group. When the bully gets together with his gang, these frat boys are portrayed on a single level, that of being irresponsible (*Animal House*, *American Pie*) drunk, sex-obsessed and reckless. Even in *Revenge of the Nerds* (Kenew 1984), although we focus on the Nerds attempts to form a fraternity, the rival Alpha Betas are there in force. Bullies, gangs and social assimilation are a standard fixture of all American high school and college campus comedies. The reason for the bullying is that our hero evidences those 'female' characteristics such as sensitivity, empathy and listening, which will ultimately make him a better mate than the testosterone-filled alpha male with his mating call of 'Spring Break!' The bully senses the competition, but does not have the wherewithal to change or do anything about it, and that which he does not understand he will attempt to crush.

The innocent but deserving victim

The butt of the joke can be a random passer-by, minor character or foil. James Finlayson in the *Laurel and Hardy* films was a past master at this. Ned Ryerson (*Groundhog Day*) just begs to get his ass kicked and 'Woogie' in *There's Something About Mary* (Farrelly and Farrelly 1998) is just plain weird. The advantage of having an oddity, a pervert or, in essence, a village idiot, is that it puts the inappropriate behaviour of the comedian into perspective. It tells us that, even though our comedian is weird, he is not *that* weird. Andy Stitzer (Steve Carrell) in *The 40-Year-Old Virgin* has become an action figure collector and an online poker player because he had no luck with women. He was *involuntarily* celibate. Phil Connors is misanthropic, cynical and a louse, but Ryerson and the other inhabitants of the town of Punxatawny are portrayed as simple folk; easily bedded waitresses, louche drunks and confused landladies; even his cameraman is mocked for his dress sense and his inability with women.

The comedian can, in this way, be a bit of a bully himself and a close examination of the psyches of stand-up comics will not always reveal a politically correct softer side. Comedy movies glorify conformity and conservatism and one way of doing this is to find someone out there who is more deserving of our derision. In mainstream Hollywood comedies, the effect is not only to equalize the social status by bringing down the bad guy (the corporation, the bosses, the bad parents), but also to place the comedian centre stage as exemplar of proper decent behaviour. The right guy gets the right girl through sacrifice, determination and struggle. The rapacious corporation is exposed and those who are too greedy (not merely rich) are punished. The law is restored and the world is brought back into balance. This echoes the former role of the court jester in that he was permitted and sanctioned by the state/king as a restorative. This is comedy as social corrective. Those whom society deems to be outsiders are punished for it. This may include foreign store owners/cab drivers, unsuitable lovers, serious alcoholics and substance abusers, extremists, fundamentalists, and others about whom it is probably best to remain silent.

Chapter 4
Plotting and Comic Scenes

Phil:

What would you do if you were stuck in one place and every day was exactly the same, and nothing that you did mattered?

Ralph:

That about sums it up for me.

GROUNDHOG DAY

Life does not have a coherent narrative. Our successes and failures, as Kipling wrote, are both traitors. Life is a stream of events that happen with scant evidence of overt cause and effect, unlike in drama where we seek to force order and meaning out of the chaos. Comedy is plotted, even when partly improvised,[1] and the resultant movie has been edited with care to ensure the clearest storyline results. Although chaotic, inappropriate and anarchistic, comedy is at its root conservative. It resets the moral dial, punishing wrongdoers and rewarding the good behaviour of the little guy with the good heart.

In vaudeville and slapstick, humans were treated as objects and perceived as such, so any amount of pain could be foisted on its stars without consequence. Chaplin was to add sentiment. In comedy drama, then sitcom, the focus was on the comedy of manners, usually of the rich or well to do. In screwball, the woman pursued a man but it did not last. Comedy began to incorporate the drama of life, leavening it with wit. The questions we ask began to form proposals for broad comedy movies. Many of Woody Allen's movies ask 'Why am I incapable of love?'

---

[1] Borat and This is Spinal Tap were plotted and scripted. The improvisation moves round this.

In romantic comedy, all is resolved, usually in a wedding celebration or feast. Comedy rarely ends in chaos. The Western parody *Blazing Saddles* (Brooks 1974) is one exception. Its conclusion features a breaking of the fourth wall where the cast invades the Hollywood Commissary, there is a pie fight, they chase Hedley Lamar to Graumann's Movie Theater and the protagonists ride off into the sunset only to climb off their horses and into a waiting Limo. Another is *Monty Python and the Holy Grail* (Jones 1975), which has the cast arrested by the police. In a sense these random endings are the best they could come up with at the time. Even The Marx Brothers' comedies achieved some kind of new order by the end.

The happy ending, as conceived by Aristotle, is one of the four conventions of comedy. The second is that nobody gets hurt for real. There is a lot of comedy pain and the physical can be stretched to its limits, (the frank and beans) but death is treated lightly. In *Austin Powers: International Man of Mystery* (Roach 1997), a henchman dies and his widow is visited with the news. Because the concept of henchmen is clichéd (they derive from the colour co-ordinated boiler-suited Blofeld henchmen in *You Only Live Twice*) they are understood to be dispensable: mere extras, as with the Keystone Kops.

Later, Dr Evil dumps another minion[2] through a hatch in his lair. He does not die but continues to protest his pain as Evil orders him shot, which again misses. We laugh at the ineffectiveness of Dr Evil's operation and at the thwarted expectation because we cannot see the 'considerable pain' he is in. Animal lover Ken (Michael Palin) in *A Fish Called Wanda* (Crichton 1988) is charged with killing an old lady. Instead, in a series of accidents, he is responsible for the death of her dogs. When she sees the last one expire, she promptly dies of a heart attack.

Third, there must be clarity of intent. Is this supposed be laugh out loud funny, amusing or wry, tongue in cheek comedy? The audience must know from the start if this is gross-out or satire. The complexity comes in the choice of genre or subgenre.

Finally, comedy is an angry art, because comedy attacks social institutions and behaviour. All comedy is a form of criticism, from the mild to the vicious. The comedy writer must ask – what am I angry about? Comedies such as *The War of The Roses or Thank You For Smoking* have clear targets, respectively divorce and the smoking lobby.

All movies begin with character. One inviolate rule is that the comedy character never sees his predicament as funny. He sees it as serious drama, as does everyone else in the movie. To them, they are at the centre of it.

---

[2]Mustafa, played by Will Ferrell.

Fish out of water

Forest Gump. Crocodile Dundee. Borat. Brüno. Big. Tootsie. The Big Lebowski. After Hours. Beverly Hills Cop. Sleeper. Back to the Future. The Jerk. Liar, Liar. The Nutty Professor. All of Me. Austin Powers: International Man of Mystery. Honey, I Shrunk the Kids.

One of the most common comedy structures is this comedy of the picaresque. It is Don Quixote tilting at windmills. The transplanting of a sympathetic character into a new environment will be the driving force for much of the humour and *Crocodile Dundee, Trading Places* and *The Hangover* all achieve this.

It need not be a place: it can be a physical manifestation of change as in the cross dressing of *Tootsie* (Pollack 1982), *Mrs Doubtfire* (Columbus 1993) or *Some Like it Hot* (Wilder 1959), or a physical alteration as in *All of Me* (Reiner 1984), *Big* (Marshall 1988), *Freaky Friday* (Waters 2003)[3] and other body swap comedies. It can be a temporal dislocation, as in *Back to the Future, Bill and Ted's Big Adventure* or *Hot Tub Time Machine*. It may be a new world such as fatherhood (*Knocked Up*) where Seth Rogen, a pot smoking loser is faced with responsibility, or *Being There* (Ashby 1979) where childlike Chauncey Gardiner (Peter Sellers) is deprived of his home and must explore the outside world.

He may be a foreigner, such as *Borat* (Charles 2006) or *Brüno* (Charles 2009), both of whom arrive in the US with no knowledge of its customs, laws or behaviour. The comedy foreigner is a well-tested comic device, effective as a fish out of water in sitcoms such as *Mork and Mindy* (Mork = Robin Williams), *Perfect Strangers* (Balti = Bronson Pichot) and *Taxi* (Ladka Graves = Andy Kaufmann). There is also Sheldon Cooper (Jim Parsons) in *The Big Bang Theory* as a reverse fish out of water. He is of this world but too smart for it. The Coen brothers are particularly fond of the fish-out-of-water device, employing the device in many of their movies.

The fish out of water protagonist has the benefit of a clear eye. The savant can see the world for what it is and is a truth teller, as in the story of the Emperor's new clothes. The art and gift of the true comedian is to make us see the world through his eyes, and they are few and far between.

The fish out of water's journey is either that of returning home or of assimilation into the new culture. There are two types, the *catalyst*, who does not fundamentally change but forces change on the new world, and the *wounded fish* (Stuart Voytilla, *Writing the Comedy Film*) who is flawed and needs to be healed. The catalyst has special gifts that will change others and the new world

---

[3]A remake of the 1976 version starring Jodie Foster and Barbara Harris, directed by Gary Nelson.

will grow because of his presence, as with Alex Foley in *Beverly Hills Cop*, or the antics of Ferris Bueller.

The wounded fish has an internal need for validation, independence, redemption or love. The world and its difficulties are what make this fish see his or her inner problems and cause the will to change – Goldie Hawn in *Private Benjamin* or Tom Hanks as Josh in *Big*. In the latter, Josh learns to value his childhood and to grow at his own pace but in order to do this he must face his worst fear. Sandra Bullock is an uptight, stuffy FBI agent who does not care about her appearance. She is thrust into a beauty pageant.

When the story is about gender shifts, as with *Some Like it Hot* or *Miss Congeniality*, the character must come to terms with the other side of him or herself. In Wilder's *Some Like it Hot*, Geraldine and Daphne are comfortable as either men or women by the end.[4] In *Miss Congeniality*, Bullock's tomboy character has learned to accept her feminine side.

Not only must the protagonist grapple with a new world, but he must also come to terms with a new order. There is a huge contrast between the old and new and this must occur early on, as in *Liar, Liar* (Shadyac 1997) where Max's wish that his dad speak the truth for one day comes into effect at 8.45 p.m. that very evening. In *Groundhog Day*, the fun begins at 6.00 a.m., every morning.

They take with them a subversive power that will help them to succeed in this new environment. The fish out of water is a kind of Holy fool, as in *Being There*, where Chauncey Gardiner's every utterance is seen as great wisdom.

Putting the character in the worst position possible is useful if not mandatory. In *Back to the Future* (Zemeckis 1985), not only is Marty McFly sent back to the restrictive 1950s but he also has to ensure that his parents meet and bond. When he fails to do so his entire existence is put in jeopardy. He must also find an ally and mentor, someone from this new world who can explain its tropes and rules before he is lynched or locked up. Mr Vic provides this in *Miss Congeniality*, Doc Brown in *Back to the Future*.

The hero will on his journey inevitably cross social boundaries, leading to insult, comedy and embarrassment, which they will not feel, since they do not know how to be embarrassed. *Borat's* inappropriate reaction on hearing his wife is dead is to high five the hotel employee, then to go off in pursuit of his impossible love interest, Pamela Anderson. As the journey progresses, the fish will come into conflict with the authorities. There may already be jeopardy in an antagonist who is waiting for him (Biff Tannen in *Back To The Future*). Rather than seeing the comic character as a harmless oddball, he perceives him as a threat to his world and rightly so, for the comic is here to right the wrongs and rebalance its axis.

---

[4] Voytilla

The comic character may have to be hidden, involving a costume change, which indicates that he is beginning to adopt the trappings of the new society. There is the need for assimilation, and in this way the fish out of water is a truly American tale. A nation of immigrants, this goal has been pursued since the Plymouth Brethren left England. The archetype is Superman, arriving in a rural setting, being taken in, adopting the language, customs and moral code, then moving toward the urban environment and becoming subsumed by it.

Plotting your comedy movie

There is no fundamental difference in writing comedy from any other screenplay, and the principles of character (Joseph Campbell's 'The Heroes Journey'), story (Robert McKee's 'Story') and structure (Sid Field's 'Screenplay') all hold true. The denouement, being comic, will end happily but how you get there is the creative part. Dark endings tend to be the preserve of black comedy and satire but otherwise the palette is light and bright with plenty of laughs and character. The latter is what sells. A character put under great stress is the comic conceit.

As with Blake Snyder's 'Save the Cat' and Keith Giglio's *Writing the Comic Blockbuster*, there are prescriptive beats and act breaks that must be hit, and these can be divided into eight sequences, two in Act One, four in Act Two (bisected at the half) and two in Act Three. Since most comedies run at ninety minutes, this can be seen as fifteen minutes apiece. Many screenwriting tutors advise that you hang the screenplay off index cards and today's lesson will be no different. Putting each scene, each beat, each character point and each Act onto index cards mean that you can *see* the script before writing it. You will never be lost inside the story and if you have planned each act, scene and sequence down to the minutest detail, the writing of the first draft screenplay ought to be straightforward.

Some writers like to carve out a rough first draft in order to find character and story, akin to the NaNoWriMo[5] method of writing a first draft of a novel as developed by Chris Baty. This is worthy if you have the time, but most of the mulch is likely to be discarded. The solid construction of character and the journey they undergo is paramount. The job of a comedy writer is the hardest of all: not only must you be able to create all the facets of screenplay but you are required to be funny as well.

---

[5] National Novel Writing Month in November, in which the participant agrees to complete 50,000 words of a novel with NO editing. This acts as seed for later drafts, fighting the common perception that most writers spend their time not writing or writing footnotes.

The comic world

In the first few pages, you must establish the comic world, the dramatic context and the tone. It is worth looking at both produced and unproduced screenplays to see if this is clear or not – if not what is missing? Screenplays begin *in media res*, so you will need to have established the pre-story. What went on before the events that are about to unfold? You must introduce the main characters visually and quickly. Who are they? What are they doing? We learn so much about them in these opening scenes that nothing can be wasted and the writer must be ahead of audience.

In *The Hangover* we start with a cold opening. There are wedding preparations and wealthy people, but something is amiss. The bride is trying to reach the groomsmen. We learn they are in Vegas. Then Phil calls. He's standing in the desert with a cut lip looking dishevelled and distraught. Where is Doug?, she asks. She is told that they fucked up and that the wedding, due to happen in five hours, won't.

Groundhog Day was reverse engineered. Producer Lewis Albert and director Harold Ramis explain on the DVD extras that the original script by Danny Rubin was like a European movie that started in the middle (Rubin agreed that you needed to establish how the magic had happened and this is what they do in the final draft). We see how cynical Phil Connors is going about his job and the Groundhog Day celebrations but fifteen minutes into the movie he is trapped by the blizzard. By minute twenty-one the magic has already begun.

First impressions in a movie are vital. Many begin with an event – *Wedding Crashers* sets up the boys and their scam before they even need to explain the rules. There may be narration or a voiceover from the main character. The IMDb script of *Bad Santa* does not have misanthropist Willie T. Stokes (Billy Bob Thornton) drunk at the bar explaining how lousy his childhood was and how screwed up his life is. The later rewrite adds sympathy for a terrible person because we do not actually see Willie do anything altruistic until late on in the movie.

There can be a framing device such as a prologue or a montage, anything to delineate the world and its inhabitants. When it comes to the lead character, a defining character action is almost mandatory. In *Sideways* (Payne 2004), we learn that Miles is lazy and a borderline alcoholic. Waking up late, he assures his buddy Jack (whom he is due to pick up from his bride-to-be's home) that he is on his way, but then proceeds to read on the can. Other best practice examples include Carl Allen (Jim Carrey) in *Yes Man* (Reed 2008), Felix Unger (Jack Lemmon) in *The Odd Couple* and Steve Martin in *The Lonely Guy*.

If characters like these are down, then they will be up at the end. Conversely, those who are at the top of their game (the rich, powerful and corrupt) will be brought down. There may also be a Greek Chorus – literally in *Mighty Aphrodite* – who will comment on the action. This can be in the form of friends or others who will stand in for the audience and explain the scenario. Narrator and balladeer Jonathan Richman does this effectively in *There's Something About Mary* (1998).

There must be an inciting incident to close the first ten minutes. Shrek wants to be left alone but is beset by fairytale creatures who arrive in the forest. In *The Truman Show* (Weir 1998), Truman Burbank lives in what appears to be Pleasantville, but is in truth a reality show based entirely around him. A paranoiac idea, but Truman is already beginning to question his life in the mirror. It is not until a stage light[6] falls from the sky that he begins to seriously examine his world. The question our protagonist must ask, and with which we must identify, is 'what is missing here? Is it sex or love, freedom or security, happiness or actualization?'

The goal

In the second half of the first act we establish the goal of the character. We have met the carpenter and now we are gathering the wood to build the house. From here, events take over and we see how the character reacts to them. In *The 40-Year-Old Virgin*, Andy is exposed. His buddies have been told of his situation and they intend to get him laid. In *American Pie*, the same pledge is made. At this time there will often be a voice of reason – a girlfriend or buddy who offers objectivity or helps to forge forward. Brian in *Forgetting Sarah Marshall* (Stoller 2008) is an online buddy to Peter who, post his naked break-up, advises him to go on vacation. How could he have known that Sarah would be there and with another man? It is easy at this point to think of the interloper Aldous Snow (Russell Brand) as the nemesis/bad guy, but it is Sarah herself, just as in the *Inbetweeners Movie* (Palmer 2011) where Simon is dumped by Carli, but then finds her on the same holiday as him and his mates. The arc of character for both is 'getting over it' as in *500 Days of Summer*.

We need to know what the movie is about and what the character wants. The dramatic question must be posed long before the end of Act One. It is also advantageous to introduce the bad guy as early as possible, although this is not sacrosanct as there are genres in which we do not see the bad guy until the second act, such as in road Movies. The enemy can be the lie (*Liar, Liar*), the curse (*Groundhog Day*) or even personal issues, as with Melvin Udall (Jack Nicholson) in *As Good As It Gets*, who asks of his Shrink, 'Dr. Green, how can

---

[6]A similar event pushes the character and plot forwards in *Birdman* (Iñárritu 2014).

you diagnose someone as an obsessive compulsive disorder, and then act like I have some choice about barging in here?'

Fun and games or brave new world

Act Two is where scripts go to die.[7] This is often because the comic premise has not been set up with due care, or the characterization has not been thought through so the idea runs out of steam. Act Two seems bulky and difficult after the clear premise of the first so it helps to break it down into four 15-minute sequences. Essentially the second act is a series of problems, which keep getting increasingly worse. The problems ought to be germane to the plotting and come out of the characters actions. The character acts in his new world, which provokes reaction from the world, which comes back at him as a set of new problems.

A scene must contain a goal, conflict and then disaster. A hero seeks something, is met by resistance and his situation gets worse. You must be prepared for your hero to lose and lose he must, over and over again, as he tries to address the problem in his life that needs fixing. If this is a lack of love then obstacles will be placed in his way – a girl whom he does love is married, taken or does not feel the same way about him. If he fears commitment then throw him no choice but to choose commitment. Although the main question must and will be resolved in the end, the audience should always be in doubt. The disaster ending to a scene propels forwards, until late in Act Two where he will have had enough. For now though, he is merely exploring his options.

This first sequence, Blake Snyder's 'fun and games', ought to be an energizing part of the writing experience. We start small, as in *Groundhog Day* – 'why is everything repeating itself?' – and go big – 'if I can do what I like without consequence, then am I some kind of God?'

In *The Hangover,* the guys wake up to find a chicken, a tiger and a baby in their Vegas apartment and have no recollection of where the groom is, how they got there, lost their teeth or got married. It is not until they arrive at the hospital that they discover they were given rohypnol (roofies), which has wiped their memory. It is only much later in a well-seeded reveal that Wolf-pack member Alan (Zach Galifianakis) confesses to spiking their drinks, thinking it was ecstasy. He just wanted them to have a good time.

Many of the big laughs will come in Act Two where we show the initial results of the comic premise. These are the trailer moments, the big sustained comic set pieces, and the comic writer will find a lot of imagery here. This is where all the permutations of the secret identity/cross dressing in *Tootsie, Mrs Doubtfire*

---

[7] Giglio: 139.

or *Some like it Hot* will throw up the biggest laughs. It is where Lawrence abuses Freddie in *Dirty Rotten Scoundrels*, where Eddie Murphy or Chris Rock will go for comic outrage in many of their movies.

In character terms, your hero will at first go for the quick and easy fix. We all do. When in trouble we try to find the simplest way out with the least collateral damage. This will not work. It is a new game with new rules. In some comedies this is patently obvious. *Galaxy Quest* has a bunch of SF actors in space – *really* in space. In *City Slickers* they are in the Wild West where the urbanites must prove themselves. In *The Internship*, Vince Vaughn and Owen Wilson are accepted onto the internship programme at Google with a hundred kids half their age. There are new appearances and new costumes. There will be enemies everywhere but also allies, those who take you at face value and want to help. The sub- or B-plot also kicks in and this too has its own dramatic question. This mini movie within the movie also has a beginning, middle and end, albeit one reduced to three events or scenes, which are directly related to the main plot. *The Hangover* is about the rights and wrongs of getting married and all four have differing attitudes towards this. The subplot mirrors and echoes the main plot, but does not get in the way. Here, echo couples and best friends try to resolve their issues in the light of the comic world illuminated by the protagonist.

In *Dirty Rotten Scoundrels* (Oz 1988), Lawrence Jamieson (Michael Caine) sees off interloper/conman Freddie Benson (Steve Martin), but soon he's back in Beaumont-sur-Mer with his own agenda. It is Lawrence's tale but Freddie, although similar to him, has differing needs.

In Act Two, you need cause and effect. Because *this* happened, *that* will occur. The danger, although these are comic sequences, is that they become simply episodic. The writer first conceived of the scenes coming off the premise and wants to shoehorn them in, rather than let them grow out of character. As Giglio notes, if a scene can be moved to anywhere in the script it doesn't belong anywhere in the script'.

Testing, testing

Here, the protagonist will make a second attempt to fix the problem. Phil Connors has tried to get away from Punxatawney. He can't, so he takes advantage of the situation, seducing women, stealing money, getting thrown in jail and then trying to attract Rita, the Ice Queen. She turns him down.

We must ask, how much is he willing to put up with? This is where a comic or dramatic character differs from us in the real world. He will try and try again, and audiences will bond with him or her. The outcome is still very much in doubt. There are scenes of anticipation and reaction, which will lead to the need for change. He is moving toward the girl, the job, the new life and here, by the midpoint, there will also be a hint of the ending. The character is beginning to grow.

Heart

The midpoint of the movie is like the curtain down at the intermission of a play. When it rises, the story slows for the part with the heart. Now, love is in the air. We have had two sequences that have focused on the comedy and it is time to seek out the heart of the picture. This is where the theme comes in, and the writer concentrates on what the movie is about. *Wedding Crashers* is a bromance between two guys, John and Jeremy (Owen Wilson/Vince Vaughn). The midpoint is when the rules are broken and the guys split up. Each pursues their women, but the theme emerges. John says it to Claire Cleary as clearly as Katherine Hepburn did in *Bringing Up Baby*. She then repeats it in her maid of honour speech – 'True love is the soul's recognition of its counterpoint in another'. John sees this in her and must do anything to win her, but love slows the story. It makes it more real and less comedic, as there is deception to be swept away. Once the tender moment is over we will be swept back into the story, but the seeds are sown. We are moving away from the midpoint and next will come transformation, recovery and growth.

Love, loss and kryptonite

There is a glimpse here of how life could be if all were resolved, but the comic is still a fool and must rescue himself from his situation. Before this can happen, unresolved issues will return – the skeleton in the closet. In character terms, the negative traits displayed in Act One are going to bounce back one more time and the comic hero is going to have to deal with them. This will be intuitive and not reasoned, because reason had been tried and found wanting.

In *Liar Liar*, Fletcher Reede's (Jim Carrey) big case comes up and he cannot perjure himself. Consequently he loses in front of his nemesis, boss Miranda (Amanda Donohue) and jeopardizes his position as partner in the law firm. However, after the divorce custody verdict is passed, he realizes that his venal client (Jennifer Tilley) has lied about her age and that her prenuptial agreement was signed as a minor, rendering it null and void. This last minute twist shows his growth. Being a lawyer isn't all about lying; it is about knowing and applying the law and its precedents. Intuition has led him to truth and away from his obsessive-compulsive disorder.

At the same point in the movie, Phil Connors gives up and tries to kill himself, repeatedly. In Danny Rubin's story, he estimated that the number of days in which Phil was trapped to be 10,000. This does not come across in the final movie, but the dark night of his soul does – and we have an emotional investment. He has tried to win Rita over and over again and failed, so he gives up. He changes his goal. This is okay; often the new goal is not so far away from the old, as in *Rocky* where he changes it from winning the World Heavyweight Championship to going the distance. It might even be a new goal, as in *Tootsie* when Michael cannot get with Julie (Jessica Lange) either as a man or as a woman, and so he decides to reveal all on his TV soap – but with a twist.

Transformation

As we enter Act Three, the story will carry itself as we head toward resolution. In character terms this means the final transformation and a shedding of the old skin. In story terms, it means the dramatic question that was put at the start will be answered.

There are three kinds of Act Three. The action Act Three, as in *Animal House*, *Blazing Saddles* or *The Blues Brothers*; The journey Act Three, as in *Due Date*, *Planes, Trains and Automobiles* or *The Hangover*; and the talking Act Three, as in *Broadcast News*, *Sideways* or *Annie Hall*.

There is often a ticking clock, a sense of urgency. The boy must get to the girl before she is married or leaves the country. The task must be completed before the magic disappears. The last opportunity to escape, to score the winning goal or to stake your claim is fast approaching, after which all hope is banished. Just before this climax, there is often another low point at which we see the humanity in the character and that he is at war with himself. There may be a final comic rant here. A mentor will give his words of advice. It is time to grow up. Big decisions have to be made.

Epiphany

Act Three in a comedy ought to be short, as it contains less comedy, more a series of reversals (*Some Like It Hot*), revelations and confrontations (*Dirty Rotten Scoundrels*).

In the final act, the viewer must not be denied the battle they have been looking forward to, be it characters arguing, running to find one another or fighting the bad guy. It is convergence and it is useful to have an arena, a symbolic location.

Sleepless in Seattle ends on the Empire State building, a crucial reference to the aborted reunion between Cary Grant and Deborah Kerr in *An Affair to Remember*. *Wedding Crashers* ends at Jeremy Grey's wedding to Gloria when John reunites with Claire, wins back his best friend and they all drive off together looking for another wedding to crash. *Bad Santa* climaxes in a shoot-out in the mall and a chase with a stuffed elephant. There is sacrifice and resurrection, the emotional death of the old self to make way for the new. There is an epiphany.

It must be a satisfying ending, the expected finale. The comedy is over and has been replaced by resolution, which is at this point more important to the viewer than laughs.

It has become common to end post credits with a series of bloopers and gags.[8] The writer is not responsible for this, however, it being tacked on by producers in the hope of saving a bomb or pushing a sequel. There are exceptions. The credit sequence at the ending of *The Hangover* was vital to the story as the photographs revealed what had actually happened in Vegas that weekend, thus filling out vital plot information.

Final twists, as with *Some Like It Hot*, are hard to come by. Its tagline, 'Nobody's Perfect' was only a working idea by writer I. A. L. Diamond and Billy Wilder until something better came up. Nothing did.

Comic scenes

The difference between comedy and drama comes at the turning point, which is to say the end of Act One. Usually, the action of the protagonist arouses the forces of antagonism, but at the comedic turning point there is surprise. The world has reacted in a way that the character (and the audience) did not expect. Instead of thrusting drama there is curiosity. Why has the world reacted in this way? What is going to happen now? The character has become victim to accident, mistake, misunderstanding or inattention.[9]

We might call it the tiger in the room. In Howard Hawks' *Bringing up Baby*, Susan Vance so upsets David Huxley that once his car has been trashed, his potential investor lost and his coat tails torn, it seems plausible that Susan is looking after a pet leopard in her bedroom. Likewise, in *The Hangover* we know that guys get up to crazy shenanigans in Vegas, so when we see the trashed

---

[8] Jackie Chan insists on it.
[9] Henri Bergson writes on this in his 1900 essay on Laughter, 'Le Rire. Essai sur la signification du comique' ('Laughter, An Essay on the Meaning of the Comic').

room and hear the chicken, taking a leak with a tiger again seems like part of a new world we might inhabit.

Each scene should move the story forwards, provide character insight or give out valuable information, ideally all three. A comic scene will do this but it is also a 'bit' – a rant, quick-fire banter, slapstick, montage or set piece.

Steve Martin, Eddie Murphy, Jack Black and Vince Vaughn are all known for delivering the **comic rant**. It has to be earned and it must come out of frustration which we have evidence of beforehand. In *Planes, Trains and Automobiles* (Hughes 1987), highly strung businessman Neal Page (Steve Martin) is trying to get home to his family in Chicago for Thanksgiving. Del Griffith (John Candy) is a talkative buffoon who interferes, causing him to lose his luggage, his credit cards and to miss every mode of transport, thus turning a short flight into three-day ordeal. Eventually, Neal blows. We laugh, not only in relief and at the transgression of social norms, but at the comic exaggeration.

Banter is the two-way back and forth cross-talk first seen on screen with Abbot and Costello and was also much in evidence between men and women in screwball comedy. Lemmon and Curtis/Matthau were masters of this (with Neil Simon's words) and contemporary examples include Mike Myers and Eddie Murphy as Shrek and Donkey in the *Shrek* films and *Wedding Crashers* stars Owen Wilson and Vince Vaughn.

Slapstick is covered elsewhere in the book. **Set pieces**, if purely there for the comedy (The *Pink Panther* films or the *Scary Movie* franchise) tend to halt the narrative drive. This is true of other spectacles such as opera, musicals and in action/adventure movies where, in the latter, the chase scene has no function other than the pursuit. The stakes are high. They will either capture or kill the antagonist or he will get away.

In a buddy action comedy, the protagonists might employ the Blake Snyder conceit of the 'Pope in a swimming pool' as characters reel out swathes of exposition while the audience enjoys the action. Set pieces are sustained comic business as with Ben Stiller in *There's Something About Mary*. It wasn't enough to get caught peeping at Mary, he traps his frank and beans in his zipper. Medical attention is sought, but this requires fireman and medics and finally a gurney as 'we have a bleeder'. Each scene tops the last, the Farrelly brothers taking the baton from the *Airplane* team (Abrahams, Zucker).

One aspect of comedy is that it does allow for coincidence and randomness. We will also accept the *deus ex machina* because it is comedy and we understand that normal rules have been bent. The laughs come with coincidence because it violates our expectations. This and random events come out of nowhere. However, too much of this and we lose interest – there is a big difference between the child who says odd things and the child who is odd.

You can also get away with giving the character an enormous amount of pain and suffering so long as you give him hope. You can even add considerable **insult to injury** and we will laugh at the sheer *unfairness* of it all, but in the end you *must* give him the prize. Your protagonist must never lose hope or, if it seems he is, then this must be his dark night of the soul for he is at the cusp of finding his inner and outer resolution. There are few exceptions to this, odd comedies with an anti-structure such as Scorsese's *After Hours*, where Griffin Dunne and Rosanna Arquette play on random coincidence. Life is indeed absurd – but that is not why we go to the movies.

When it comes to pitching, it ought to sound like the best kind of comic story. You tell it scene by scene, getting across a flavour of the physical jokes and the best lines. The twists, turns and reveals are the funniest parts. The humour must be established in the set-up, which is why a neat 'what if?' is so crucial. Once the idea is out there, it makes the punch almost inevitable. It is worthwhile for the writer to spend most of his creative energy on this because the idea must arouse emotion. A strong set-up is a reservoir of comic energy. Once you have set it in motion, a great comic idea will flow by itself and then you can introduce the reverse or inversion, flipping it around. You can step on the laughs for a bigger one at the end as you build each comic scene and set piece. You can time the gags to when the emotion is at its flood, and only when you reach an emotional waterfall do you release it.

Chapter 5
Performative Comedy

Most movie comedy relies on narrative, and much of this book is devoted to understanding how each subgenre is constructed and the tales they tell. Being comedy, there is always the aspect of performance and how overt it should be. Can this be evidenced in the script? Should the script be written for the performance aspect of the movie? Whilst a star comedian will always be looking to put his or her stamp on a role, there are those who perform comedian comedy, those who are subsumed in a comic character and those who do a little of both, sometimes (unwisely) in the same movie.

Slapstick is the province of the pratfall, playing on the sadistic value of physical pain. The name derives from the Italian tradition of *Commedia dell'Arte* where one performer beats the other with two wooden sticks that made a slapping sound. Mack Sennett based his entire career on it; the *Keystone Kops* proved that what is funnier than one person falling over is a dozen of them falling over. In the sound era, the Three Stooges and Abbott and Costello fought to keep the art alive by poking each other in the eye. Slapstick does not have to be exclusively about violence and falling over, but that is its main province, along with a lot of kicking people in the pants. Rising above this, Charlie Chaplin (*The Great Dictator*, *Modern Times*), Buster Keaton (*Sherlock Jnr*, *The General*) and Harold Lloyd (*Safety Last, The Freshman*) had a social message to impart, whereas Abbot and Costello, Laurel and Hardy and the Three Stooges did not.

Although the advent of sound reduced the number of slapstick comedies, its tricks have been used to great effect in Jacques Tati's Monsieur Hulot films, by Mel Brooks, and by Woody Allen in his early comedies *Take the Money and Run*, *Bananas* and *Sleeper*. The Zucker/Abrahams/Zucker films – *Naked Gun* and sequels rely heavily on slapstick, as do their successors the Farrelly brothers (*Dumb and Dumber*), as well as the films *Home Alone*, *Flubber* and *Mousehunt*. Multiple Oscar winner *The Artist* (Hazanavicius 2011) harked back to, and borrowed from, the comedy of the silent movie era.

Chaplin's universal appeal was that of the immigrant experience.[1] He played the stranger in an alien and hostile environment. Slapstick was appropriate to a culture where the important encounters were with physical danger from the mechanized urban or country environments and fantasy methods for avoiding that danger. Many waves of immigrants came from the less urbanized parts of south and Eastern Europe and would have related to this. Also, his brand of comedy did not depend on any local or specific meanings rooted in language. Cinema had yet to establish its ground rules and many of these were technical, the placing of the camera and the edit, many of which are still used today. A director will always read what is written in the script with an eye as to how it is to be played, in effect 'seeing' the script – so you need to write for the eyes as well as the mind.

The grammar of the shot

Due to the static nature of the camera (too heavy to move), early films were made in a single long take. Wherever the camera was placed, the actors had to act using the frame as a proscenium arch. The simple recording of actions was enough for documentary footage but for the more experimental, the new medium tempted its artists to get creative. You could edit, you could tamper with the film, or you could use what was *not* seen in the frame.

Demolition D'un Mur (1895) was the first movie to use reverse photography where, played backwards, a wall seemingly reassembles itself. The next trick was to effect a transition from dream to reality in *Let Me Dream Again* (Smith 1900) and also in the Pathe brothers' *Reve et Realite* (*Dream and Reality*, 1901). In both films a man enjoys a drink and revels with a lady, but on waking (dissolve out and move back into focus), he finds himself in bed with a less attractive one. Trick editing was developed in *Explosions of a Motor Car* (1900) where cinematographer Cecil Hepworth would stop the camera and use a cloud of smoke to substitute a carful of people with wreckage. Later, George Melies was to develop the double exposure and superimposition.

The first use of unconventional framing was in *A Chess Dispute* (Paul 1903), where a chess game becomes a tussle and the pair end up below the frame. The comedy is implied as we see clothes and legs thrown up from the fight below. This is a good comic device, rather like radio comedy, in the sense that the laughter comes from what is imagined rather than what is seen. Implication is stronger than realization. So long as we do not *see* the agonies foisted on a character, physical extremes have few limits.

---

[1] Mark Winokur (1991), *Black is White/White is Black*, cited in King: 169.

Under-cranking the camera was used by Mack Sennett with *The Keystone Kops*, which had the effect of speeding up the action. This, combined with upbeat piano playing in the auditorium, created the idea of panic on fast forward. Rapid editing was another way to increase the pace to a farcical degree. In *Double Cross* (1914) there are edits lasting just three seconds, the equal of today's action movie.

Montage came next. Juxtaposition is a vital feature of comedy. Director/ playwright David Mamet insists that shots in a movie ought to be uninflected, conveying information and intention, but no inherent emotion. Meaning is imparted in juxtaposition. If we see a man with a bunch of flowers, it tells us no more than he is in possession of the flowers. We may assume that he has bought them, that he is a florist or that he wishes to give them to someone but we do not have enough information to go further. If he stands alone with the flowers in a busy street then the implication is that they are for someone. If the next shot is of a woman approaching, we assume that she is to be the recipient. This will be confirmed if he then takes a step towards her.

Juxtaposing can be used in many ways. Putting together unexpected reaction shots is one, and the development of the reverse shot allows for many interpretations. You see one person talking and assume the recipient is listening. In the reverse shot they may be doing something different or inapposite, we might cut to another listener, such as a chimpanzee. Any number of violations of expectation can work in this way. *Dead Men Don't Wear Plaid* has many reverse shots of real actors spliced with Steve Martin's gumshoe.

The reveal (or pull back to reveal) was only possible once the camera could be focused with a long lens or a placed on a dolly so as to be able to pan out. In *Sherlock Jnr* (1924), Buster Keaton provides multiple reveals, and in *Cops* (1922) he appears to be in prison behind bars but is then revealed to be waiting outside the gates of a mansion where his inamorata resides.

The long shot too might impart humour. Nowadays we are used to rapid quick-fire editing and whip cuts, which mimic the rapid movement of our eyes as we take in information. To see one continuous shot is unusual, and we start looking for the comedy or the drama in it. The longer take allowing a slow unfolding of action was a theatrical device loved by Chaplin and Keaton as it allowed them to give a similar frontal performance as they had done on the Music Hall stage. One such is in *One A.M.* (Chaplin 1916) Chaplin's first standalone single reeler where a drunken Chaplin tussles with a fold-up bed for more than five minutes, broken only by thee mid-shots to add emphasis.[2]

---

[2] The critic Bazin praised him for the greater realism afforded by the 'straightforward photographic respect for the unity of space' (Bazin 1967: 46).

In Jacques Tati's *Playtime* and *M. Hulot's Holiday* the frame is kept wide to allow for multiple events to occur simultaneously, thus building a complex comic narrative. He uses the off-screen space too. In *Holiday*, he trips with a heavy suitcase through an open hotel door, then delays the fall, crashing out the back as we *hear* the comic impact. Tati's oeuvre was filled with character detail: not only sight gags, but aural ones too, where the sound track has been carefully manipulated.

A similar protracted comic set up was used to perfection in *Borat,* where Borat exemplified the phrase 'a bull in a china shop' as the horrified owners of a tacky suburban mall gift emporium watch as he proceeds to destroy most of their stock.

The camera can lie too, holding off the reveal as in Laurel and Hardy's Oscar-winning *Musical Box* (1932) in which the pair struggles to deliver a piano up an insurmountable number of steps. Their Sisyphean task is stymied by the belated revelation that they could have driven said piano up by road. This idea of delayed narrative has been used more recently in the work of the Farrelly Brothers. In *American Pie*, seminal fluid is delivered to a cup of beer and left as a comic time bomb, thus literally seeding a gag. A later scene in which Stifler and his girl are making love in the same room is fraught with comic tension. Who will drink the liquid and when? It is no more than the same pay-off in the 1895 comedy *Watering the Garde*ner, simply held off. Planting a gag can be seen in *Dumb and Dumber* with laxative, in *There's Something About Mary* with more rogue sperm, and in *Along Came Polly* with more toilet action.

Gags vs narrative

Early movie comedy was restricted by the inflexibility of the medium. The single reel meant that it had to be all about performance and contained little narrative. As the medium developed, and took on the stage play, narratives began to appear in the work of Chaplin et al. Other comedies of the time[3] were in the main a string of gags based on absurd behaviour and *deus ex machina* conclusions. Some comics made a virtue of breaking the fourth wall, as they would have done on stage, most notably Groucho Marx who acted as narrator and accomplice for the audience. Julius Henry ('Groucho') Marx's moustache and exaggerated eyebrows originated in the early 1920s when, prior to a vaudeville show, he did not have time to apply the pasted-on moustache and so added greasepaint to his fake one and his eyebrows (he did not need spectacles either). The exaggerated walk with one hand on the small of the back and torso

---

[3]The Marx Brothers, *The Crazy Gang*.

bent almost ninety degrees at the waist was a parody of a fad of the 1890s when fashionable upper-class young men would affect a walk with their right hand held fast to the base of their spines. Groucho's schtick was a cynical connection between the cardboard characters of the narrative and the audience, a role he carried through to his later TV performances as host of the TV game show *You Bet Your Life*.

Bob Hope would also question the 'reality' of the plastic medium. In *Road to Morocco* (Butler 1942), Hope turns to the camera as they are freed from being trussed up and asks, 'How did we get loose with our hands tied and everything?' Bing Crosby croons 'If we told anybody, they'd never believe it.'

The first feature length comedy was *Tilly's Punctured Romance* (Sennett 1914), in which Chaplin, a con artist, attempts to get the savings and inheritance of a country girl (Marie Dressler). This demanded a narrative, playing to a middle-class audience for profit on an industrial scale.[4] 'The mode that governs this type of comedy is described as "performative" or "presentational" based on a performance played directly out to the audience whose presence is openly acknowledged' (*Film Comedy*, King 2002).

Slapstick came to be seen as a lower cultural form based on crude and violent behaviour. For producers and directors there was a trade-off between respectable narrative-led drama and these crude spectacular attractions. Sennett's Keystone Company was seen as sideshow, a support act, but when Lloyd, Keaton and Chaplin began to move to features it legitimized them. Keaton even wrote about the abandonment of 'impossible or cartoon gags.' In the 1920s, romantic comedy began to displace slapstick.

Frank Capra, later to become a master of narrative screwball comedy, had evolved as a joke writer for Mack Sennett. 'It was not unusual to reverse the general order of story preparation and work out plots to embody a series of gags which had been worked on independently' (*The Film Comedy Reader*, Capra [1927] 2001).

Gag-centered comedies never died out, and enjoyed a resurgence in the 1960s with *It's a Mad, Mad, Mad, Mad World* (Kramer 1963), *The Great Race* (Edwards 1965), *Those Magnificent Men in Their Flying Machines* (Annakin 1965), *Casino Royale* (Various 1967) *and Monte Carlo Or Bust* (Annakin and Itzkovitch 1969), which contained huge set pieces and musical numbers in an attempt to stall the falling audience numbers. They reappeared with the *Scary/Epic/Date/Teen Movie* parodies of the last decade, in a similar response to technological innovation, this time streaming and free download. These spoofs are highly performative.

---

[4] The four-reel narrative framework was begun by Chaplin in *Shoulder Arms* (1918), then developed further in *The Pilgrim* (1923). *Duck Soup* was a narrative comedy undermined by slapstick. There is more narrative in *A Night at the Opera* (1935).

Comedian comedy

Comedian comedy is based on the immediacy of the star performance. In short, it is a showcase for his talents. A fictional universe is built around the comedian and plot is an excuse for the main attraction. They are playing themselves or a version of their comic persona and are entirely goal driven. Often there is a romantic subplot but the main plot will be all cause and effect. *All of Me, The Mask, Good Morning Vietnam* and *Coming To America* are all comedian movies.

'The operative modality is not just that of comic inconsequentiality' (King 2002: 33). They also play on the needs of vulnerable children to seek the emotional allegiance of the viewer. In *Liar, Liar*, Fletcher Reede is already an eccentric. In *Mrs Doubtfire*, Hillard is a voiceover artist who inserts his own improvisation into animated cartoons which impacts on his kids. Both *Parenthood* and *Grown Ups* contrast the adult with unruly children who must be pacified. This is not new. In *The Kid* (Chaplin 1921), the boy (Jackie Coogan) could be used as foil, for pathos, as accomplice or as whipping boy.

Children were more hardy then, un-cosseted or bred with a sense of entitlement, but as the Silent Age dwindled, the abuse of children (exclusively boys – girls were permitted to be trussed to a railway line) was reduced to a kick in the pants or slap around the head. In today's climate the idea of punishing a child on screen is unthinkable. Today, childhood is sacrosanct unless it is other children doing it to them as with Nelson and his bullies in *The Simpsons*. In animation, children are always smarter than adults. In *Home Alone* (Columbus 1990) eight-year-old Kevin outwits a trio of burglars who suffer horrendous slapstick injuries: it could never be the other way round no matter how much one might desire it.

In a comedian comedy, the choice of shot is often a mid-shot where the star partially faces the viewer but is still acting within the diegetic universe. The effect is to emphasize the virtuoso skills of the performer. Like a musical, which makes no bones about breaking the fictional frame to burst into song, we accept the artifice.

There are many examples of comedian comedy worldwide, including France (Tati's Monsieur Hulot), Italy (Roberto Benigni in *Johnny Stecchino* [1991]), Mexico (Cantinflas, who created a nonsense language), Egypt (Adel Imam), Iran (Alireza Khamesh), Japan (Kiyoshi Atsumi's wandering peasant Tora San) and China (Stephen Chow playing the bumpkin who obtains success in the city). In each case, the comic prevails against all odds through luck, innocence, guile or intervention. Chaplin's *Little Tramp* will win out. Keaton's blithe indifference will carry him through (*The General* 1927) and Bob Hope will always bluff it out. In The UK, George Formby and Norman Wisdom played the 'little man' beset by society. In the US, Jerry Lewis[5] predated Steve Martin and Jim Carrey, but today's comedians tread a path between broad comedian roles, cameo comic parts and characters that are fully integrated in the narrative. Ben Stiller is wholly performative in *Zoolander*, but not in *Meet the Parents*. He is full on in *Dodgeball,* but the schlemiel in *Along Came Polly*. Paul Rudd and Jason Segal have alternated romantic lead and comic support roles, and Will Ferrell and Adam Sandler have tried this with varying degrees of success.

Does one write for the comedian? In essence the material makes the choice. If you are writing spoof or parody then by its nature you are taking off a pre-existing form and are therefore writing sketches. If your subgenre is gross-out, you are looking for extremes of physical discomfort in which to place your character, thus overriding narrative. Comic set pieces may also dominate in a high-concept comedy, but they ought to come out of a character piece. The writer's aim is an integrated character and story, but what the director and star comedian choose to do with the material is out of the writer's hands.

---

[5] In Lewis' *The Bell Boy* (1960), narrative was displaced in favour of extended comic business. There was even a warning by the head of production, who admitted that there was no story and no plot. *Casino Royale* (1967) would have benefited from the same.

Chapter 6
Narrative Comedy

The love impulse in men very frequently reveals itself in terms of conflict.
SUSAN VANCE, *BRINGING UP BABY* (1934)

Screwball

Intolerable Cruelty. My Man Godfrey. The Awful Truth. Bringing Up Baby. It Happened One Night. How To Lose a Guy in 10 Days. The Palm Beach Story. Raising Arizona. His Girl Friday. The Lady Eve. The Seven Year Itch.

Screwball comedy is an American genre, which arrived after the advent of talkies, ran approximately between 1932 and 1944 and was characterized by rapid-fire dialogue, frenetic pacing, smart one-liners, sublimated sexuality and cross-dressing. Uninterrupted speeches were rare and verbosity was used to cover the sound of the camera machinery. It featured for the first time women unafraid to flaunt their sexuality and leading men who were content to be the butt of the joke (Clark Gable, Cary Grant). These women were equal in wit, energy and resourcefulness to their male partners. Screwball has been paid homage to in more recent movies such as *When Harry Met Sally, A Fish Called Wanda* and *Intolerable Cruelty*.

The progenitor, *It Happened One Night* (1934), starred Clark Gable and Claudette Colbert, combined a road movie with issues of class conflict and mistaken identity, garnering five Oscars for Best Picture, Director, Actor, Actress and Screenplay.[1] The term 'screwball' has been traced to a Paramount studios

---

[1] A feat unmatched by any comedy until *As Good As It Gets*.

publicist working on *My Man Godfrey* (1936) using a baseball term for[2] 'an unconventional pitch that moves in the opposite way to a conventional curve ball' (McCabe 2005). Its principal directors were William Wyler, Gregory La Cava, Leo McCarey, Howard Hawks, Frank Capra, Ernst Lubitsch and Preston Sturges, with writers Ben Hecht, Charles MacArthur, Billy Wilder, Sturges and Robert Riskin. Comedy fans should familiarize themselves with their work.

During the Great Depression there was a demand for films with a strong social class critique and escapist themes, such as the minor misdeeds of the elegant rich. The screwball format arose largely as a result of the major film studios' desire to avoid censorship. As such, they were able to incorporate adult risqué elements, such as pre-marital sex and adultery into their plots, which were a more realistic and satirical type of entertainment than the musical. Later, audiences wearied of the genre, 'concerned as it was with the misadventures of ditzy socialites and the idle rich' (McCabe 2005). Hawks' *Bringing Up Baby*, now seen as a classic, received a lukewarm response at the box office.

There had been a cultural shift in America. Divorce had doubled by 1910 and a new conservatism had evolved with a move toward marriage based on loving companionship as opposed to arranged ones. The 1920s heralded sophisticated comedies about infidelity among married couples or marital farces: there were even comedies of remarriage such as *Bluebeard's Eighth Wife* (Wood 1923) and *The Awful Truth* (Powell 1925). These pictures offered a kind of cultural escape valve: a safe battleground in which to explore serious issues like class in a non-threatening framework. In screwball, the upper class tended to be shown as idle and pampered and having difficulty in getting around in the real world, as with the heiress Ellie Andrews in *It Happened One Night* or movie director John Sullivan in *Sullivan's Travels*. Paradoxically, lower-class people attempting to pass themselves off as upper class were able to do so with relative ease (*The Lady Eve*, *My Man Godfrey*).

The stylistic device of fast-talking, witty repartee (*His Girl Friday*) can also be found in other Hollywood cycles such as the gangster film. It has links with theatrical farce and elements can be traced back to stage plays such as Shakespeare's *Much Ado About Nothing, As You Like It* and *A Midsummer Night's Dream*, as well as Oscar Wilde's *The Importance of Being Earnest*. Other comedy genres associated with screwball are its successors, romcom, bedroom farce and sitcom.

Plots ranged from 'road movie' to 'Cinderella' often involving mistaken identity or circumstances in which the characters tried to keep some important fact a secret. Sometimes they featured male characters cross-dressing, further

---

[2]A pitcher for the New York Giants developed a throw that struck out Babe Ruth.

contributing to the misunderstandings (*I Was A Male War Bride, Some Like It Hot*) and a central romance in which a mismatched couple are hostile to one other at first, but overcome their differences in amusing ways that lead to romance (a romantic comedy staple). Often this mismatch came about because the man was further down the economic scale than the woman. Sometimes, the women had planned the romantic union at the outset, as in *Bringing Up Baby*, where Katherine Hepburn announces, 'He's the man I'm going to marry, he doesn't know it, but I am.' They also often turn on an interlude in the state of Connecticut[3] as seen in *Bringing Up Baby, The Lady Eve and The Awful Truth*. Perhaps producers owned properties there.

Film critic Andrew Sarris defined the screwball comedy as 'a sex comedy without the sex' (Sarris 1996). When the Hays Production Code was adopted in 1934, there were a great many restrictions on what you could and could not show or imply on screen (see Appendix 1). They were nevertheless comedies about sex and romance. A subgenre was the comedy of remarriage, in which characters divorced and then remarried one another (*The Awful Truth, The Philadelphia Story*) although in many cases the divorce proved to be a mistake.[4] Courtship, as seen in screwball, was a time of ordeal but was not resolved in marriage, unlike in romantic comedy. Marriage was seen as a condition of discord, something of a throwback to the genteel, respectable world of middle-class sobriety. The screen portrayal of the downtrodden husband had debuted way back in 1912 with comedy double act (John) Bunny and (Flora) Finch, where Bunny played the henpecked husband and Finch his shrewish wife. It had become a pervasive cliché.

Within a month of the release of *It Happened One Night*, audiences were flocking. With a key scene set on a bus, the ailing *Greyhound Bus Company* was brought back from near bankruptcy. Conversely, the makers of men's undershirts lost a lot of business when Clark Gable went bare-chested under his shirt, scaring previously fulsome and feisty Colbert to her side of the 'Wall of Jericho' – a blanket hung between their beds so as to avoid any impropriety. The eagle-eyed viewer will note a clever production trick that indicates the turning point of Act One. As the lights go out, Peter Warne (Gable) keeps talking – from the heart now, as he cannot be seen. All we see are her eyes and they *sparkle*. Practically, all that was done was to move a light behind the camera but the moment conveys all – her first moment of thawing toward him.

The Production Code was established in the same year, reflecting the growing desire of the clergy to censor and control the unhealthy influence of

---

[3] As noted by philosopher Stanley Cavell in *Pursuits of Happiness*.
[4] For the effect of *It Happened One Night,* see Kay Young (1934), 'Hollywood 1934: Inventing Romantic Comedy': 262–3.

movies. There were big fines if films were released without the Code's stamp of approval and actresses Mae West, Jean Harlow and Marlene Dietrich were all forced underground. Brassy women and platinum blondes came to be portrayed as working women or independent heiresses. If Chaplin, Keaton and Lloyd saw the male comic as victimized in an indifferent malevolent world, the talking comedy had the lovers do it with words. They bickered and fought and the 'talkie' was just that, a film about talking. Screwball delighted in the intimacy of speech, a trope used to the fore in *Annie Hall* and *When Harry Met Sally*. It also moved on to talk of marriage, but only in its exploration of the aspect of play (Spencer Tracy/Katherine Hepburn movies, most notably *Adam's Rib*). The state of marriage in these comedies is one without financial worry or children. It is state of privilege with no responsibility – a fantasy.[5]

Modern screwball tends to mean warring partners and a loopy coincidence-based plotting. The Coen brothers are huge fans of early screwball and its influence can be seen in *Raising Arizona, The Hudsucker Proxy* and *Intolerable Cruelty*. Post screwball, this style of writing mainly decamped to TV, producing a golden age for the American sitcom in *The Jack Benny Program*, Jackie Gleason's *The Honeymooners* and Lucille Ball's *I Love Lucy*. Modern sitcom uses some of the tropes of this golden age and the comedy writer can learn much in terms of pacing, rhythm and characterization from screwball movies.

Romantic comedy

Four Weddings and A Funeral. Sabrina. The Apartment. Sleepless in Seattle. As Good As It Gets. When Harry Met Sally. You've Got Mail. Bridget Jones's Diary. Pillow Talk. Breakfast at Tiffany's. What's Up, Doc? The Shop Around The Corner. Annie Hall.

In romcom, there are mistaken or unrevealed identities, there is reconciliation and transformation and real world issues are frittered away by romantic love. To write romantic comedy you must believe in the primacy of love. You must imbue the work with the certainty that love conquers all and that it will convert the most ardent cynic into a romantic. This is the comic dimension of whimsy where the worst physical mishap is a beating but the emotional knocks are far greater. For this there is the eternal reward and that is finding your soul mate, as in *The Wedding Crashers*.

---

[5]Fred Astaire tells Ginger Rodgers in *Top Hat*, 'You see, every once in a while I find myself dancing'.

If the Old Comedy of Aristophanes was about satire and political criticism of the state, then the New Comedy of Menander was about marriage,[6] or at least the union of younger couples against opposition by an older generation. It was a social theme that made reconciliation possible and set in motion the happy ending of marriage, festival, feast or dance, which become the *Hollywood Fantasy Model*. In the HFM, the division of class and power are secondary to common humanity. It is magical escapist entertainment and wins a global audience.

The comedy of romantic attraction has been a motivator for comic action from the advent of sound. It began as a device rather than being explored in its own right. Originally, female roles would simply be as 'The Girl'. Edna Purviance filled this role for Chaplin, being an abstract, idealized figure secondary to the male. 'Romance' is a more integrated form of comedy involving narrative as the primary function of character and relationship.[7] The fact we know they will end up in each other's arms offers relief. This outcome is never in doubt and audience expectations would be frustrated if this was not the result, tipping the story out of genre and over into the complexities of drama. Instead, we can sit back and enjoy the accumulation of intervening obstacles and complications and be sure of the result. In romantic comedy this may be shown as a mixture of performative routines such as those of Sally Albright in *When Harry Met Sally*, Bill Murray in *Groundhog Day* or Seth Rogen in *Forgetting Sarah* Marshall and the adversarial roles of the lovers.

Placing the lovers as adversaries highlights the fact that they are the embodiment of different qualities sought by the participants. Each represents what the other needs most, thus the antagonist becomes the partner. There is a strong will they/won't they? (get together) attraction. They are at once repulsed (this person reflects what I so sorely need, but I have gotten along without it up until now) and attracted (they will complete me, but I am scared to change and blossom).

This opposition is shallow however, as with Susan and David in *Bringing Up Baby*.[8] David Huxley, tightly wound in his lab coat and cracking jokes about putting dinosaur bones 'in the tail' is waiting to be freed from his stern fiancée who does not wish to see any 'romantic entanglements' get in the way of his work. Tom Hanks as Joe Fox in *You've Got Mail* is far too nice to be an evil businessman for a rival bookshop (aggressive takeovers not usually being

---

[6] King: 54. Northrop Frye.

[7] 'The romance is foregrounded and treated lightly but not as melodrama. There will almost always be a happy ending'.

[8] Or prime minister (David) and cleaner (Natalie) in *Love Actually*, or Peter Warne and Ellie Andrews in *It Happened One Night*.

stalled by love). Antagonists Hugh Grant and Colin Firth in *Bridget Jones' Diary* have a very English, and somewhat pathetic, coming to blows.

In today's movies the heroine expects equality with men, as was true in screwball times. The attainment of marriage has ceased to be the goal. The state of marriage in romantic comedy is still accepted as an institution but it will do to end on the kiss or the consummation. Emotion is based on sexual attraction rather than a feeling that a man is the total fulfilment of a woman's social and economic needs. It has been a long road, however, as the Code had a strong effect on movies and the 1950s put feminism back in the box as far as the silver screen went. It wasn't until a decade later that the roles of women onscreen began to shift. Once the Code began to wane (with the societal changes of the 1960s) there was more of an open discourse on sex and sexuality in such films as *Pillow Talk* (Gordon 1959) *Sex and the Single Girl* (Quine 1964) and later, *Bob and Ted and Carol and Alice* (Mazursky 1969), the latter being a sex comedy.

Romcom had always been based on patriarchal and heterosexual ideologies, but with renewed assertions of feminism, gay rights and gender discourse, by the late 1980s it looked like it was becoming impossible to do anymore. The heart, though, will always find a way, and the ideal of seeing two rich, white people fall in love is very much in evidence today and other countries have adopted the Hollywood Fantasy Model. These Cinderella stories involve rags to riches (*Pretty Woman*) and have roots in many cultures. It is almost a monomyth. The girl is born of noble parentage or has some unrecognized qualities of inner beauty that must come out.[9] Her life is one of toil in a backbreaking job in publishing or as an intern in the media. There are forces which keep her there, some caused by herself. Along comes a suitable character but she must go on the journey of self-discovery in order that he see and pursue her for her hidden beauty. There have been minor modifications. Woody Allen's romances were postmodern and ironic. In both *Annie Hall* and *Manhattan* the central characters did NOT get the girl. The former is a romcom in reverse and is remarkably honest in its assertion that he gets the girl in the play because it never turns out like that in real life. This meta-fictional comment and the devices he employs (voiceover, direct address, tweaking of time and time scales) shift this toward performative comedy. The latter is more of an ensemble piece, being Allen's first foray into drama with comedy.

Nora Ephron's *When Harry Met Sally* took as its premise the romcom concept that men and women cannot be friends (without sex getting in the way) until they fall in love, and had antagonists Sally Albright and Harry Burns fight it out over several years. This conceit was seen again in *Groundhog Day*, *50 First*

---

[9]Or she's just really, really attractive.

Dates and *One Day*, all of which goes to prove that fate and kismet are constant tropes and that there isn't much new in movies.

In *Four Weddings and A Funeral*, the protagonists empathically did not want to get married, but ended up together forever and that was what counted more. In *My Best Friend's Wedding* (1997), friendship was offered as a rival source of emotional bonding. The *Sex and the City* crew took up the idea of the importance of female friendship over sex or inappropriate love. In *Bridesmaids* (Feig 2011), female jealousy rose once more but all came right in the end. In modern romcom, so long as there is love and a feast at the conclusion then you can stray all you like.

Beware of trying to tinker with the formula. *Forget Paris* (Crystal 1995) featured a couple, Mickey (Billy Crystal) and Ellen (Debra Winger) who meet in Paris and fall in love. However, on their return to reality they find they cannot forget the affair (echoes of Richard Linklater's *Before Sunrise, Sunset* and *Midnight* trilogy), and reunite in order to marry. They do not live happily ever after, dealing with failed conception, antagonistic relatives and difficult career choices. The story is told in flashback, starring and directed by Billy Crystal. However, where *When Harry Met Sally* succeeded in portraying a romantic and a cynic coming to terms with one another and falling deeply in love, *Paris's* theme of keeping the romance alive is not compatible with romcom. While it adopted some of the tropes (and was perhaps intended to be his *Annie Hall*) you cannot go against the natural conclusion of the kiss or the betrothal – the happy-ever-after myth.

These are urban tales, barring the odd excursion back to the sticks (*Sweet Home Alabama*). They are set in a buzzing urban metropolis, almost always New York or its simulacra, San Francisco or London. As with the sitcom *Friends*, the singletons will live in impossible apartments and will have rich and or powerful relatives. They are slumming it (echoes of the heiresses in screwball) as they wait for the right guy or girl to come along. The man will work in business, Wall St, a top law firm, medicine, advertising, architecture (always architecture), auctioneering or publishing. Artistic (poor) men, painters, writers, musicians and the like will never win the girl, being relegated to unsuitable bad boy roles and nemeses, such as Aldous Snow. She in turn will be struggling with a job to which she is unsuited. Somehow she has obtained a lowly job in publishing (always publishing), the media, the arts, fashion or real estate where she dwells, the office Cinderella. Alternatively she may be on a break, waitressing or caring or working with animals or for charity whilst she 'finds out what to do with her life'. These aspirational people are much better than you or I. Equally as flawed, just a lot more beautiful.

The romantic calendar is framed in dates that are significant for outpourings of sentiment such as Christmas, (the holidays) New Year or Valentine's Day

– gathering dates when love is in abundance and they can be lonely and alone and then later succeed in finding love and communal acceptance.

Romcom, because of its longevity as a genre, allows for an exploration of its clichés even within a movie. *Sliding Doors* (Howitt 1998) has couple Helen (Gwyneth Paltrow) and James (John Hannah) almost kiss, but allows them to remark on how this ought to be the movie kiss moment and therefore they shouldn't. What were once Kodak moments are now movie moments (or Smartphone, YouTube or Vine moments). Of course they later do consummate the kiss, thus fulfilling the expectation of genre.

Chasing Amy is different (Smith 1997). Here, the love object Alyssa is gay, or at least bisexual. She sleeps with the lead (Ben Affleck) and the movie twists into a blend of bromance, comedy and drama. The guy does not get the girl and the idea of pining over a loved one (Amy) is resolved in mournful looks at Comic Con. The fine line between romcom and romance, which allows for loss and emotional tragedy, is crossed. It is inviolate that romantic comedy concerns a mismatched couple who need to figure out that they were made for each other, the plot being a map of all the possible ways of keeping them apart via internal or external sources.

The comedy is the icing on the cake. It is a romance with comedy rather than a comedy with romance, as many other comic genres have a romance in them. In those genres the romance is inferior to the concept as the comedy comes first: the characters illustrate a high concept and populate an altered comedic universe where anything can and probably will happen. In these we have buffoons, idiot savants, morons and shysters, all of who may *earn* our respect and sympathies by the end. In romantic comedy, we must care about our characters from the outset. That is not to say that they aren't flawed but we must relate intimately to them. To enable us to laugh we require identification. Whether it's cute uptight Sally Albright or foot-in-mouth Bridget Jones,[10] we identify. We may not be able to carry out a heist or go shoot up the hood, but we can all be terrible in love and in matters of the heart. This is vital to how the comedy plays out. If the lead characters were mere figures of fun, we would not go with them on the journey.

Today's leading actresses have branded definable character roles for romcom, with Julia Roberts as the glass princess, Reece Witherspoon or Jennifer Aniston as the girl next door, Sandra Bullock plays uptight and prickly and Cameron Diaz cute but ditzy, although she and Drew Barrymore also play tomboy roles. Their actual dramatic range is wider than this but these are templates, shorthand for

---

[10]Or equally with the men – neurotic, anxious Woody Allen, nebbish, gauche Ben Stiller in *There's Something About Mary* bumbling Hugh Grant or latterly, Simon Pegg in *Man Up* (2015).

the mass audience. There is always the next year's blonde or homecoming queen and newer actresses are always breaking through, so lately we have Emily Blunt, Rachel McAdams, Isla Fisher, Mila Kunis and Lake Bell, to name but five.

Clearly defined roles are also true for the men, ever since Cary Grant turned from comic klutz into a suave leading man. Gregory (John Gordon Sinclair) in *Gregory's Girl* walks this line carefully. He's young, gauche, acned, gawky, desperate and Scottish. What's not to love? As soon as he sees Dorothy (Dee Hepburn), who is young, beautiful and better at football, he willingly gives up his position as centre forward for her and we love him for it. Many do not go for Woody Allen's nebbish persona, but they do want to discover how brains might win a shiksa goddess such as Diane Keaton or Frank Sinatra's ex-wife, Mia Farrow. Hugh Grant is the embodiment of the posh, tongue-tied Englishman, the inverse of his namesake, the urbane Cary.

Romantic comedy characters must have just enough flaws to keep them eligible. They must be pitied but not pitiful. They are stymied by loss, fear, inactivity or social exclusion, as in the *40-Year-Old Virgin* (Apatow 2005). Either they cannot find love or have chosen the wrong love object. Promiscuity has in the past always been punished and this is still the case, as in the postmodern and knowing *Friends with Benefits* (Gluck 2011), where, in trying to avoid the clichés of Hollywood romantic comedies, Dylan Harper (Justin Timberlake) and Jamie Rellis (Mila Kunis) discover that adding sex to their friendship only leads to complications. They follow the curve that sex must ultimately become subservient to love and end up in a passionate, loving kiss.

Being about to marry or married to the wrong guy is an oft-used device to keep the couple apart. Carrie (Andie MacDowell) marries Hamish in *Four Weddings*. In *10* (Edwards 1979), Dudley Moore falls for Bo Derek only to find out that it is her wedding night. Maid of Honour Claire (Rachel McAdams) in *Wedding Crashers* is betrothed to Sack (Bradley Cooper) and Maggie Carpenter (Julia Roberts) has abandoned three men at the altar in *The Runaway Bride* (Marshall 1999). This not only puts a price on them and makes them desired but also takes them off the market or adds a ticking clock for anyone interested in a last minute auction, as the wedding looms.[11]

Incomplete people

The fundamental difference between romantic comedy and other genres is we are laughing *with* the protagonists and not *at* them. This requires empathy

---

[11] Another might be being trapped in Time, as in *Groundhog Day* or *About Time* (Curtis 2013).

with the characters, an emotional engagement that is not a prerequisite of other kinds of comedies, therefore romantic comedy is character writing and (aside from some external contrivances) the action and plots come from these flawed characters.

Unlike early screwball, where the characters were secure in their social standing, they attempt to be urbane, self-aware, faithful, sober and fully-functioning adult humans, but are slightly less. The romantic comedy is an examination of those parts, asking: why do fools all in love? How is it that love conquers all? Is there such as thing as Fate? Is there The One?

Romantic comedy is optimistic. It suggests that we need another to complete us, and that if we watch these movies we too will learn how to get a partner who will love us properly and forever. The comedy comes in the gap between image and reality, between hope and expectation and between fear and commitment. The comedy is that of the klutziness, worry and general foolish actions we make when faced with our object of desire. It is about vulnerability.

Pessimism can destroy its fabric. A movie that played with the form, *Down with Love* (Reed 2003) was a pastiche and homage to 1960s romantic sex comedies. It concerned a feminist (Renee Zellweger) who had written the eponymous book of the title, which purported to free women from love and to teach them to enjoy sex without commitment. Following her rules would help to give women a boost in the workplace and the world in general. She became entangled with a lothario (Ewan McGregor), there were deceptions and hidden identities as the theme of love vs sex was explored but ultimately a middle ground was agreed upon; for him, 'somewhere between a blonde and a brunette' for her, acceptance (or capitulation) as she dyed her hair red.

How To Lose a Guy in 10 Days (Petrie 2003) also plays with the anti-love motto but, as ever, the warring couple Andie (Kate Hudson) and Ben (Matthew McConaughey) revert to type. It is impossible to make a romantic comedy about the end of love. *The Wars of The Roses* is a dark satire about divorce. *Me, You and Everyone We Know* (July 2005) is a quirky ensemble comedy drama. *Eternal Sunshine of the Spotless Mind* is a comedy drama about the memory of love and the non-linear narrative, *500 Days of Summer* (Webb 2009) is a coming-of-age movie where Tom breaks up with Summer, only to meet a girl named Autumn, the lesson being the same as in *Gregory's Girl*, that you must learn to love, and that love will find you someone, even if it isn't the one you set out for.

'Getting over love' is a recent development in romantic comedy and this has been played out in *Forgetting Sarah Marshall* and *The Inbetweeners Movie*, but in general, because romantic comedy deals with hope, it can only deal with minor hopes dashed and with temporary break-up. The real drama of heart-break is often avoided.

The narrative thrust of the story is propelled by desire, failure, obsession, doubt, incompetence and hope. The actions of the protagonists will result in embarrassment, shame or slapstick. The dialogue will be based on wit, where one person is funny, and banter, where two people bounce off one another. The subtext of romantic comedy is always ironic because we know more than they do. We know that they are well suited and no matter what they say or do, they will inexorably be drawn together.

In romantic comedy people rarely tell jokes unless it's a particular flaw of their persona. Woody Allen does, and he puts one-liners into the mouths of his characters, as did Neil Simon (*The Odd Couple, Barefoot in the Park*). This theatrical wit derives from vaudeville. The wisecrack, the snappy retort and the withering put down is an American, Jewish style of comedy exemplified in the films of Groucho Marx. However, in romantic comedy the protagonists are fundamentally not all that funny. The comedy comes out of the situations and the minor characters surrounding them. We are given a superior position as they are kept in the dark.

Interruptions are crucial to romantic comedy. The moment the protagonists achieve catharsis or epiphany and want to tell each other about their feelings, events, objects or people will get in their way (e.g. *Notting Hill*) so as they cannot tell one another the truth. They must be kept in the dark about their true natures and in this sense *Groundhog Day* and *Lost in Translation* are similar stories, differing only in tone. Romantic comedy is homogenous and white. Interracial relationships have so far been thin on the ground, with *Romauld et Juliet* (*Mama There's a Man in Your Bed*, Serreau 1989) being one sole (French) exception.

Romcom sees singledom as a disease that must be eradicated and treats outsiders, be they gay, ugly or obese, with disdain. There is rarely a death in romcom unless it is unbearably poignant, as in *Four Weddings*, where it is used to shock the leads out of their torpor. Andy McDowell's character is as deluded in her way as Hugh Grant is in his. The comedy is about the betrayals and minor disappointments of being in and yearning for love, focusing on the behaviour of the putative lovers. Both are blind to the fact that they are or will soon be in love with one another. They are deluding themselves in one of the following ways:

- Fear commitment (*Four Weddings and A Funeral, Friends with Benefits*);
- Desire impossible beauty (*10, Weird Science, The Sure Thing*);
- Too self-obsessed to see true beauty or love (*Forgetting Sarah Marshall*);
- Too intransigent to accept change (*When Harry Met Sally, Wedding Crashers*).

The comic character

The character is driven by a blind desire. This desire is not always for the love object as the need can be to NOT commit or to remain in inertia for fear of being hurt, but it is usually for the partner or the idea of love. Whereas the dramatic character can step back and be aware of his situation, the comic one cannot. He lives in the here and now and has no real idea of his flaws. Even if he does have some inkling of them, as in the films of Woody Allen, he is still unable to address a solution. Inspector Clouseau was obsessed with being the world's best detective. The comedy arose from the reality that he wasn't. Once a comic character gets what he wants then the comedy is over, hence the clichéd running scene. He has understood and acknowledged his flaw and there is no more comedy to be had.

In *Groundhog Day*, it is not until Phil Connors acts with altruism that things start to change. Once he does something solely for Rita (and the townsfolk of Punxatawny), he is redeemed and his life begins to move forwards once more. In *Wedding Crashers*, John Beckwith (Owen Wilson) faces up to the fallacy of his dogma, as represented by mentor Will Ferrell, nullifies it and then moves toward love object Claire. In *Gregory's Girl*, Gregory is obsessed with Dorothy and does anything to win a date with her. However the obsession is misguided, because he is infatuated with being in love, so when he fails to win her and is offered a more realistic alternative in Susan (Claire Grogan) the infatuation evaporates in the Scottish mist.

In a comedy with two equal protagonists, it is usually the woman's story, but a rough rule of thumb, as in Greek comedy, is the first person on stage is the protagonist, the second the antagonist.

Opposites attract

Often the protagonists are the illustration of opposing points of view and are almost two halves of the same character, the romantic and the cynic, the practical and the impulsive, the conventional and the rebellious. That opposites attract is a conceit which romantic comedy plays up to, but the couple are not diametric opposites but compatible parts of the same person. They need one another to make a whole. If one is ditzy, the other will be organized, if one profligate, the other parsimonious, if one is shy, the other will be gregarious – homogeny is the goal. Many relationships contain an introvert and an extrovert and whilst it is true that the marriage of similarity (extrovert-extrovert celebrity marriages often break up) is difficult to manage, difference is important. In *Annie Hall*, Jew and Gentile attempt a modern relationship but ultimately fail because their cultures are too different. A decade later, Harry is a cynic, Sally a romantic. Both end up in the middle where love flourishes.

In *Bridget Jones's Diary* (Maguire 2001), Bridget is desperate, both Mark Darcy and Daniel Cleaver are easy in their skins, confident and powerful. Does she get the right one? She is equally wimpish, yet possesses an inner strength, whereas Cleaver is amoral. In *Four Weddings*, Carrie (McDowell) is more liberated and sexually active than Grant, but they are a dovetailing pair, as both are portrayed as outsiders. Contrast this with *Notting Hill*, where Anna Scott (Julia Roberts) and William Thacker (Hugh Grant) find true love at the end, but are fundamentally different people. The question – can a famous movie star fall for the man in the street? – is superb high-concept so long as that street is Hollywood Boulevard or London, W11, but would it have lasted?

Romantic comedy plots

1. Not being who you truly are: this is the comedy of pretension on an emotive level. The character is pretending to be something that is alien to his or her true nature. If we pretend, we will get found out. Before that happens, our pretension is undermined. What is required is a partner who does not accept us at face value and who relentlessly undermines the façade. This can be done through wit, insult or slapstick.

2. The attraction of chaos. Love equals the loss of power and the relinquishing of control. We are all scared of this, but the single person who has decided not to let love in is vulnerable to attack. Contrast a desperate person with one who is certain and there will be fireworks. Again there is the undermining of the status quo. One partner says they need no one and the other goes all out to prove that this is a false position.

3. The fear of commitment. We are conditioned to believe that out there is a Mr or Mrs Right for all of us. The truth is that there are many possible and potential Mr or Mrs Rights and today's method of trawling through Tinder or Match.com proves that the search might be endless. Love means having to compromise, but romcoms suggest that THIS is the one. It says that we will marry within our class and close-knit work or social group. The comedy comes out of prevarication and there are rarely more than two options.

4. The familial desire to ensure your children mate like for like. As long as they don't and keep choosing inappropriate partners, the more fun you can have with authority figures (e.g. *Meet the Parents*). In modern romantic comedy the need

for marriage has in some cases been supplanted by the desire to bond or to have children and to ensure their safety with a suitable provider.

Echo couples and stock characters

There is often an echo couple or chorus, who are a pair of puppets who ape the main protagonists relationship. Bruno Kirby and Carrie Fisher *in When Harry Met Sally* are a couple who get together as mutual best friends of the pair but end up bickering over a wagon wheel table. The template is *Some Like it Hot* (Wilder 1959) where Joe (Tony Curtis) is the lead as he pursues Sugar Kane (Marilyn Monroe). Jerry (Jack Lemmon) as Daphne is one half of the echo couple with much-married millionaire Osgood Fielding III (Joe E Brown). *The Hangover* and *Bridesmaids* are full of them. The friends of the couple (almost the entire supporting cast of *Four Weddings* or *Notting Hill*) can be silly, flawed, sluttish and arrogant and it is often these traits that define them. The romcom cast often consists of variations on the following.

The male best friend who is inept in love; lustful, old, settled or cynical. He may be a lothario or go the opposite direction and be a geek, wimp or overweight. His character is usually far too talkative or plain weird (Rhys Ifans in *Notting Hill*) and his advice is always wrong, being entirely in his own interest and opposed to love.

The girls' best female friend will be either overweight or yo-yo dieting, leading to easy dieting or fat gags. She may be older and married, giving rise to jokes about male potency, or sluttish, in which the angle is male failings (they're all the same), lesbian (they are scum) or may be her sister, thus jokes about the female protagonist's useless love life. Common too in urban romantic comedy is the **gay male best friend**, allowing for camp jokes about heterosexuality, fashion or interior design. Gay men are invariably portrayed as stylish and cultured and never misogynist or promiscuous.

Disapproving parents or authority figures (*Romeo and Juliet*). This can also be workmates (*The 40-Year-Old Virgin*). Any authority figures in comedy be they police, parents or teachers represent maturity and stuffy normalcy. They have 'never been in love': nowadays the reverse is true, where the parents are more liberated than the offspring. Whereas *Meet the Parents* (Roach 2000) was true of the former trope, *Meet the Fockers* is true of the latter, they being a product of the Baby Boomer generation.

Background characters. Because the principals are so angst-ridden about being in love, the minor characters lighten the tone. Much like the above, they can be weird workmates, endearingly flamboyant friends, roommates, comedy vicars and bumbling Best Men.

Scenes

What follows are a series of almost obligatory scenarios and characters in romantic comedy. By no means are all of these used but most romcoms employ a selection of them – the art being to pour in fresh emotion and insight. The parodist kills what he once loved but the romantic comedy writer is challenged not to lose sight of love and to twist the scenes afresh: better yet, invent new scenarios, characters and concepts, although there is nothing wrong with homage.

- The meet-cute, in which the pair are thrust together in adversity and awkwardness, leading to comical misunderstandings. This is as old as *It Happened One Night* and as new as *Man Up* (Palmer 2015).

- The boy cannot ask the girl out. Blinkered by love, he is unable to express himself in a straightforward manner. He either sends an envoy whose message is misinterpreted or fails abysmally, reaping only humiliation. There is the risk of rejection with which we all empathize. Think about the location. Who is around them and what can affect the timing of this? Romantic comedy is all about misunderstanding and failed communication.

- The girl does not simply ask for or agree to a date, instead falling back on an atavistic mating ritual dance that states that the man must ask her. This is subverted when Mary (Cameron Diaz) accepts so quickly in *There's Something About Mary*.

- The first date will be disastrous but there will be one spark of recognition, even if that spark is apparent hatred. It will involve humiliation, often in a restaurant, where food equals sex. His inability to order food implies sexual inadequacy (*Along Came Polly*). A take on this is Sally Albright's pernickety personality when ordering food.

- The man fails to phone back or is prevented from doing so by circumstance. This is post-date, thereby setting up anxiety and capsizing the relationship before it has begun. Again this is a communication issue and our saturated technology era this paradoxically means even more opportunity for screw-ups.

- The dumping of an unsuitable partner. This is a 'comedy' dumping in that it is not love that is destroyed but only the removal of habit. It is a strengthening of character for the dumper, with the additional benefit that the dumped can now become an adversary and return for later ramifications (*Four Weddings and A Funeral*).

- A disguise may be employed (*Cyrano, Roxanne*) in order to discover the true feelings of the love object. One or both partners will be misadvised by friends as to the nature and motives of the other.

- Circumstances will keep the couple apart. These may include becoming lost in a crowd, at a high-profile social event such as the opera or an art opening, book launch or company event.

- There will be a family gathering or ritual.

- A conscious choice is made to go with a wrong partner. This otherwise unsuitable element permits contrast with the right guy or girl and permits the breaking of taboos and a lot of inappropriacy.

- Sex will not happen. If coitus is about to occur with mutual consent, then there will be some event that prevents it. Sex is only funny when it is not happening. The preparation for the date and the paraphernalia of it is a rich seam. No one will ever forget the scene when Ted (Ben Stiller) cleans the pipes in order to prepare for his date with Mary (Cameron Diaz) and she mistakes it for hair gel. That she is genuinely a nice girl keeps this from being crude and only adds to the comedy. The need for a private space, a bed, contraception, mood, lighting, clothing, temperature and sobriety or lack of it are all factors that can be played with to find the comedy. Once the sex happens it isn't funny anymore. You laugh someone into bed and that's where it stops. Trust me.

- The break-up. After several permutations of closeness they will break up, thus testing the relationship to its limit. Often time is sandwiched in romantic comedy and we only see up to the point of consummation, but there is a long way to go between here and the wedding, the official sanctioning of that state.

- There are clear markers in adult relationships beyond first, second and third dates – the first month, the sixth month and crucial eighteenth month barrier marked by the 'serious talk'. This and potential infidelity are all roadblocks to happiness.

- The running scene. Once one or both partners realize they have made the wrong decision, they will endeavour to get back into the arms of the love object – but it's too late: a symbolic end and a new journey for the other is in sight. Anything and everything will be put in their way as they rush to the airport or train station. There will be no cabs (which previously appeared from nowhere), movie rain will drench them, the car won't start, the train has gone and the gate has closed. This is a dramatic scene because the epiphany has been reached and the character has matured enough to pursue the love object (which reveals itself in terms of conflict).

Chapter 7
Comedy About Sex

Oz Ostreicher:
You ask them questions, and listen
to what they have to say and shit.

Steve Stifler:
I dunno, man, that sounds like a lot of work.

AMERICAN PIE

Teen comedy

Gregory's Girl. 10 Things I Hate About You. Pretty In Pink. Weird Science. The Sure Thing. Clueless. Mean Girls. Ferris Bueller's Day Off. The Breakfast Club. Animal House. Porky's. Beach Blanket Bingo. Fast Times at Ridgemont High.

Teenage comedy is a mainstay of Hollywood production, its target audience being the prime demographic at which most movies are aimed. Teens have independence and spending money and their major activity is dating, therefore teen movies are highly commercial and must therefore appeal directly to this (conservative) market.

The state of adolescence is one of turbulence and flux, partly rebellious and anarchistic, but also desperate to be cool and to fit in with a social peer group. This is the rite of passage into adulthood, beset by sexual desire, a time when we are at our hormonal and emotional peak. Teen movies reflect this by ramping up the excitement to fever pitch. Gatherings, parties and music are central events around which the movies are structured, with music being used to drive an emotional stake into the heart and memories of the viewer.

Teen movies tend to be written by people who are not too far off this period, or who are living a protracted adolescence. Once you have matured, as with the events of your own youth, they seem embarrassing and faintly ludicrous. We re-live our own angst when we watch a teen comedy. It is exaggerated in terms of its hardship, which must be presented visually, so all the depression and heartache is shuffled away in favour of slapstick, gross-out humour and emotional moments. Subcultures, such as Emos or Goths are portrayed not as a group, more as one cute Goth girl or lone Emo boy. They are, unless placed in a period setting, of their time, so the fashions and trends can date alarmingly (1980s pearls, 1990s jeans).

Teen movies have been around since the teenager was invented in the 1950s, where for the first time in history, American youth had spending power and time on their hands. Radio, TV and rock 'n' roll spread like wildfire as a new generation learned to dance, to make out and to become aware of the evils of 'reefer madness'. Movies soon caught on, reflecting these trends – *Rebel Without a Cause, The Wild One, The Girl Can't Help It* and *Rock Around The Clock* were huge successes, and as each new generation came along, they had their accompanying movie. The 1970s had *American Graffiti, Meatballs* and *Animal House*; the 1980s had *Porky's* and John Hughes films (*Ferris Bueller's Day Off, Pretty in Pink*) and so on.

Teen movies usually have a high-concept premise that can be summarized in a sentence. *American Pie* (Weitz 1999): four buddies determine to lose their cherry by graduation; *16 Candles*: a girl's parents forget her birthday. *Clueless*: Shakespeare re-done in LA; *The Breakfast Club:* a group of teens in detention.

These character types have become cliché – so much so that they were parodied in *Not Another Teen Movie* (Gallen 2001) where, at John Hughes High School, 'students are the same as just about every other teenager in a teen movie'. The popular jock, Jake, takes a bet from Austin, the cocky blonde guy, that he can transform Janey, the pretty ugly girl, into the prom queen before the prom. But two people are trying to stop Jake from succeeding: his evil sister, Catherine, the cruellest girl in school, and Priscilla, the bitchy cheerleader. Their friends are types: Areola, the naked foreign exchange student, Les, the beautiful weirdo, Malik, the token black guy, the desperate virgins, Amanda Becker, the perfect girl, Ricky, Janey's obsessed best friend, and Sadie, the VERY old undercover reporter.' There are clearly elements here from both *Pygmalion* and *Scream.* The ubiquity of movies centred on the American teenage high school experience has had an effect worldwide, with the UK introducing Prom Night events in many of their schools as well as much of the slang teenspeak[1] infiltrating

---

[1] Most conspicuously, Californian Valley Girl speak from TV shows *Beverley Hills 90210* and others.

successive generations of British and Antipodean teenagers. Essentially the coming–of-age comedy is about three things.

- The guy wants the girl or the girl wants the guy;
- The guy/girl wants to be accepted for who they are;
- The guy/girl crosses the threshold into adulthood or adult behaviour.

As their lives are centred on school or college, the setting will be based around these institutions. Added to the stock characters listed above there is also the jock (who will be humiliated), the nerd (whose mental skills will help him/her to triumph), the virgin (the prize), the frump or ugly duckling (who will transmogrify into a swan), the stoner dude (who may or may not mature) and the rebel (who ends up subsumed by the system, or dies, or leaves the group). These also form the basis for slasher movies and slice 'n' dice horror of the 1980s and beyond, *Halloween* (or *Black Christmas*) being their progenitor. Wes Craven's postmodern horror hit *Scream* (Craven 1997) employs comedic elements as well as rite-of-passage and coming of age.

Teen Movies are about gender, identity expectations and social hierarchy. The rituals are sexual, social and moral, a continuing exploration of each successive generation of American teenager. Since *American Pie* and its successors, the norm has been to go for gross-out. The tropes are well defined, one major element being the end of term passing-out ceremony, Prom night, divided into Junior and Senior Prom. Obtaining a date for this occasion has created huge social pressure and subsequent stigma for the teenager, making it a significant and specific goal.

In teen movies there is plenty of conflict. There is the inner desire to be understood and the compromise necessary to become popular. There are real goals (the girl) and false ones (those established by the peer group). There is the pressure of that peer group – the desire of the crowd versus that of the individual, who may not want to engage in underage sex or drinking but feels that he/she has to. The lure of the gang, initiation rituals and keeping in with the cool kids is all that matters at high school. There is the tension between the hero, his love interest and love rivals, who will create a triangle. There are authority figures – parents and teachers, the former who wish to curtail the urges of the teen player or, more embarrassingly, to be over sharers or 'down with the kids', the latter imposing sanctions and controlling their behaviour. There may also be encounters with the police over minor crimes of vandalism, speeding and/or underage drinking.

It is wish fulfilment. In real life we do not win the cheerleader, the prom queen or the nice girl, causing years of sullen, bitter resentment and dreaming of the magic pixie dream girl. In reality, we will do anything to get into and to hang onto the gang and to remain cool. The message here is that being different is okay, but you must still be useful to society. James Dean did not offer anything substantially different when he offered to rebel. Rather than offering a new societal structure, he only asked what they had for him to rebel against. He asked for a target.

Teen comedies are also all about heart. There is almost always a happy ending. Despite being ensemble comedies, the tale is most often about a lone boy or girl dealing with crossing the threshold into maturity. In this, he or she will come into conflict with parents, school friends and/or siblings. The issue is made worse by public humiliation, embarrassment or misunderstandings. Jim is caught masturbating in *American Pie*, leading to a cringing fatherly chat. Later, the facts of his premature ejaculation are broadcast to the whole school.

There may be gossip and rumour to add to social ostracization. The kinds of coven in *Heathers, Mean Girls or Clueless* are as real to the female teen experience as the male bonding in *Porky's, American Pie* or *The Sure Thing* are to the male.

There will be a number of obstacles in the way of getting the girl or achieving independence. The romcom model is used but if the boy does not succeed in getting the girl, his desperate efforts may be stretched to farce. As an audience we expect to see a scene of triumph, in which the hero proves that the forces holding him back were wrong. It will prove that teen intuition is correct, rather than logic. This too is referenced in many teen slashers in which the final girl conquers through animal instinct, not reason, for reason cannot kill the monster. Here the monster is an overly strident definition of conformity, not to that of his parents' generation, but to the desire of the crowd. He or she will find her own way, which is a precursor to how they will later function in the real world. The reward for this is a passing-out ceremony, be it graduation, escape or consummation (the kiss) – a passing on to the next stage, which is adulthood. Sometimes, in order to franchise these movies (*College Trip*) the lessons learned are kept minimal and maturity is not reached, allowing for a sequel.

Frat boys

Diner. Animal House. Old School. Swingers. Boys' Night Out. Stripes.

The Boy's Club or fraternity is nothing new. *Boys' Night Out* (Gordon 1962) featured three married men who were not getting enough out of their marriages, so they hired a divorced friend (James Garner) to set up a woman in an apartment (Kim Novak) for each of them to 'see'.[2] Unbeknownst to them she was a sociology student studying married men for her thesis on 'the adolescent fantasies of the suburban male'. She slept with none but let each believe she had slept with the others. She provided what they really needed in their marriages, which was to eat, to talk or to tinker. The wives become suspicious and hired a private eye to expose the sham. The divorcee (James Garner), who did not take his 'night', won her over and the boys' night was over.

The idea of men being on a leash is a predominant one in cinema, as is the idea of liberation being that of freedom from the control of women, and yet, women are what they desire. Also set in 1962 was the king of frat boy comedies *National Lampoon's Animal House* (Landis 1978). Here, two freshmen sought a Fraternity at Faber College, ending up at the worst, Delta Tau Chi, which Dean Wormer wanted to remove from campus for conduct violations and a poor academic record. As a tale of the underdog triumphing over 'the man' it is pure comic anarchy and a counterculture take on the American college system. It was also one of the most profitable movies of its time, garnering an estimated gross of more than $141 million in theatrical rentals and home video. This and Landis' freshman effort *The Kentucky Fried Movie* (Landis 1977) define the gross-out genre.

Old School (Phillips 2003) finds three guys who miss their adolescence too much to let it go, so they start a frat house. They are quickly unshackled from their partners and return to their adolescence ('all of the fun, none of the education'). There are echoes of *Boys' Night Out* here in that they throw open the fraternity for those who are bored with the nine-to-five treadmill and also of *Animal House* with the Dean (Jeremy Piven) being a boy they used to bully and who will try anything to stop them.

The characters in frat house comedies tend to be extensions of male traits with simple through lines: as with most gangs there will be a charismatic and unpredictable leader and his lieutenant. Followers will include a corpulent or loser type, a lovelorn romantic and a turncoat who can act as an internal shape shifter. The true nemeses will either be the Dean and his forces of academia or a rival fraternity. The latter will be super rich with a sense of entitlement and the wherewithal to control the legal, fiscal and collegiate bodies. The frat boys resort to being lords of misrule, being puerile and juvenile and refusing to obey any strictures placed upon them. Ultimately the powers that be will box them in on all sides and they must seek out hidden skills, be they a legal loophole, or an unforeseen angle, which will allow them to triumph. This is often a pyrrhic victory and by the credits they are seen to conform, or if not, to find a lifestyle

---

[2]Shades of Billy Wilder's *The Apartment*. Marital infidelity was the hot topic in early 1960s comedy.

that makes them happy. The conflict is that of the individual vs the system. Again it is a conservative view, College years are seen as a last opportunity to be truly free and irresponsible before maturity kicks in. Another aspect of arrested development is stoner comedies.

Stoner comedies

Harold & Kumar Go to White Castle. Dude, Where's My Car? Jay and Silent Bob Strike Back. Pineapple Express. Up In Smoke.

Comedians Richard 'Cheech' Marin and Tommy Chong took a decade's worth of live work and parlayed it into the stoner classic, *Up In Smoke* (Adler 1978), followed by *Cheech and Chong's Next Movie* in 1980. Cannabis was the main recreational drug of that period and their Fat Freddy cartoon style of massive consumption and evading the law struck a cord with the counterculture.[3] The 1980s engendered a different breed – the yuppie (Young Urban Professional) who could have what he wanted when he wanted it in the new emergent free market economy. Greed was good (*Wall Street* Stone 1987) and cocaine became the drug of choice. Conspicuous consumption gave way to different lifestyle and drug choices, but since the 2000s there has been a return to dope as an acceptable high in movies and stoner comedies have proliferated. It is not hard to make stoned people laugh and these comedies either concern the pursuit of drugs, or guys on drugs in pursuit of a simple goal, be it burgers, munchies or their car. A girl may also be involved.

These movies tend to be watched at home on rental. A stoned audience is not likely to follow a complicated plot or deep characterization and these things tend to be of less importance than random surreal oddities and quotable catchphrases. The comedy is broad, and in *Dude, Where's My Car?* the tattoo sketch is a clear nod to Abbot and Costello's 'Who's on first?' cross-talk classic ('What does mine say?' 'Sweet.' 'What does mine say?' 'Dude!' etc.). This is comedy for a specific audience.

In the more popular examples, such as the *Harold & Kumar* franchise, it is interesting to note that their addiction is a leisure rather than a lifestyle choice. This may be because they are Korean and Asian American and both cultures

---

[3]*Easy Rider* is the progenitor of drug films. Not a comedy, the movie, starring Dennis Hopper, Peter Fonda and Jack Nicholson, brought the conspicuous consumption of hallucinogenics to a mass audience and (along with Woodstock) heralded the end of the Hippie movement. It is discussed at length in Peter Biskind's seminal *Easy Riders, Raging Bulls*.

are known to have a strong work ethic. *Pineapple Express* mixes the stoner subgenre with action comedy over a witness to a murder and a misplaced roach – the protagonists must get out of town pursued by bad guys (echoes of *Some Like it Hot*). *The Big Lebowski* concerns the plight of the Dude (Jeff Bridges), a carpet and a marmot but has the Coen brothers at the helm, creating a noir plot and some visual flourishes as well as mad cameos. Other than these notable exceptions, the problem with stoned people, as with people who tell you their dreams, is that it only really matters to them.

In plotting and character terms there is also the problem of inertia. The principal desire of the drug addict is to lie around and take drugs, with his secondary need being to score more drugs. This means there is little here to work with in plot terms and so, coincidence, misunderstanding and *deus ex machina* are employed to get the show on the road. There is no appreciable character growth save that of maturity.

The outcome of these plots is invariably that the stoner was right all along, and that he saw more clearly despite his befuddled state (there are few female stoner comedies[4]): thus his lifestyle triumphs over the bad guys, authorities and the Man. They are anti-resolution, hoping to get the girl or the munchies and retain their lifestyle. Not being able to mature appeals to their target demographic who has invested in remaining in a state of stasis. The stoner comedy works with cannabis sativa and hallucinogenic 'milder' recreational drugs but not with harder ones such as heroin or crack: open drug use of this kind would lead to unrated status. They also seem to be restricted to Californian locales or simulacrums thereof, where, it can be assumed, this kind of lifestyle is acceptable and encouraged.

Gross-out

Brain Dead. Evil Dead II. American Pie. Dumb And Dumber. There's Something About Mary. Me, Myself and Irene. Porky's.

If the John Landis films of the 1970s were the progenitors of the gross-out subgenre, it is the Farrelly brothers who have made the most impact and revitalized it with *Dumb And Dumber* (1994), *Kingpin* (1996), *There's Something About Mary* (1998), *Shallow Hal* (2001) and *Dumb and Dumber To* (2014). Semen in hair, explosive diarrhoea and disabled schtick is their shock in trade and they never fail to delight and appal in equal measure. Gross-out is a return to the slapstick of Laurel and Hardy and the anarchy of The Marx Brothers, but more extreme

---

[4]*Smiley Face* (Araki, 2007) starring Anna Faris.

and base. 'Dumbing down' was a slang expression coined by screenwriters in 1933 to mean: 'revise so as to appeal to those of little education or intelligence', which illustrates that there are movies that have always appealed to the broad demographic. The quandary over comedy for the heart or the gut is best explored in Preston Sturges' satirical *Sullivan's Travels*, in which director John Sullivan seeks to make a meaningful picture ('but with a little sex in it', he is advised) but once he undergoes real hardship he realizes that there's a lot to be said for making people laugh as, for some, it's all they have.

Come the early 1990s, commercial pressures and a trend for family-friendly movies meant that Hollywood hadn't made an R rated comedy for years, but *Dumb and Dumber* opened the floodgates and soon came *American Pie* (now a five-movie franchise), *Road Trip* (2000), *Old School* (2003) and much less. Box office proves that there is an ongoing market for this type of comedy – but how far can one go? Critic Mikhail Bakhtin wrote of carnival during the medieval times (literally to 'put aside meat' for the period of Lent) where the hierarchical order and rank was suspended. Carnival was a celebration of change and renewal where the high was rendered low, a world turned upside down. It is a form of degradation where the unruly male breaks the rules of the uncontrollable biological urge for food and sex; he loses control of his body parts – a lack of physical control often seen in the comedian comedy of Steve Martin or Jim Carrey. This comedy concerns the lower stratum of the body, the belly, the anus and reproductive organs. Bakhtin presents the human body as a source of the grotesque, of defecation, copulation and birth. The fool or court jester was ideal for the role.[5]

Many of the comedies of Chaplin and his contemporaries were concerned with the anal, a kick up the arse being a common comedic device – see *City Lights* (Chaplin 1931). The sophisticated early talkies aimed to rise above this, creating a schism among audiences between the masses and the emergent urban city dwellers. The Hays Code put paid to sex, violence and smut, but in 1966 Jack Valenti, newly elected President of the MPAA, deemed it to be out of date and bearing the 'odious smell of censorship'.

To avoid the intrusion of government into the movie arena he devised a set of advisory ratings, the voluntary MPAA ratings that took effect on 1 November 1966. G was for general, PG for Parental Guidance. PG-13 films may contain stronger language (e.g. bitch, shit and tits) and one uncensored use of the word fuck, provided that it was used as an insult and not for sexual intercourse(!). If said expletive was spoken more than once or used sexually, it became routine for a film to receive an R rating.

---

[5] Trickster figures can be found in many myths, especially in Native American Indian stories.

Gross-out slapstick crosses the taboo of privacy. In most societies it is unacceptable, embarrassing and inappropriate to lose control of our bodily waste or functions. Critic Julia Kristeva has written extensively on the abject and the pleasure of disgust. The delight comes in transgression. As children, if we are injured, the scab fascinates us, and the desire to pick at it is hard to resist. This is the *abject* – that which is both alive and dead, still a part of us and yet no longer living. In this way, faeces, vomit, urine and ejaculate, boils and pus have the ability to fascinate. Gross-out examines this and the involuntary rebellion of our internal organs. The question is 'how much can you take?', is a rite of passage for the young, who are still exploring their bodies to see what they can do with them. A recent online fad, *Neknomination*, had teenagers and idiots of all persuasions nominating others to consume the most potent and dangerous of cocktail beverages. Its peak resulted in the deaths of participants and it has now passed into the past labelled 'stupid'.

The most extreme film in motion picture history is *Salo, or the 120 Days of Sodom* (Pasolini 1975) based on the writings of the Marquis de Sade, which contains rape, torture, coprophagia, multiple penetrations and underage group sex. This is pure disgust with no comic dimension. Comedy has to make its rules clear from the start that no matter how black, it must be 'safe' in that the viewer is aware of the comic distance. The key here is repulsion, the social test for adolescents. These are movies to watch in a pack, a challenge to the weaker members of the fold, an initiation rite – the mechanics of disgust are energetically discussed as if pawing through the augers.

This is not restricted to adolescents. One of the most outrageous displays of corpulent comic disgust was the Monty Python sketch in *The Meaning of Life* (Jones 1983) with an obese character named Mr Creosote, who keeps eating until he explodes in a rain of blood, guts and vomit ('Just one wafer thin mint M'sieur?').

Verbal disgust was pushed to the limit in the documentary film *The Aristocrats* (Jillette 2005), in which a number of famous comedians and writers told their version of the same obscene joke. It begins with a man walking into a talent agency to propose a new act. He describes the act, improvising a series of scenarios that includes incest, graphic violence, defecation, coprophilia, necrophilia, bestiality, child sex abuse or any other taboo – the more graphic the better – before the bewildered agent asks the name of the troupe, to which the punchline is the title, *The Aristocrats*.[6]

To make the comedy work, there must be an element of naivety, as there was in the work of Laurel and Hardy or Chaplin. In *There's Something About Mary*,

---

[6]Presumably, the agent then books them and takes 15 per cent.

Mary (Cameron Diaz) mistakes ejaculate for hair gel and places it in her hair but it is testament to her portrayal of innocence that this is neither pornographic nor cheap. It seems sweet because neither protagonist has lustful intentions. Stiller is merely 'cleaning the pipes' before their date. That she mistakes it for hair product (visual displacement) flatters us because we are in on the joke, and he is even more anxious.

There is also comedy in dislocation, placing semen in hair or in a beer glass. The offending object is placed in the limbo of comic irony. The audience knows that its consumption will result in disgust, but does not know when this will happen or who the victim will be. Teenage revenge, often involving bodily fluids, has been a feature of teen movies since *Carrie* (De Palma 1973) where the soaking of prom queen Carrie (Sissy Spacek) in pig's blood caused a vast telekinetic reaction. Palma's adaptation of the Stephen King novel took the teen comedy clichés, parodied them (the soft porn opening in the shower, the comedy sports team) and spat them back as horror.

In these comedies, what will never happen is honesty, which is Kryptonite to teenagers. Parents and school staff see through lies easily but teens, when dealing with their peer group, do not. Much of the bragging is taken at face value. There is often a group leader (Jay in *The Inbetweeners*, Stiffler in *American Pie*) who professes to greater knowledge and wider experience despite his clear naivety. As in the theatre of Shakespeare, Gogol, Wilde or Coward, lies and deceptions are useful comedically because they set up the suspension of belief. The comedy works by suspending normality and NOT saying what ought to be said. Once the lie is challenged, another is proffered and a web is spun. 'Truth' is referred to as 'the simple truth' because it is sequential, a series of unbroken events that are incontrovertible. Lies are so much more fluid and the fantasist has a world to choose from, as in the Danny Kaye/Ben Stiller movie *The Secret Life of Walter Mitty* or the play/book/film *Billy Liar* (Schlesinger 1960)

In testing our public and private cultural boundaries the question is, does this undermine or confirm to the social norm? Is this liberation or safety valve? A major theme of Henri Bergson's essay on laughter states 'Laughter has often been seen as a means of enforcing conformity through ridicule of that which does not confirm to dominant expectations' (King: 68). What is culturally acceptable to one nation – eating with your fingers, using toilet paper, or removing your shoes when you enter a house – might be anathema to another.

Sasha Baron-Cohen's *Borat* delights in trampling American social norms, confronting feminism ('listen pussycat'), racism ('a genuine chocolate face') and toilet behaviour (he appears at a party with his soil in a bag) because, as a naïve (but driven by lust) foreigner from a country about which no one knows a thing, he simply misunderstands. This and *Brüno* (his follow-up film which button-pushed American homophobia to the limits) were examples of the main character engaging directly with gross-out. This is rare, as often it is committed by secondary characters such as Bluto in *Animal House*, making them easy to sideline as marginal.

When writing this form of comedy, the loss of control of bodily functions can be racked up in comedic terms by making it occur at some prestigious event, such as a ceremony, meal or exclusive wedding dress boutique, as in *Bridesmaids* (Feig 2011). Put simply, people do not like to be reminded of where their food is going or what is happening to it as we eat, which is why we do not like to be located near the toilet in a restaurant. The food/shit connection is universal. So too is the loss of bowel or bladder control whose gateway is the fart.

Farting is funny, full stop. The sound (the Whoopee or fart cushion was always a No. 1 seller in comic books) and the propulsion of air from the posterior is something we all try to keep silent. It is a basic transgression and an obsession from child to adult. Salvador Dali wrote a treatise called 'The Art of Farting'. Actor Leslie Nielson was known for his scatological japes, and in the UK it is almost a national obsession: much of the British *Viz* comic's *Roger Mellie's Profanisaurus* is devoted to synonyms for letting rip and exclamations such as 'sew a button on that.' There is even a character called Johnny Fartpants.

Vomit too is always funny in cartoon form. *Family Guy*, whose vignette 'Who wants chowder?'[7] has Peter, Brian, Stewie and Chris in a fountain of puke. Notably, the women, Lois and Meg are not involved in these pranks. It is a boys' club and from the evidence it seems that women neither perspire nor emit wind, which is why the transgressions of Melissa McCarthy and Kristen Wiig in *Bridesmaids* are so funny – they violate the expectation that women ought to behave with a degree of decorum.

We pity those such as tramps/hobos who have no basic level of self-control but this can be played for laughs, as in the hilarious portrayal of Ruprecht, Michael Caine's idiot 'brother' (Steve Martin) in *Dirty Rotten Scoundrels*. It has been established that he is a danger to himself (cork on fork), but then, when invited for a meal with Caine's putative fiancée, he apes good behaviour by asking 'May I go to the bathroom?' Silence follows and the audience does not need to see the pool at his feet. A sight gag without the need for the visual, we do not need to see, only to *know* that he has soiled himself.

Where does gross-out go next? It seems there are few boundaries left that have not been shown on screen. It is possible to see the most obscene acts on

---

[7] Season Four, Episode Eight.

the Internet (*Two Girls, One Cup*) where there is currently little to no censorship. Pornography inevitably follows new technological developments[8] and online everything is permitted. Perhaps there is no way but back.

Sex comedy

Alfie. Shampoo. Bob & Carol & Ted & Alice. The 40-Year-Old Virgin. The Sure Thing. Friends with Benefits. Confessions of a Window Cleaner. Euro Trip. Hot Tub Time Machine. Fast Times at Ridgemont High. The Graduate. Sex is Zero.

Sex comedy proliferated originally in England. It began with Geoffrey Chaucer and continued with Restoration theatre (*The Country Wife*, *The Rover*), and in the bawdier elements of Shakespeare's comedies. In movie terms, the *Carry On* series of films (*Carry On England* and *Emmanuel*, in particular) and the run of *Confessions Of* movies were popular in the 1960s and 1970s. Even the Boulting brothers, famous for their social satires, produced *Soft Beds, Hard Battles*[9] (Boulting 1974) with Peter Sellers playing six roles including Hitler and the president of France in a brothel full of girls helping the war effort.

Sex and censorship in the movies go hand in hand. In 1949, rivalling the Hays Code for strictness, the BBC issued the *BBC Variety Programmes Policy Guide For Producers and Writers*[10] banning among other elements jokes concerning lavatories, effeminacy in men, immorality, suggestive references to honeymoon couples, chambermaids, fig-leaves, ladies' underwear, lodgers, commercial travellers and the vulgar use of words such as 'basket' (for bastard). The N word was banned, although the phrase 'Nigger minstrels' was still tolerated. This hegemony was challenged by a radio show *Round The Horne*, where comic actors Kenneth Williams and Hugh Paddick played two effeminate characters named Julian and Sandy. They spoke a dialect called Polari (from the Italian 'to talk'), a cockney slang used by actors, circus folk, Punch and Judy puppeteers and those in the merchant navy. Radio was an extremely popular medium – over half the population tuned in regularly – and Polari[11] became a part of popular discourse. The gay liberation movement of the 1970s abandoned it as being politically incorrect, but the need for secrecy had declined with the

---

[8] The invention of the camera led to naked photography; the moving pictures led to 'What the Butler Saw' – peep shows.
[9] Known in the US as *Undercovers Hero*.
[10] Known as 'the Green book'.
[11] The words 'naff' (useless) and 'zhoosh' (to freshen up) are Polari.

Sexual Offences Act (1967).[12] In comedy terms, the need for subtle innuendo had passed.

Film production was aided by the Eady Levy (named after Sir Wilfred Eady), which had been established in 1957. Under the Levy, a proportion of the ticket price was to be pooled, half to be retained by exhibitors (i.e. a rebate on tax) and half to be divided among qualifying British Films in proportion to UK box office revenue.[13] To qualify as a British film, no less than 85 per cent of the film had to be shot in the United Kingdom or the Commonwealth. This led to the success of the James Bond franchise, as well as many US and European directors working in the UK such as Kubrick, Lumet, Huston, Polanski, Truffaut and Godard. Comedy became broad and lewd in this climate of liberal sexuality, with the Eady Levy providing funding for the boost in British pornographic film production in the 1970s. The Thatcher government terminated it in 1985, stalling the British Film Industry for a decade until the Lottery Funding of the mid-1990s.[14]

British sex comedies were similar to stage farces (*No Sex Please, We're British* was both a play and a film) in which unlikely lotharios found themselves ensconced with buxom nubile ladies, running from room to room to avoid angry husbands. The films included randy workmen such as plumbers, window cleaners or milkmen forming the basis of spurious pornography scenarios ever since. The new X rating was an incitement to view, but the quality of the comedy was *Carry On* slapstick farce at its most flaccid.

A finer British comedy about sex was *Alfie* (Gilbert 1966). An adaptation by Bill Naughton of the titular novel and play, it concerned womanizer Alfie Elkins (Michael Caine) who beds and cheats on several women until his comeuppance at the hands of an older woman Ruby (Shelley Winters) with her withering put down, 'Don't you get it? He's younger than you are.' Both sex comedy and ironic satire, it is notable for breaking the fourth wall and was the first film to receive the 'suggested for mature audiences' classification by the MPAA.[15]

R-rated *Bob & Carol & Ted & Alice* (Mazursky 1969) was a huge US hit, gaining four Oscar nominations. Bob (Robert Culp) confesses an affair to wife Carol (Natalie Wood) and she accepts it. Best friends Ted (Elliott Gould) and Alice (Dyan Cannon) are shocked, but then Bob and Carol both have affairs. Ted has an affair and when he reveals it to Alice; she demands that it be taken to its conclusion, a partner swapping foursome in Vegas. All four climb into bed

---

[12]Decriminalizing private homosexual acts between men over the age of twenty-one in England and Wales.
[13]With no obligation to invest in further production!
[14]And the concomitant rise of independents such as *Working Title* and *Film Four*.
[15]In 1966, Jack Valenti became Head of the MPAA and introduced voluntary ratings. NC-17 replaced the X rating, which came to be associated with pornography or extreme horror, in 1990.

and the women kiss but after a few moments the four stop. They dress, ride the elevator and walk out of the casino with their original partners. It pulls its punches but it was instrumental in other 1970s explorations of love versus sex as a topic for comedy.

Shampoo (Ashby 1975) was a breakthrough movie for Warren Beatty with a conceit in which the lothario is the only straight hairdresser in town, allowing him access to many female clients. The movie – also a political satire of the incoming Nixon administration and of Beverley Hills manners, forces George (Beatty) to face his philandering. He proposes too late to his true-love Jackie (Julie Christie), losing all his women but gaining moral maturity.

Sex as recreation as opposed to conception is also mocked in *Everything You Always Wanted to Know About Sex *But Were Afraid to Ask* (Allen 1972). A series of vignettes, it is based on the sex manual by physician Dr David Reuben which became part of the sexual revolution. Each sketch used questions asked in the book such as 'do aphrodisiacs work?' or 'what happens after ejaculation?'

These are comedies about sex, as opposed to sex comedies and the difference is in the focus. The frat boy sex comedy is a coming-of-age ritual played out in *Meatballs*, *Animal House*, *Porky's* and *American Pie*. This same trope, about guys getting it, is also the focus of *Superbad* (Mottola 2007), *Road Trip* (Phillips 2000) and *Euro Trip* (Schaffer/Berg 2004). The plots are uniform and linear: the chase, the seduction and, if you succeed, the hunt for more. Either way, the consecration of the sex act or the discovery of infidelity is the fulcrum at which the man succumbs to love, which trumps sex every time.

The tone comes in the variation of the mechanics, rather like sex itself. If romantic comedy is all about love, and ends with sex, then the sex comedy is its inversion. Consequences are rarely addressed and the teen pregnancy comedies of *Knocked Up* or *Juno* are no longer about sex. The mechanical question (as in gross-out) is what you can get away with. Secondary sexual organs are permitted but not primary ones, although Peter Bretter's (Jason Segel) junk is seen in his break-up in *Forgetting Sarah Marshall*, which is rated R for sexual content, language and some graphic nudity. Full frontal nudity will get an R, whereas explicit or violent sex, including rape and assault, gets NC-17. Most of these movies are Unrated.

R-rated comedy became popular as a reaction to what is not free on TV. Kevin Smith's *Zack and Miri Make a Porno* (Smith 2008), while purporting to take things to the next level, conforms to type as lifelong platonic friends Zack and Miri look to solve their respective cash-flow problems by making an adult film together. As the cameras roll, however, the duo begins to sense that they may have more feelings for each other than they previously thought. The aim is always to restore love and romance and this is seen in *Friends with Benefits* and *Sex Tape* (Kasdan 2014) where married couple Cameron Diaz and Jason

Segel speed through dating, marriage and childbirth and, exhausted, look to re-energize their marriage by making a drunken sex tape. The tape is one that, in *Hangover* style, is seen only at the end and whose camera angles are unusually flexible for a stationary iPad. As with all sex comedies, it proves the adage that other people having sex is not funny or sexy unless it actually is porn. The voyeuristic element is the downfall of sex comedies. Too prurient and it will be pornographic, too coy and it will be cute.

Chapter 8

Mocking Society: Parody, Mockumentary and Satire

A parodie, a parodie! To make it absurder than it was.
BEN JONSON, *EVERY MAN IN HIS HUMOUR* (1598)

Parody

Parody is one of the easier forms of comedy, as it starts out with something in existence, that which we look on as stale. It is easy to laugh at the SF/Horror movies of the 1950s (big, hairy monsters) or yuppie movies of the 1980s (big hair and phones), but what will we find risible about the movies of the 2010s? Some genres are more prone to parody than others: who has not watched an action movie and wondered why the hero only ever gets shot in the shoulder or why there is always a crawlspace big enough for a man to crawl through? Why is it the red or the blue wire and what if you are colour-blind? The action genre is physically preposterous but resilient, so much so that it can incorporate self-parody, as with the Bond movies, or because stars like Bruce Willis and Arnold Schwarzenegger are willing to send themselves up so long as their fee is met.

Genre develops in four stages: the primitive, when its characteristics are established; the classical, the genre at its peak with its qualities refined; the revisionist, which scrutinizes and revaluates the conventions; and the parodic, where genre is satirized in a conscious and self-reflective manner. To be parodic, there must be an existing form – a target of formal or aesthetic value with conventions and representational devices. Even though parody attacks and debunks, it reaffirms the object of its mockery and in this way pays tribute. To be parodied is to have achieved a certain status and recognition, as parody 'needs to appeal to a target familiar to a sufficiently large audience' (King: 112) (Harries 2000).

The principal function of parody is to expose what has become clichéd. It is an affectionate form of comedy and an ambivalent one, using the material of its target as its structure. This is something satire need not do, as it takes a more distanced attitude. Parody lacks this critical approach: It copies closely, sometimes shot for shot, and because of this it apes the genre with a clear understanding of the form.

History

According to Aristotle (*Poetics*: ii, 5), Hegemon of Thasos was the inventor of parody. By altering the wording in well-known poems of the time he transformed the sublime into the ridiculous. In Greek literature, a *parodia* was a narrative poem that imitated the style of an epic but featured light, satirical or mock heroic subjects. The word derives from 'counter' and 'song' – but can also mean 'besides'. Old Comedy contained parody where even the Gods would be mocked. In Aristophanes' *The Frogs*, hero-turned-god Heracles is portrayed as a glutton and Dionysus (the God of Drama) is cowardly and unintelligent. The trip to the Underworld is parodied when Dionysus dresses as Heracles in an attempt to bring back a poet to save Athens.

Parody has existed in film almost since its inception. *The Little Train Robbery* (Porter 1905) was a sequel to the 1903 drama, *The Great Train Robbery,* and featured a cast of children (shades of *Bugsy Malone*). D. W. Griffith's melodrama *Intolerance* (1916) was spoofed by Buster Keaton in his feature length *Three Ages* (1923). *Mud and Sand* (Pratt 1922) was a vehicle for Stan Laurel, a lampoon of Rudolph Valentino's *Blood and Sand* (Niblo 1922) and Laurel later went on to star in other parodies such as *Dr Pyckle and Mr Pryde* (Pembroke/ Rock 1925) and to direct spoofs such as *Yes, Yes Nanette* (1925), a play on the popular Broadway show of the time.

During the War years and beyond, the *Road To...* movies, starring Bob Hope and Bing Crosby, were parodies of the film genres of the day, using settings such as the jungle, the Arabian nights, Alaskan adventures and the High Seas. Their final film together – *Road to Hong Kong* – spoofed the spy films of the 1960s.

There is a difference in parodying Hitler and the rise of Nazism.[1] Charlie Chaplin spoofed both in *The Great Dictator* (1940) but, as we shall see, this was only possible during the early years of the war. Before the true nature of the final solution was understood, Hitler could be mocked for his unusual Chaplin moustache and goose-stepping gait. British comic film star George Formby appeared as Adolf in an extended dream sequence in *Let George Do It* (Varnel 1940). Will Hay too appeared as Hitler in The *Goose Steps Out* (Dearden 1942) and there was even a Donald Duck animated propaganda short, *Der Fuhrer's*

---

[1]See Satire.

Face (Kinney 1943). The best example is perhaps Ernest Lubitsch's sublime *To Be or Not To Be* (1942), later remade by Mel Brooks, who also parodied Hitler in *The Producers* in 1968 (a sufficient distance from the war).

Indeed, Brook's output consists almost exclusively of parody. *Blazing Saddles* deconstructed the Western, to be followed by *Young Frankenstein* (1974), attacking the Universal horror films of the 1930s and *Silent Movie* (1976) whose sole line of dialogue was given to Marcel Marceau, a mime. *High Anxiety* (1977) spoofed Hitchcock. *Spaceballs* (1987) was all about Star Wars and *Robin Hood: Men in Tights* (1993) is self-explanatory.

Woody Allen also began his movie career by turning out spoofs of popular movie genres, with *What's Up Tiger Lily?* (1966), a dubbed spy spoof;[2] *Take The Money and Run* (1969) was the first mockumentary; *Bananas* (1971) spoofed Latin American politics, *Sleeper* (1973) attacked Californian culture and science fiction movies and *Love and Death* (1975) debunked the European Art movie and Russian literature.

Parody suffered in the post-war period due to a combination of economic instability, a growth in revisionist Westerns (the leading genre at that point) and the demise of the B movie.[3] Many of these supporting movies moved to television, which also started to produce skit and sketch comedy shows – the most famous being Lorne Michaels's *Saturday Night Live*, which spawned a legion of comedy acting superstars (see Sketch Comedy).

In the UK, many of the thirty-one *Carry On* movies had parodic elements, primarily *Carry On Spying, Cowboy, Screaming* and *Emmanuelle,* which spoofed the spy genre, Westerns, horror and soft porn respectively but acted more as a starting point for the ensemble cast of stock comic characters to do their turns.

Austin Powers: International Man of Mystery is the most recent in a long line of spy movie spoofs.[4] The massive success of the James Bond franchise, beginning with *Dr No* in 1962, had created an industry. There was the *Matt Helm* series of films starring Dean Martin, and on TV *Get Smart* (1965–70) written by Mel Brooks and Buck Henry and its subsequent movie version (Segal 2008) with Steve Carell. *The Man from UNCLE* (Rolfe 1964–8) also

---

[2] Allen was hired to rewrite the original film *Kagi no Kag* (*Key of Keys* 1964), a Japanese Bond film, and subvert it – the new dialogue simply being dubbed on top. The lead character's name became Terri Yaki and the McGuffin was the search for the perfect egg salad.

[3] Although it continued to thrive in animated cartoons.

[4] Len Deighton's spy creation, Harry Palmer, was the inverse of James Bond, a cockney instead of a public school-educated playboy, he lived in an apartment in Notting Hill, liked to cook and was beset by departmental politics and fights over a pay hike. By contrast, Bond's salary is never mentioned, but he must have had a massive expense account. Michael Caine starred as Palmer in *The Ipcress File* (Furie 1965), *Funeral in Berlin* (Hamilton 1966) and *Billion Dollar Brain* (Russell 1967), reprising the role in the 1990s.

used spy tropes and Bond author Ian Fleming as a consultant. More movies appeared: *Our Man Flint* (1966) and *In like Flint* (1967) starred James Coburn in an obvious parody of Bond. *Modesty Blaise* (1966) was a prototype for a female Bond. The original *Casino Royale* (Various 1967) featured six Bonds including David Niven, Ursula Andress, Woody Allen and Peter Sellers. By the time the Zucker brothers got a hand in with *Spy Hard* (1996) the genre was well into self-parody. More recently, the French period spy movies *OSS 117: Cairo, Nest of Spies* (Havanavicius 2006) and *OSS 117: Lost in Rio* (Havanavicius 2009) introduced Jean DuJardin as a suave French Bond with a fluid sexuality.

It was *Airplane!* (Zucker, Abrahams, Zucker 1980) that revitalised the parodic form, taking off the disaster movies of the mid-1970s and putting several nails in their coffin. The team was a product of the video generation, having shot and edited sketches which had been played to audiences as part of their *Kentucky Fried Theatre Company* in the early 1970s. They moved from Wisconsin to LA and came to the attention of John Landis who re-versioned the best of the material into the *Kentucky Fried Movie* (1977). This allowed them creative control and a $3 million budget for *Airplane!*[5] It defined two trends – first revitalizing the genre parody, and second, the careers of a number of TV character actors, such as Robert Stack, Lloyd Bridges, Peter Graves and Leslie Nielson.[6] This led to *Top Secret!* (Zucker 1984) and the *Naked Gun* movies, parodying spy and detective thrillers. More recently, the *Scary Movie* (Wayans 2000) franchise has aped the teenage slasher subgenre – though later sequels adopt a more scattergun approach. *Date Movie* (Friedberg/Seltzer 2006)[7] and *Epic Movie* (2007) are self-explanatory and both were box office hits, recouping over four times their £20 million budgets. They have continued to parody genres with *Meet the Spartans* (2008), *Vampires Suck* (2010) and *The Starving Games* (2013).

In 1986, theoretician Rick Altman wrote of the three axes of genre. First, there is the semantic or lexical (the setting, characters and objects); second, the syntax (the narrative based structures); and third, the style (the conventions of genre). Parody must anchor itself to these and yet display itself through an incongruity toward them. In his book, *Film Parody*, Harries suggests that there are six methods of creating similarity and difference, thus leading to parodic humour. These are

---

[5]Which went on to gross $80 million domestic.
[6]McCabe 2005: 65.
[7]A parody of romcoms, *My Big Fat Greek Wedding*, *Bridget Jones's Diary* and *When Harry Met Sally*, *Date Movie* spins us into the arena of comedy-about-comedy, which has limited pay-offs.

- Reiteration;

- Inversion;

- Misdirection;

- Literalism;

- Extraneous inclusion;

- Exaggeration.

Reiteration concerns the setting and the props. In *Blazing Saddles* (Brooks 1974), this means establishing the received idea of the Western frontier town, or as in *Galaxy Quest* (Parisot 1999), the spaceship as clear imitation of the bridge on the Starship Enterprise *in Star Trek*. It is also useful to familiarise the viewer with the form as parody by employing actors from the original films, such as using Linda Blair in *Repossessed* or John Hurt in *Spaceballs*.

The *Family Guy* hour-long spoof *Blue Harvest* (Polcino 2007) which opened Series Six, parodied *Star Wars Episode IV: A New Hope* and whole scenes were lifted from the original and used as plot dynamics. Parody does not need to travel far from its source to be amusing. *Young Frankenstein* (Brooks 1974) used the original sets from Universal Studios and was shot in black and white in a German expressionist style to match the original.

Inversion comes when the expected is corrupted. Neither Austin Powers nor Hubert Bonisseur de la Bath (a.k.a. French Secret Service agent OSS 117) are the super spies they think they are. Likewise, *Spinal Tap* are a third-rate heavy metal band.[8]

Misdirection sends us off into unexpected realms, as with almost all of *Airplane!*, including the air-traffic controller at the end of his tether, the pilot with a fondness for boys and the sick child being tended to on board the plane. Also there is **literalism**, as in 'Don't call me Shirley' or Austin Powers' Basil Exposition who is based on the Q character in the Bond movies. Another example of this is when the new sheriff in *Blazing Saddles* rides into town accompanied by a stirring orchestra – which is then revealed to be Count Basie and his band in the desert.

Extraneous inclusion accounts for the police showing up at the end of *Monty Python and the Holy Grail* (Gilliam 1975) or the persistence of Dr Evil's henchmen to not be killed but mortally wounded. It can also be the inclusion of other movies within the subgenre (or even out of it) as in *Scary Movie*, which includes spoofs of *I Know What You Did Last Summer* and *The Matrix*.

---

[8]Ironically, a documentary was made about *Anvil* – a genuine 1980s metal band, skating close to Spinal Tap, whose reputation was only enhanced by the movie.

Exaggeration is rife in parody, with size or duration as its mainsprings. The Zucker brothers and Abrahams were masters of this, making things bigger than they ought to be or closer to us, or having the frame cut a tall person's head off or putting the comedy in the background – all learned from the silent movies of Keaton, Lloyd and Chaplin.

Parody must be played straight and the actors must never be conscious of the audience. The characters must believe in their reality and be committed to their goals. Having said this, parody plays with the artifice of movies and is often obsessed with this aspect, leading to a degree of style over substance and thin characterization. However, it ought not to be merely a string of jokes. *Galaxy Quest* (Parisot 1999) is a movie that apes science fiction tropes but creates narrative and real depth of character in its human and alien participants.

Because we know the conventions, we can twist them. *Scream* (Craven 1997) was not a spoof, as neither Wes Craven nor writer Kevin Williamson were looking for laughs. They did, however, use exposition to parody what was tired and jaded about the subgenre,[9] and in introducing the 'rules for sequels' they had it both ways. The audience was simultaneously able to enjoy the original because this *was* a horror movie and also the deconstruction of it. Once the novelty of using comedy had worn off, *Scream* played out the real scares as well as the fake ones. This too is in evidence in *Cabin in the Woods* (Goddard 2012) and *An American Werewolf in London* (Landis 1981).

Parody can devolve to silliness, as in the cowboys and beans scene in *Blazing Saddles* (Brooks 1974) or in the 'throw him to the floor, Centurion' scene in *Life of Brian.* It can become episodic; being more a series of sketches suited to TV, as in the later *Scary Movie* franchise movies where the fictional frame is broken one too many times.

Parody can also skate on the thin ice of offense. *Blazing Saddles*, whilst being a lampoon of a genre well into its fourth stage of pastiche, tackled racist views in America, its conceit being that of having a black sheriff in a frontier town. Notwithstanding comedian Richard Pryor's work as writer on the film[10] the use of the N-word is used liberally by black and white alike. This seems shocking but only until the context of each utterance becomes evident. The townsfolk first use it but it is interrupted by church bells, then by Brooks as Governor Petomane, where it is truncated. A gang of roughnecks use the term but are then tricked by the black railroad gang into a neat reversal, that of singing the slavery song, *Camptown Races*. It is then used by Cleavon Little

---

[9] The original title of the movie was *Scary Movie.*
[10] Although it is stated in the DVD extras that he worked mainly on the 'Mongo' character.

as Sheriff Bart, who *is* black then later as invective by an old lady, who later recounts and offers him some pie. All bases are covered. There is no overt use of the word without justification.

Life of Brian (Jones 1979) moves beyond a mere parody of Bible stories and Hollywood epics (the original logline being 'makes Ben Hur look like an epic') into the area of blasphemy: so much so that it was banned in the Republic of Ireland, Norway and by thirty-nine local UK Authorities. Following a thirty-year ban in Aberystwyth, it was due to be screened in 2009 with Palin, Jones and Mayor Sue Jones-Davies (who played Judith Escariot) present. Just before the screening, a student discovered that it had never actually been banned (Yapp 2009). Although *Brian* takes a sketch format – almost every scene stands alone – in taking on the greatest story ever told, it moves into a wider take on religion, fundamentalism and the concept of belief. *Brian* uses *elements* of the Life of Christ, but artfully so, never naming him as the source and always remaining in parallel. *Brian* therefore moves beyond parody to satire, an area where there is critique and artfully delivered offence.

Writing Parody

Woody Allen and Mel Brooks started out writing parody on Sid Caesar's *Your Show of Shows* (1950–4). The new comedy writer attacks what he considers dated and thus in this way parody is a kind of circuit breaker, a re-setting of the cultural dial. The target audience for parody is now the same as that for the original product, meaning there is a pre-sold market, which is 'Another characteristic central to the contemporary Hollywood economy of˜ risk aversion' (King). There are parodies of individual films, such as *Repossessed* (Logan 1990), *Silence of the Hams* (Greggio 1994) or *Stan Helsing* (Zenga 2009) of subgenre, *Fatal Instinct* (Reiner 1993), or of late a mash-up of any number of movies, such as *The Hungover Games* (Stolberg 2014) and *30 Nights of Paranormal Activity with the Devil Inside The Girl With The Dragon Tattoo* (Moss 2013).

Parody has become ubiquitous. In our postmodern state, culture has turned in on itself, recycling and reworking and becoming a collage where juxtaposition is seen as originality. The general public is film literate and free streaming means instant access to any cultural source. We can parody anything, and put together any number of film genres to do it. The art is in getting there first, in mining the subgenre that takes itself too seriously. The seam of comedy, once tapped, can be extremely lucrative.

Mockumentary

Take the Money and Run. A Hard Day's Night. All You Need is Cash (The Rutles). This is Spinal Tap. Naked Gun. Zelig. Best in Show. Waiting for Guffman. Borat.

The feature-length documentary began with *Nanook of the North* in 1922 (Flaherty), the word being coined by John Grierson in his review of Flaherty's film *Moana* (1926). It grew via newsreels in Soviet Russia, in the West as propaganda (Leni Riefenstahl's 1935 *Triumph of the Will*) and later as Cinema Verite. As a televisual format it established itself with *Civilisation*, *Whicker's World* and Mike Apted's *7UP*. Today the documentary is ubiquitous, particularly in the false narrative of reality TV. In comedy terms, television had reached the end of modernism by the end of the 1960s with the Monty Python troupe spoofing the documentary in a sketch called *Whicker Island*.

Early examples of the use of mock or fake documentary might include Luis Bunuel's *Land Without Bread* (1933) and Orson Welles' 1938 radio broadcast of Well's the *War of The Worlds* – although this was done for dramatic rather than comedic effect.

The '*Swiss Spaghetti Harvest*', was perhaps the first proper televisual spoof, created for April Fool's Day and shown on BBC One's *Panorama* in 1957. The Beatles' first feature film *A Hard Day's Night* (Lester 1964) was also mock documentary. This and subsequent Beatles films were later spoofed in *All You Need Is Cash* (The Rutles) (Idle 1978). Although this predates Rob Reiner et al., the term 'mockumentary' was coined in the introduction to the seminal *This is Spinal Tap* (Reiner 1984).

By its insistence on 'reality', documentary is a form that invites play. Rather than recreating reality, mockumentary is a parody of the televisual idea of real life. It uses commonly understood techniques and formats and is a unique and special world. It attempts to be the most real of all comedy genres, working on the level of comic irony where the audience knows it is not a real documentary, but its participants don't. They in turn are convinced the documentary is real and behave accordingly. The comedy comes in the juxtaposition, the editing and the reveal. Often a character will give a version of events, usually to camera but sometimes in voiceover, which will be visually or aurally contradicted as the camera pulls away to show the lie, or a cut to illustrate the untruth.

Mockumentary has specific targets. In *This is Spinal Tap* it was the outrageous demands and behaviour of self-aggrandising rock stars. Its writers/stars later parlayed this idea into folk music (*A Mighty Wind*), dog shows (*Best in Show*) and amateur theatricals (*Waiting for Guffman*). More recently, *Borat*

(Charles 2006) took an innocent from Kazakhstan and traced his journey across America – his targets being the gullibility, racism, homophobia and sexism of the Great American Public. Comedian Sacha Baron-Cohen also used mockumentary elements for *Brüno* (Charles 2009) and for *The Dictator* (Charles 2012). Mockumentary tropes include:

- A narrator, often someone with gravitas, a voiceover artist who commonly does 'straight' documentaries, thus establishing verisimilitude;

- Pieces to camera where a character speaks earnestly. They must be convinced of the truth they tell. Sometimes the comedy is in the background;

- Mocked-up archive documents/historical footage, artificially aged film stock as in the *This is Spinal Tap* 'New Originals' and the recreations of historical events in *Zelig*;

- Interviews with 'experts' and 'expert witnesses' – often spurious types whose claims to veracity are suspect;

- Handheld, hidden fly-on-the-wall camera, so that what is said in secret can be later revealed and played on to humiliate;

- Improvisation from an ensemble troupe of actors;

- Shot on digital video thus enabling multiple takes over a long period of time;

- The participants want entry to the celebrity class, looking for a sense of self-worth through acceptance (e.g. *Brüno*);

- Running gags, such as *Spinal Tap's* thirty-seven dead drummers;

- Minute obsessions, such as Nigel Tufnell's problem with sandwiches;

- Exaggeration and caricature. Derek Smalls has a huge silver-foil-wrapped cucumber in his pants;

- Understatement (litotes) – 'Too much perspective'.

The mockumentary is the straight man, allowing us to find the comedy in what is presented to us as reality. If we cannot believe the news then what can we believe? In this way it is subversive. It also glorifies the trivial. Why should we be interested in these people simply because they are on our screens? Mockumentary shows us how easy it is to fake these codes and conventions.

It can also take us into more edgy arenas. The Belgian film, *Man Bites Dog* (*C'est Arrivé près de chez vous* or *It Happened in Your Neighborhood*) (Belvaux 1992) is a black comedy in which a documentary team follows a serial killer about his day only to become complicit with and engaged in his murderous rampage. The viewer is drawn in, as are the film crew (played by its writers and directors) ending in a blood bath as the film makes strong comment about complicity. When do we stop filming and take action?

By contrast, filmmaker Michael Moore makes humorous documentaries, not mockumentary. The difference is clear. He has a political and social agenda and uses unsuspecting members of the public to hold up institutions to ridicule, but he is not parodying the form and none of his participants are actors.

Sacha Baron Cohen's *Borat* (2006) and *Brüno*, both stretch the form to excess. There is a naked fight in *Borat* between the protagonist and his obese manager, which starts in a hotel room and continues to a convention on the ground floor. Hilarious though it is, would this have really been caught on film, and by whom? In fact they used two different hotels, but the comic sequence is so outrageous and transgressive that we hardly stop to question it. In *Brüno*, social and sexual conventions are trampled from using Mexicans as furniture (in order to unnerve Paula Abdul) to full frontal nudity and gay sex. It is an assault on our senses but not as transgressive as John Waters' *Pink Flamingos*, in which camp icon Divine's act of canine faecal mastication goes all out to be 'real'.

Mockumentary has been co-opted by TV sitcom, its progenitor being the British show *The Office* created and written by Ricky Gervais and Stephen Merchant[11] which made its lead, David Brent – inadequate, self-serving, unable of censoring himself – into a comedy icon. The American *Office* uses the same format, as does *Parks and Recreation* and *Modern Family*, and in the UK, there is *Twenty Twelve* (mocking the Olympic Committee), *W1A* (the machinations of the BBC) and *People Like Us*. It is an effective way of establishing the veracity of a situation and of introducing an oddball cast, but the writer must keep things fresh and not rely on the tried and trusted clichés of the form.

Satire

Gentlemen, you can't fight in here! This is the War room.
President Merkin Muffley, Dr Strangelove (1972)

Bulworth. Dr Strangelove. Bananas. Bob Roberts. Broadcast News. Network. Wag the Dog. Dave. The Truman Show. Thank You For Smoking. M*A*S*H.

---

[11] There had been others who parodied the TV formats – *The Day Today* Team and Chris Morris' satirical work – but *The Office* was a huge and influential hit.

Satire says something about the way we live *as a whole*, identifying corruption, injustice, immorality and incompetence at the highest levels. It tells us that something is wrong but society is in itself too broad a target to hit with a scattershot approach. The satirist must isolate the particular area of what enrages him and people it with symbolic figures to represent what is ineffective about that group. It might be the medical establishment, big business, government, the military or the media: it cannot be 'economics', 'fair trade' or 'global terrorism'. To succeed you must be specific. *The Dictator* (Charles 2012) opens with the skewering of Western ideas of Middle Eastern potentates, stretching and making the truth absurd and reducing the unacceptable to ridicule.

There is comedy that seeks to entertain and there is comedy with a point, a disaffected voice that attempts to affect change. If parody is simple mockery then satire has a deeper aim and an august tradition from the writings of Jonathan Swift and the art of William Hogarth, to the extremes of *South Park* or *Team America*. It takes derisive wit, ridicule, scorn, exaggeration and irony and applies them to our social institutions. It has a target and a point. If the laughter of gross-out teen comedies and slapstick is that of the gut, then satire appeals to the head.

We have several expressions for the kind of comedy that has us breathless and silly with laughter: splitting our sides, busting a gut, even wetting ourselves – the aim to literally be helpless, reduced to a childlike state where you dissolve in paroxysms of glee. This is about the loss of control, the desire to purge and cleanse and in that unguarded moment to shuck off the robes of adult behaviour. Satire however, is the laughter of the mind; it is the wry grin, the knowing smile, the glowing satisfaction that your darkest and most cynical views on society have seen expression. Satire is our night watchman, but rather than being the guardian at the gates, he is one who turns inwards to look at the inhabitants of the castle, gazing at the king and his court, his priests and judiciary and finding them wanting. Satire is about truth, or the truth as we see it. We *know* that the politicians, bankers, media, corporations and big business are lying to us, but we accept it. What can we do? What you can do is to speak out, as Senator Jay Billington Bulworth did in *Bulworth* (Beatty 1999) or Howard Beale in Network (Lumet 1976):

Howard Beale:

So, you listen to me: Television is not the truth! Television is a goddamned amusement park! Television is a circus, a carnival, a traveling troupe of acrobats, storytellers, dancers, singers, jugglers, sideshow freaks, lion tamers, and football players. We're in the boredom-killing business! So if you want the truth … Go to God! Go to your gurus! Go to yourselves! Because that's the only place you're ever going to find any real truth.

But, satire tells us, reveal the truth and you will end up mad or dead. Someone has to say something and when comedy becomes satire, this is what it does, albeit in an exaggerated way. We laugh at the truth because we so often do not hear it. We are used to obfuscation and filibustering, the evasions of the rich, the powerful and the famous. To hear a bald truism, as Senator Bulworth offers at the altar in a church in South Central LA, is shocking – but wins respect.

> Angry black woman:
> Are you saying the Democratic Party don't care about the African-American community?

> Bulworth:
> Isn't that OBVIOUS? You got half your kids are out of work and the other half are in jail. Do you see ANY Democrat doing anything about it? Certainly not me! So what're you gonna do, vote Republican? Come on! Come on, you're not gonna vote Republican! Let's call a spade a spade!

Satire must seek out its target and spear it remorselessly. Mild satire is as useful as wet toast. Satire can also be used to attack external enemies, as Chaplin did in *The Great Dictator* (Chaplin 1940) or it can create internal social and political criticism as in Soviet Russia. Most comedy pulls its punches and this is true of Hollywood in general (remembering the fantasy model). True political satire is rare. *Bulworth* and *Wag the Dog* go some way toward it, and both protagonists end up dead.

'The pattern of great eras of satire parallels eras of public excess, hardship, impropriety, and aberration, notably post-Republican Rome, Britain's Restoration era, and America's Prohibition era and Great Depression' (Snodgrass 1996).

These are times when satire is needed – perhaps we are there now. The targets of classic satires, government warmongering (*Duck Soup*), political manipulation (*The Great McGinty*, 1940) and press accountability (*Ace in the Hole* (1951) or *Sunset Boulevard* (1950), are as relevant today as they ever were.

Animated satire

Animation is an effective medium for satire. The fact that it is seen as being for children allows for a lot of social commentary to slip under the radar. Both *The Simpsons* and *South Park* have taken advantage of this, but in other countries, animation has been used to raise political sensitivity. Czech puppeteer Jiri Trnka made *Darek* (*The Gift* 1946), which satirized Hollywood and consumer society, then *Pérák a SS* (1946), lampooning the German occupation of Czechoslovakia.

Ruka (*The Hand*) (1965) is perhaps his best-known work. Made before the Prague Spring of 1968 it created satire out of state oppression with an animated hand that terrorized the creative endeavours of a potter, forcing him to make sculpture in the hand's own image. An attempt to flee led to imprisonment and death.

Eastern Europe too was a source of satire as political dissent, with The Zagreb school of Yugoslavia producing *Ceremonija* (1965) and *Zid* (*The Wall*) (1965).

Max Fleischer (the inventor of the Rotoscope) who was best known for *Betty Boop*,[12] *Koko the Clown* and *Popeye*, had a great satirical opportunity when his studio made Swift's classic *Gulliver's Travels* (1939), but it ran over budget and they were trying to compete with Disney. In the UK, *Animal Farm* (Halas 1954) was more in the spirit of Orwell. More recently, Parker and Stone's *South Park: Bigger, Longer & Uncut* mocks media culpability and political correctness and *Team America: World Police,* employs foul-mouthed *Thunderbirds*-style puppets to mock US foreign policy. Although expensive to produce, animation is a powerful route for the budding satirist (see Animation).

Political satire

In the US, political satire is best exemplified by *Wag the Dog* (1997),[13] which concerns a president who allows a fake war to happen in order to get re-elected. Hollywood producer Stan Mots (Dustin Hoffman) is hired to create a war, but is placed in a position where he wants to decide how it ends, his decisions becoming as morally dubious as those of his paymasters. This was not Hoffman's first foray into satire, as he had previously made his name in *The Graduate* (Nichols 1967).

> A satire about ennui, it discovered an audience that for the majority of the decade Hollywood had lost and/or ignored. Post-World War II, the young had come into their own. They looked for movies that spoke to them, movies that knew where Haight Ashbury was. *The Graduate* got that. It related to a disenfranchised audience, told them their point of view was relevant and ultimately, helped define their point of view. (McCabe 2005: 104)

When newscaster Howard Beale threatened to kill himself on air in *Network* (1976), the ratings went through the roof. The movie later descended into farce when faced with a Marxist leader arguing over distribution rights. Beale

---

[12] Whose lively, sexy flapper character fell victim to the Hays Code.
[13] Also *Bob Roberts and Bulworth*.

becomes a prophet of the airwaves ('I'm mad as hell and I'm not going to take it anymore'), and is later killed by said revolutionaries. *Broadcast News* (1987) attacked news hypocrisy, corporate takeovers, audience chasing and media manipulation, but was ameliorated by having a love triangle at its heart.

Perhaps the most successful military/political Cold War satire is *Dr Strangelove: or How I Learned to Stop Worrying and Love the Bomb* (Kubrick 1972) where the futility of war is examined from several perspectives. As in the dramatic version, *Failsafe[14]* (starring Henry Fonda), at the start of the movie the bombs have already been launched and only diplomacy can prevent their impact. Kubrick drafted in novelist Terry Southern for scriptwriting duties and the film was slated to end in a massive custard pie fight. This was abandoned and instead its darker ending has Dr Strangelove, a wheelchair bound Kissinger/Nazi, offering an Aryan solution where the most beautiful women are apportioned out to surviving members of the bunker.[15] As this happens, the Russian delegate continues to take covert photos of the installation as Slim Pickens rides a falling nuclear bomb to Vera Lynn's wartime song 'We'll meet again'.

The 'no fighting in the War Room' line may be a nod to another satirical buffoon, Colonel Blimp. Originally a cartoon strip by David Low, the story was made into a film by Powell and Pressburger[16] (*The Life and Death of Colonel Blimp* 1943). Its opening depicts Blimp, a senior commander in the Home Guard being captured in a pre-emptive strike before a training exercise in a Turkish bath '[The] War starts at midnight!' he howls. The film satirized the British army and its leadership or lack of it.

Continuing to ridicule the futility of War are *M*A*S*H* and *Catch-22*, the latter being an absurd surreal comedy with Alan Arkin in a dark satire of capitalism and business ethics where parachutes and morphine are replaced by share certificates.

Satire relishes 'dark', as in *Heathers* (1989) or *Serial Mom* (Waters 1994) and is not restricted to North America. There is Cuban satire *Too Afraid of Life* (1988) and *El Viaje* (*The Voyage* 1993) from Argentina. Britain too has a satirical tradition in the films of the Boulting brothers – a trilogy beginning with *Private's Progress* (1956) satirizing the military, *Lucky Jim* (1957) targeting academe and *I'm all Right Jack* (1959) mocking the Trade unions and management. There is also Sidney Gilliat's *Left Right and Centre* (1959), which has two political opponents (of each sex) falling for one another. Ealing Studios made *The Man in the White Suit* (Mackendrick 1951) starring Alec Guinness, which posited the usefulness of a fabric that never

---

[14] *Failsafe* was released at a similar time and suffered as a result.
[15] Ronald Reagan asked to be shown to this same War room with its 22-foot circular table. It was a set.
[16] The directors deny this source.

needed washing. *The Mouse That Roared* (Arnold 1959) was a vehicle for Peter Sellers in which The Duchy of Grand Fenwick, the smallest country in the world, declares war on the US when they find that Californian producers have undercut them on wine prices. The plan is to lose the war in less than a day with no casualties, after which the US will provide vast financial aid to rebuild the country.

Director Lindsey Anderson produced a satirical trilogy for the 1970s with *If...* (targeting public schools), *O Lucky Man* (capitalism) and *Britannia Hospital* (the NHS and privatization) which featured the same protagonist, Travis (Malcolm McDowell). The 1980s produced *How to Get Ahead in Advertising*, wherein Richard E. Grant literally grows another head. More recently the political sitcom *The Thick of It* has spawned the satirical movie, *In the Loop*.

Peter Cook, creator of the Establishment club, starred in *The Rise of Michael Rimmer*. His protégé Chris Morris, long a thorn in the side of the establishment with Channel Four's *Brass Eye* show, produced *Four Lions*, the first satire on radical fundamentalism.

Satire seeks to destroy and rarely suggests a new order. It is enough to leave the subject of your ire in ruins. It needs to be extreme, sometimes to the point where the audience is unsure if it is satire or not. Two movies that cross this boundary and which are only intermittently funny are Quentin Tarantino's *Natural Born Killers* (Stone 1994) and Mary Harmon's *American Psycho* (2000) (see Transgressive Comedy). Rather, 'in Hollywood, the norm is to dilute the satirical edge or force to cut, ultimately, in the direction of established comic or social norms' (King 2002).

Satire is the preserve of the angry and embittered, the cynic not the romantic. It is the comedy of the moralist and rationalist over the sentimental. In order to write satire, you must choose a target to suit you. Be it military, media or government, it is important to do your research and know your subject. Historically, insiders have written most satire; those who know the processes and formulas only too well: BBC bureaucratic sitcom satire *Yes Minster* was written in part by former political advisor Anthony Jay.

Satire relies on a 'what if?' that is at once outrageous and yet somehow feasible. What if a president were to start a war in order to improve his ratings? What if one decided to tell the truth? What if a patsy were placed in the workplace to cause dissent? What if America sent armed forces into other countries and did more damage than they saved lives? In order to mock these ideas, satire uses analogy, such as in *Gulliver's Travels* or *Animal Farm*. It takes the norm and displaces it. By dislocating the set of circumstances, we obtain objectivity and ironic comic distance. It is funnier to create a place called Fredonia, which is small, remote and autocratic (*Duck Soup* 1933) where all our ills can be placed rather than refer to the real.

A fish-out-of-water character as lead is a common trope. He is often naïve and comes into the world or employ of evil men and does not know it. He is a go-ahead guy who stumbles onto a secret but, though morally dubious, it is presented to him so as he stands to gain more than lose. Compromise is the fulcrum of satire. The lead is gradually corrupted or otherwise paid off. In Act Two, he will suffer a change of heart and perhaps attempt to become a whistle-blower, but it will be too late. Once on board, he is part of the gang, and his first duty may be to remove old friends and allies as a test of faith. He is to be pushed to the limit. The new world will offer benefits but it is a Faustian pact. Once underway, the plan (government policy, war or media manipulation) cannot be stopped. It is bigger than any component part. Miscommunication also features, in that disinformation will be passed on to further complicate matters. Those who are running the show must believe totally in what they are doing and their undoing will never breed sympathy (*Trading Places*, Landis 1983). The satire will exaggerate and thus ridicule the establishment, pouring scorn on it by having characters behave as badly as is humanly possible.

Sometimes in satire, the protagonist escapes by the skin of his teeth; sometimes it simply gets worse, the darkness of the palette depending on the depth of cynicism. The hero will ridicule authority and sometimes, like Hawkeye Pierce in M*A*S*H, make a sacrifice, in his case his golf game in order to defeat a military idiot and save a Korean child's eyesight.

There are also terrible ironies, as in *Brazil* (Gilliam 1985) where Sam Lowry's attempts to fix the simple typing error ends in his being incarcerated and operated on by long-term best friend Jack Lint (Michael Palin). Only madness and death lie at the end of the bureaucratic system.

Satire provokes laughter and the wince of truth and recognition. It is aggressive and tough. It desires a return to basics or a new world order but it never states what that might be. This is comedy for a sophisticated audience who likes to have its beliefs challenged. Satire ought to have you leaving the theatre angry yet somehow satisfied. Your views have been expressed but the world is still a crap-hole. It is comedy's call to arms.

Chapter 9
Dark Comedy and Farce

Tragedy is when I cut my finger, comedy is when you fall down a drain and die.

MEL BROOKS

Dark comedy

A Clockwork Orange. Swimming With Sharks. The War of The Roses. Kind Hearts and Coronets. Ruthless People. Throw Momma From The Train. Arsenic and Old Lace. The Ladykillers. Raising Arizona. Bad Santa. Bad Teacher. Cheap Thrills. Horrible Bosses. A Simple Plan. Harold and Maude.

Black comedy is where people die but it doesn't matter. The characters in dark comedy are viewed with comic distance, so all the deprivation and violence inflicted on them is safely in the comic realm. An example of this is the finale of *Monty Python's Life of Brian* (Jones 1979) where, following Brian's crucifixion, his friends do not come to his aid but instead leave him to a martyr's death. Fellow Crucifixionee, the ever-chirpy Eric Idle then leads the chorus in one of the best-known comic songs of all time – 'Always Look on the Bright Side of Life'. The toe-tapping number lifts the tone from sombre to silly – take this away and you have an ending that, whilst poignant, would be too bleak for the irreverent tone of the movie.

The term 'gallows' or 'black humour' (*humour noir*) was first coined by the surrealist Andre Breton in 1935, taking the scepticism and cynicism of satire and pushing it to its natural conclusion. Breton cites its originator as being arch satirist Jonathan Swift, who in his pamphlet *A Modest Proposal* (1729) suggested that the solution to the Irish famine ought to be cannibalism: they should eat their young, a child being delicious either boiled or fricasseed. This was a direct attack on the British landowners who had already prized every morsel out of Ireland. The black comic approach says, 'you have taken my arms; you might as well take my legs as well'.[1]

Like satire, black comedy can be a propaganda force for channelling anger into a drive for change. At its best it is unruly and hostile. It is not funny as in laugh-out-loud funny, but takes swipes at attitudes. It is stinging. It suggests we have false Gods in our authorities and conventions. It picks on elements such as the institution and sanctity of marriage, the military, judiciary, government, the rich and their exclusivity, even Hollywood itself. *Wag the Dog* and *The Player* (Altman 1992) are blackly satirical and both involve death, the latter of a screen-writer at the hands of a studio executive.

It is also about taboos. It says the unsayable and mocks political correctness, pushing at the boundaries of taste and decency. Topics such as paedophilia, (*Happiness*), domestic violence (*The War of The Roses*) and murder (*Horrible Bosses, Throw Momma From The Train*) are all acceptable targets. Black comedy can even be wrapped up as a Christmas film, as in the Spielberg produced *Gremlins* (Dante 1984) – outwardly a cross between *It's A Wonderful Life* and *The Blob* with cute animatronic animals, but readable as an anti-authoritarian take on the sanctities and niceties of American society.

As black comedy has a desire to change the system, it is in this way idealist and often the preserve of the younger writer, one who has come up against the intransigence of faceless bureaucracy and who has not yet learned that all is lost.

The screenplay, a wish fulfilment, takes the hero on a dangerous journey, one of which we might ask, is this a sensible idea? Will the hero win? Perhaps he is doomed to failure? Sometimes the hero will fail to learn the lesson, but we will. In this case, his failure transfers the anger and puts the onus on us. In order to do this, black comedy uses absurdity and exaggeration. It takes things to ludicrous extremes. Its aim is to reveal the target as absurd.

In divorce comedy *The War of The Roses* (DeVito 1989) the movie looks at how both parties (Michael Douglas and Kathleen Turner) believe themselves to be in the right, but takes their justifications to ludicrous and deadly extremes. Director Danny DeVito offers a cameo as the divorce lawyer providing bookending narration, the final outcome being the deaths of the two participants. In the end, only the lawyers win, so was it worth it?

---

[1] Cf. The Knights of Ni! (*Monty Python and the Holy Grail*).

A lighter tone is taken in the Coen brothers' black screwball comedy *Intolerable Cruelty*, again taking divorce as the target[2] but adding avarice. Divorce lawyer Miles Massey (George Clooney) is a man who knows the price of commitment and who has developed the cast iron pre-nup. He however falls into the clutches of serial gold digger and divorcee Marilyn Rexroth (Catherine Zeta-Jones). It plays its satire tongue in cheek, exposing the folly of chasing money and its incompatibility with love.

If black comedy dwells on the negative, it tries to illuminate the positive. Human behaviour could and might sink to this level of absurdity, but when it doesn't perhaps there is something to be salvaged in terms of humanity. The veneer of manners keeps us from acting so cravenly, so naked in our desires, the enjoyment being in the comic distance we have as an audience from these awful people.

Character

We approach the black comedy in a wicked frame of mind. The scenario cannot be taken at face value (as with other forms of comedy), as it is a heightened reality. It means the protagonist must be charismatic and passionate, as with Louis Mazzini (Dennis Price) in *Kind Hearts and Coronets* or Elizabeth Halsey (Cameron Diaz) in *Bad Teacher* (Kasdan 2011). We root for the bad guy or girl, although we are aware that their triumph is hubristic and cannot be allowed to stand. Even though they transgress, they must arrive at a logical way of presenting their modus operandi to the audience. In their world there must be no other way of getting the money or justice. They present us with a *fait accompli*, the comic departure coming as the audience separates from them. Whereas we would give up, they take the next step toward black comedy and farce. *Horrible Bosses* (Gordon 2011) examines this in the world of work with Kevin Spacey, Jennifer Anniston and Colin Farrell playing craven employers. Three employees are in thrall to them via bullying, sexual harassment and the son of a boss intent on destroying the company. None can afford to give up their job, or has too much invested in it, or is trapped by a spurious criminal record. Their only option is to hire a hit man to end their misery.

In *Bad Teacher*, Elizabeth Halsey is an amoral gold-digging teacher who after being dumped by her wealthy fiancée needs $9,300 for plastic surgery in order to snare her next, Scott (Justin Timberlake). Unable to raise enough by dubious scams, she moves onto blackmail. The comedy comes in her obsession to stick with the goal to the bitter end.

---

[2]With a wonderful tagline, 'They can't keep their hands off each other's assets'.

In *Heathers* (Lehmann 1988), a Lynchian high-school comedy, the question is – how important is it to be popular? The heroine, Veronica Sawyer, (Winona Ryder) has recently been made a member of the popular clique the Heathers, but hates it and wants to end their tyranny. In this movie, the adults are aloof, self-serving and insincere, a reflection of the yuppie trend of the time. At school, teenage concerns are amplified and there are class discussions about how a teenager might go about killing herself and on mourning rituals (how long is appropriate to grieve for a cheerleader?) Veronica's wish is then granted when Jason (J. D.) Dean (Christian Slater) helps her to dispatch them. Appalled and fascinated by his actions, she goes along with it. A crisis of the heart occurs when she discovers that J. D. intends to take out the entire student body with a bomb, pushing the plot beyond justice to annihilation. She stops him and J. D. blows himself up instead of the school.

This martyrdom element is common to black comedy where the anti-hero falls on his sword.[3] Veronica is redeemed by this and relieves the last Heather of her badge of honour, a red scrunchie. She negates the toxic influence of the clique and turns her back on prom night, preferring to stay in and watch movies with one of the nerds.

Even black comedy fights shy of an actual high-school massacre. It has been seen in *Carrie*, but this was down to supernatural causes. Perhaps it is the frequency with which these terrible events occur in real life that makes it hard to sell as a prospect. It may also be in the choice of target. Giving access to firearms to teenagers is a hot topic and the debate goes right to the heart of the Constitution. A time may come when aspects of this kind of outrage can be treated comedically – but not yet.

Plot

In black comedy, the hero's goal is a negative one, often concerning monetary gain or revenge. Sometimes he does not obtain this and there is another, saner character who sneaks out at the end with a degree of knowledge if not fiscal benefit. In any case, the money/McGuffin is not the aim, for it often gets lost (*A Simple Plan*, *Lock, Stock and Two Smoking Barrels*). The currency is seeing sense. The point of such movie narratives is wisdom and maturity.

There might also be an antagonist who offers a second option, giving the protagonist the chance to root for the lesser of two evils. There may be an ally who will try to demonstrate that what is happening is absurd, but this voice of reason will be ignored. We may have a narrator, who puts the story into context.

---

[3] E.g. Peter Finch as Howard Beale in *Network*.

Louis Mazzini's (Denis Price) confession bookends the story of *Kinds Hearts and Coronets* and explains his failure: 'It's so difficult to make a neat job of killing people with whom one is not on friendly terms.' *Heathers* uses Heather's diary and in *The Opposite of Sex* (Roos 1998), Christina Ricci is full of self-awareness as a cynical narrator. This device tells the audience what they will learn and how they will feel.

The plotting of black comedy takes us into areas where we ask, 'what's the worst that can happen?' and then explores this result. Once the character has established his Faustian pact, all bets are off and he will follow his obsession to the bitter end. If this leads to the utterly ludicrous and fantastical, it is termed black farce.

Allies will be co-opted into helping with the plan, but once involved they may turn tail and become a liability. Often, the staunch ally is abandoned shortly after the midpoint where, steeped in blood, our comic Macbeth soldiers on. Antagonists will become more dangerous once it is understood that the protagonist intends to poach their spoils. Subterfuge is played out and revealed and a final plan is put into action, the financial result is unimportant: what counts is whether it is a redemptive or a tragic tale. The question is 'what is the personal cost to the protagonist?' The answer is usually his life.

In *Bad Santa* (Zwigoff 2003), Willie T. Stokes is first seen in a crowded bar at Christmas, miserable and drunk in his Santa outfit. His voiceover explains why: an abusive father, a terrible upbringing, no optimism and no hope. It is the antithesis of the Christmas spirit and we are co-opted into his bleak comic world. The next few minutes seek to establish his negative goal and modus operandi. He and Marcus, his elf ally, rob a shopping mall but the rewards are short-lived. He goes to Florida with a dream of running a beach bar but cannot escape his addiction to sex and alcohol. In a nod to *Groundhog Day,* the clock comes around to that time again, (Christmas) when Marcus has lined up another scam. This time it is the last chance saloon. Arriving drunk in Phoenix, it is apparent to Marcus that Willie is sexually and physically incontinent, and keeping up the subterfuge of being a jolly store Santa until they can affect a break-in is going to prove difficult. Enter the antagonists, prudish mall manager Bob Chipeska (John Ritter) and store detective Gin (Bernie Mac), who are both on his case. If they expose or fire him, it will stop the flow of money that Willie needs to support his lies. Their only saving grace seems to be Marcus who, being a black midget, has all the cards to cry discrimination.

Into this comes Thurman, a simple child who believes that Willie *is* Santa, a ray of light in this desolate universe. His mother has died, his father is 'away'[4]

---

[4] In prison.

and he lives with his senile grandmother. Willie proceeds to rob the house and steal the family car but Thurman's incessant questions are the first that Willie responds to. It is this response that lets us know that the child's innocence has punctured the bubble of his selfishness and misanthropy.

Moving in with the boy, he brings a waitress back for sexual exploits, leaving Marcus to despair about how low he will sink. Meanwhile, his nemesis, Gin has discovered the truth about Thurman's father and confronts Willie and Marcus, demanding half the proceeds to keep silent. Here, both protagonist and antagonist are similarly motivated by greed. Willie, being weak, gives up and attempts suicide, giving Thurman a note to give to the police, confessing all and pushing him further along the redemptive path.[5] Before he can execute his plan, he notices that the local bullies have beaten up the boy. This stirs something in him and renewed purpose has him train the boy to defend himself. Meanwhile, Marcus succeeds in killing Gin, and the plan is back on.

The heist takes place on Christmas Eve, but Marcus has had enough and pulls a gun on Willie – thus having the ally turn nemesis. Willie is pursued by police as he heads back to Thurman's house with a last-minute Christmas gift. Here the ordeal is all. He is shot in the back on the doorstep, but his death is a spiritual one, for an epilogue voice over reveals that shooting a Santa was such an embarrassment for the police that he escapes censure. His waitress girlfriend is given guardianship over Thurman and the implication is that they will form a family unit. Willie has learned to change. In performing an act of altruism it has released him from the curse of his life. It is a redemptive ending – the only option in a world painted this black.[6]

Farce

Arsenic and Old Lace. Some Like It Hot. The Producers. Grand Budapest Hotel. Duck Soup. The Ladykillers. A Shot in the Dark. Women On The Verge Of A Nervous Breakdown. La Cage aux Folles. Home Alone. Anchorman. Date Night.

Farce relies on labyrinthine plotting and coincidence more than character. It allows for deception, slapstick and physical comedy, exaggeration, mistaken identity and lightning-fast pacing. At its best, it is a corkscrew of comedy that tightens until it pops. Farces can be light – a comedy of lies, manners and social behaviour, or dark, as in the black farce of *The Ladykillers* or *Arsenic*

---

[5]A similar plot point to *Kind Hearts and Coronets*, in which a confession is also vital to the final twist.
[6]Also see 'Christmas Movies'.

and Old Lace, which involve murder and death. Guy Richie is a modern exponent of this: his gangster movies, *Lock, Stock and Two Smoking Barrels* and *Snatch* have a dark thread of cruelty running through them.[7] In general, however, farce fights shy of satire and black comedy, which is more cruel and cutting and denies us the last minute reveal and tying up of loose ends that makes farce so popular. More often, farce depends on a comic situation, skilfully manipulated by the cast so as to extract the maximum of laughter and chaos.

It is theatrical, its origins firmly planted on the stage with Shakespeare's *A Comedy of Errors*, Oscar Wilde's *The Importance of Being Earnest,* Noel Coward's *Hay Fever* and *Blithe Spirit*, Moliere's *Tartuffe* and *The Miser,* Feydeau's *Le Dindon* and the modern French farces of Francis Veber, many of which have now been filmed, such as *La Cage aux Folles* (*The Birdcage*), *Le Placard* (Veber 2000) and *Le Diner les Cons*.

Blake Edwards too, has successfully created farces for the big screen, much of his early work starring Peter Sellers, including *The Party, A Shot in the Dark* and *The Pink Panther* series. The English stage farce tradition is going strong too in the works of Alan Aykbourne; Michael Frayn's play *Noises Off!* (Bogdanovich 1992) and Richard Bean's adaptation of *Servant and Two Masters* (Carlo Goldoni 1743) remade *as One Man, Two Guvnors.*

In farce we maintain our comic distance. Little knowledge is required to understand the initial setting or to get the joke, certainly when it involves cross-dressing and slapstick. It is universal and at its most raw, the basic scenario is man vs his environment. Objects wilfully take on a life of their own and can change purpose, being used as weapons or as a disguise or for anything other than their original purpose. There may be abuse too, both physical and verbal. This is often against a clear comic antagonist with whom we have little sympathy, as with the characters in *There's Something About Mary*.

Character

At heart, the farcical character is selfish and self-obsessed, akin to the character comedian with a blind obsession. Inspector Clouseau does not see the chaos he causes all around him, too concerned is he with being France's greatest detective. They have exaggerated traits and points of view. The farcical hero may be overconfident or otherwise deluded and bewildered and must

---

[7] Also, the darkly comic Belgian *Man Bites Dog,* which takes a look at a day in the life of a serial killer, has farcical elements.

be faced with obstacles, tests and ordeals. There is often love unrequited, if indeed love is the object. All too often it is lust, desire and bawdiness. In a sense, farce acts as a kind of pornography for the theatregoer. It is based on pure spectacle and performance, satisfying our baser instincts and avoiding any moral dimension.

There is often a large cast to cover up the lack of characterization and each will require a unique perspective and a defined goal. Each character must treat the situation with utmost seriousness (playing for laughs is strictly for pantomime) and because they are utterly selfish, this makes them antagonistic, surrounding the lead with opportunities for evasions, deceptions and conflict. The characters will go to any lengths to get what they want. In black farce, this will be life or death, as in *The Ladykillers* or *A Fish Called Wanda*.

The deception of cross-dressing involves sustaining a huge lie, and is well suited to farce, as in *Some Like It Hot, Mrs Doubtfire* or *Tootsie*. In each of these, there are high stakes. In *Mrs Doubtfire*, Daniel Hillard wants to see his children, in *Tootsie* it's the last acting job in town, in *Some Like It Hot* the boys are witness to the St Valentine's Day murder. Assuming a disguise offers liberation but also the fear of discovery. The strange new comic world has new rules that must be mastered quickly and it is often these behaviours that provide much of the comedy. In *Some Like It Hot*, once Curtis and Lemmon have mastered walking in heels ('she's like Jell-O on springs') and are accepted by the other girls, they must then deal with members of their own sex (*fresh!*) leering at them and providing an ironic mirror on their previous faults as men about town. There is also the comic fare offered by the fear of being caught during the transmogrification from man to woman and back again – then later the delicious sizzle as the two (the actor and his animus) are by chance placed in a situation where they are supposed to be in the same room together. Learning the rules of the new farcical world is like jumping on and off a carousel. Each time it turns, it is different.

There are often roles for a femme fatale, or certainly a love object as in *There's Something About Mary* in which everybody wants Mary. There are compound deceptions and many motives. In Veber's *Birdcage* (*La Cage aux Folles*) the farce elements are brought together when a gay couple discovers that their son is in a straight relationship and that he is bringing home his fiancée. The conceit is intrinsically farcical.

Characters in farce have simple needs. Bialystock and Bloom want to get rich in *The Producers*, Wanda in *A Fish Called Wanda* wants $13 million worth of diamonds. In order to get this there will be alliances and helpers but these alliances are temporary. The lead must be put in a situation where he faces his worst fears and his greatest desires, for example Ken (Michael Palin) in *Wanda*, the devoted animal lover who ends up accidentally killing three dogs.

Plot

Farce is a comedy of errors where anything that can go wrong will go wrong. So long as you establish a true motivation for the character, we will go with it. Farce must begin with a character in a world that we can recognize. In *Home Alone,* even though there are questions we might ask about how Kevin came to be left alone at Christmas in New York City (you didn't spot you were missing a child at the airport?), we accept that he is indeed alone and the events that follow have some degree of causality.

In Veber's *The Closet*, Francois Pignon, a man on the brink of being fired, is encouraged by a neighbour to reveal that he is gay, therefore making his sacking a matter of sexual discrimination. Farce works on a series of hidden gears that, once started, are impossible to stop. One absurd situation and/or ludicrous deception breeds another and soon reaches fever pitch and teeters into chaos, where it will remain for as long as possible until the structure collapses in on itself. Unlike other comedies, which are forged out of character, coincidence and implausibility reign supreme.

Act One is all about the set-up. As with a good con, all the seeding and plotting must be done here so as the reveals and pay-offs which come later will seem organic and germane. Comedy logic dictates that even though there are many coincidences, we do not see them as such. In Act Two, the lead has moved into a world of deception and has fewer choices. As lie piles upon lie, the less room he has to move as he paints himself into a corner. The ensuing chaos of the third act leads to truth. Sacrifice must be made in order to break through to the truth and what must be sacrificed are the lies you have told. In *A Fish Called Wanda,* Otto pretends to be a CIA agent giving a debriefing, but the person to whom he speaks – Archie's wife, (who has superior knowledge) knows this cannot be true, thus creating embarrassment and capitalizing on the lies.

The big reveals come at the end when all the plots and subplots come together. The house of cards collapses and the character comes clean. Often, as with a parent scolding a child for lying, the truth is enough to provoke forgiveness, and the comic law is enforced whereby, after throwing rocks at your character for an hour and a half, the suffering is over and you simply give the prize to him. It is his reward for undergoing all manner of degradations. Alternatively, as in *The Producers*, Bialystock and Bloom end up in prison, planning a new theatrical production. It has not been a redemptive curve. There will be more scams.

Farce should be kept to a short, tight timescale with an intimate cast of characters bound together via avarice, lust or obsession. *Dirty Rotten Scoundrels* pits two conmen against one another as they fight over the same patch and ultimately the same woman, who bests the pair of them. Each has a simple goal, to rinse the wealthy widows and heiresses who frequent Beaumont-sur-Mer each season, differing only in their methodology. Whereas Lawrence Jamieson (Michael Caine) has perfected an impersonation of a prince seeking funding to restore his kingdom, interloper Freddie Benson (Steve Martin) is a more mundane conman, playing on sympathy and hard luck stories. Sensing a rival, Lawrence sends him off and then has him arrested (he is in cahoots with the local police chief). Freddie however, sees through the scams and returns to carve out his own patch. Lawrence then takes him under his wing as protégé, hoping to disillusion him so much that he will tire of the game. This is not to be as the arrival of a naïve American soap heiress (Glenne Headly) forces a winner takes all wager – later to be finagled when she plays on their heartstrings and weak points. It is elegant farce, one so robust that it has been made into a hit musical.

Chapter 10

Sketch Comedy and Television

Monty Python's Flying Circus. Saturday Night Live. Kids in the Hall. Robot Chicken. Kentucky Fried Movie. In Living Color. MADTV. The Muppet Show.

The joke is the basis of all comedy, be it one-liner, pun, wordplay, quip, pointed comment or witty riposte. The joke is elegant and simple, a combination of the set-up, which contains only the information required for the joke, and the punchline, which ought to be as brief as possible and must contain the element of surprise and thwarted expectation.

From an early age we get used to the rhythm of jokes. As toddlers, English children are introduced to the 'Round and round the garden' game, in which the palm is first stroked ('round and round the garden, like a Teddy bear'), after which the finger play continues onto the wrist and inside elbow ('one step, two step') followed by a tickle under the armpit ('tickle under there'). This illustrates the premise of the rule of thirds[1] – *omne trium perfectum*, which states that things in threes are inherently funnier, more satisfying, or more effective than other numbers. An audience is more likely to consume information if it is written in threes such as slogans (*South Park: Bigger, Longer & Uncut*) and in folk and fairytale characters such as the Three Bears, Three Little Pigs, The Billy Goats Gruff or the Three Musketeers. Goldilocks samples three beds and three bowls of porridge. There are always three wishes, no more, no less. This creates the progression of set-up, confirmation and twist and introduces the element of surprise, a comedic mainspring.

That the game of 'Round and round the garden' becomes predictable is of no consequence to the child. He knows the result is coming but the fun lies in delicious anticipation. We know there will be a twist to a joke and we revel in

---

[1]Which later becomes the verbal set up for the 'Englishman, Irishman and Frenchman' joke, or other combinations of race and racism.

not only the certainty of this, but also in the anticipation of how cleverly we have been diverted. A joke is often told in question form – 'what do you call a ...? What is the difference between ...?' or it might be question and answer 'Knock, knock' or even a declamatory statement 'A man goes to the doctor ...'.

If a joke is poorly written or timed (or is a pun), it conjures a groan. If it is smart, it gets a smile and a peal of laughter. Comedy *demands* a reaction. A comedian never watches but *listens* to his audience, timing his delivery by their response. Stand-up is like waves that ebb and flow: as the joke reaches back to the rear of the room, the next one is already coming. The directness of the art form is unparalleled. If someone laughs, it's funny. If they don't, you have to re-write, re structure and edit or simply drop it. Sketches, when performed live, can be honed in this way, as was the work of the *Second City Comedy Troupe* (1959 onwards) or in the UK, *The League of Gentlemen* as well as the numerous sketch groups who attend the Edinburgh Fringe festival each year.

In the UK, short form or sketch is known as broken comedy. There is no narrative, only one set and scene and the comedy is self-contained. It is a single comic idea, with no more than two speaking parts. Here, the fledgling comic writer learns to stretch his wings. There are sketches (some of which blend into character comedy) that have become classics. In the US, after the madness of Sid Caesar's *Your Show of Shows* and *Rowan and Martin's Laugh-In*, SNL brought us *Olympic Restaurant, Coneheads, Gumby, Samurai Delicatessen, Pathological Liars Convention, Nerds, Superhero Party, Bassomatic, The Festrunk Bros* amongst others too numerous to mention, while in Britain, *Monty Python* gifted the world with *Cheese Shop, The Dead Parrot Sketch, Nudge, Nudge and Room for an Argument*.[2]

The basic situation is to have one man who wants something and the other who does not want to give it to him. This is in essence the straight man and the feed, but it can be played either way. In the British *Two Ronnies* classic *Four Candles*, the performance of poor bewildered, antagonized shopkeeper (Ronnie Corbett) is every bit as vital and comedic as the idiot farmer (Ronnie Barker).

On the page, a sketch can be half a page long or it can run to five minutes. If short it is a quickie, a pull back to reveal idea based on verbal misunderstanding or visual displacement. In this case, the audience's suspension of disbelief will only last as long as it takes for them to guess the trick. If you only have the reveal (we are not where we say we are or one person has misunderstood who the other is) then the hand must be played quickly. Character deception in movies (*Roxanne, Coming to America*) can sustain the whole narrative but in the short form we are always looking for the gag.

---

[2] All sketches referenced are currently available to view on YouTube.

The sketch is comprised of three parts, *Set-up, Complication and Resolution*. The set up establishes the idea, which ought to become evident in the first few lines, as in the 'Argument sketch' (Monty Python):

> I have come to a place where I can pay for an argument. I walk into the wrong room, where I am subjected to abuse. I then walk into the correct room, but the man tells me that he has already told me once – whereupon we argue over this. After a short period of argument he demands money to continue the argument. When I pay, he denies having had the money.

In this way the initial premise escalates into flights of fantasy and worlds of absurdity. The resolution is the capper that tops it all off and brings us to a satisfactory comic conclusion.

> I continue to argue over whether we have paid (pointing out that since we are arguing, I must have paid) until my interlocutor informs me that he may be arguing in his spare time.

This classic sketch continues on past this neat reversal, but the Pythons, as with the SNL writers, often milked their ideas or even mocked the idea of having a punchline. The problem is that life does not have a punchline. Comedy is an artificial construct. Sometimes the Gods of Comedy smile down upon you and you conceive of the punch first and simply write backwards, but this is rare. More often you have a great notion; you develop it and sweat blood to get to some semblance of an ending. The benefit of pair or team writing is having many comedy minds working on one idea. Being 'good in the room' is a useful skill for a comedy writer.

The sketch has its roots in vaudeville and music hall. Abbot and Costello, The Marx Brothers, The Crazy Gang and Flanagan and Allen all performed sketch comedy on stage before it was transplanted to the one and two reeler – the comic bits and businesses being honed and perfected by Chaplin, Lloyd, Keaton and Laurel and Hardy. The comic performer has here a simple goal – that of achieving resolution to a single problem. Beat the bad guy, win the day or get the girl. The characterization was not deep or complex enough to support the longer narrative, their desires being little more than a need expressed. Sketch comedy found its natural home in television, where the hour or half-hour programme format suited the shorter form. There are films, which are a series of sketches, the most successful of these being *Airplane!* (Zucker, Abrahams, Zucker 1980). Born out of the Zucker brothers' history of writing sketch comedy, its running time (eighty-seven minutes) is short enough to sustain a series of brilliant parodic spoofs, one-note characters, running and visual gags, violated expectations and general chaos. This format of pile 'em high, sell them cheap has proven to be successful in other genre parodies, such as the *Scary Movie* franchise and its successors.

The Monty Python films too are sketch comedies bolted together. This is self-evident in *And Now for Something Completely Different* and *The Meaning of Life*, but also in *The Holy Grail* and *Life of Brian*. A glance at the chapter headings for the latter illustrates this, each one representing the germ of the comedy sketch idea.

1   The Baby in the Manger;

2   Life of Brian;

3   The Sermon on the Mount;

4   A Stoning;

5   The Ex-leper.

The Python team wrote in pairs, Michael Palin and Terry Jones, John Cleese and Graham Chapman, with Eric Idle adding sketches and songs and Terry Gilliam the visuals. They would read out the work in committee with only the strongest sketches surviving. *The Life of Brian of Nazareth* is unique in that what was a number of strong sketches achieved more than the sum of its parts. The character (more so that Arthur: King of the Britons in *Holy Grail*) was born in the wrong place at the right time and is given a degree of characterization. His desires become manifold: to escape the Romans, to join the Judean People's Front, to be with Judith, to prove he is not the Messiah and to avoid being crucified. Admittedly, these are reactive (the love interest is barely developed), but it is a stark satirical depiction of bureaucratic hopelessness. The final song is bittersweet, its catchiness mitigating against the darker tone of the fact that he has been left to die on the cross.

If Monty Python[3] was the parent to British comedy, then that role in the US goes to the brainchild of Lorne Michaels, *Saturday Night Live*. A show that runs for 90 minutes and debuted on NBC in 1975, its premise was to combine rock 'n' roll with comedy, late at night and live. Michaels, a Canadian who had been part of a comedy double act before turning to TV production, figured that by 11.30 p.m., audiences would be stumbling out of bars and be up for the 'Not Ready For Prime Time Players'. Chevy Chase was its first star and he left after one year to appear in *Foul Play* (1978) opposite with Goldie Hawn, then went on to star in *Caddyshack,* the *National Lampoon Vacation* series (1983–) and

---

[3]With a tip of the hat to Spike Milligan and his radio creation, *The Goon Show*.

Fletch. Bill Murray, a graduate of the Second City Improv troupe in Chicago, replaced him. SNL's first golden age added Dan Aykroyd, often paired with the late John Belushi – they went on to star in *The Blues Brothers*. Later members were Eddie Murphy, Mike Myers, Billy Crystal, David Spade, Chris Farley, Tim Lawrence, Gilda Radner and Tina Fey.

When a sketch is more about the catchphrases and behaviour of a pair of characters, this is character comedy. They may be aliens, foreigners or fish out of water, but these repeating characters have provided a stepping off point for several movies, such as *Coneheads* (Steve Martin, Dan Aykroyd), *The Blues Brothers.* (Aykroyd, Belushi), *This is Spinal Tap* and *A Mighty Wind* (Harry Shearer, Christopher Guest), *Mr. Saturday Night* (Billy Crystal) *and Wayne's World* (Mike Myers, Dana Carvey) each adding a narrative device to develop the comic idea to feature length.

This can have its problems. What was designed to amuse solely on the level of repetition now has to do a lot more heavy lifting. As in the British films *Kevin & Perry Go Large* (Harry Enfield and Kathy Burke's teenage creations) or *Ali G Indahouse* (Sasha Baron Cohen's 'Wigga' character), this can serve only to point up flaws in character. It is hard to develop TV characters into feature length ideas. The audience expectations of sketch comedy are lower; the quick hit being more disposable. A movie has to build on character, requiring depth and back-story. This is anathema to the sketch character whose sole function is to deliver or repeat the joke.

Sitcom

This is also true of sitcom. In the UK, *The Inbetweeners* has spawned two hugely successful movies and *Alpha Papa* put Alan Partridge (character comedian Steve Coogan) in a hostage situation. The first *Inbetweeners* movie (Palmer, 2011) took four teenage characters and put them on holiday together. Its prime motivator was getting laid but in terms of characterization, it neatly parcelled out the emotions so that you had Simon being lovelorn and in thrall to Carly (a girl who did not care for him), Neil, who was just dumb, Will, who thought himself better than the others, and Jay, who was all teenage bullshit. It gave them an arc, pulling together and simultaneously pulling apart. Even though it took them out of the sitcom environment of home and school, it did not tinker with the character dynamic. Its sequel was set in their gap year.

In the US, sitcoms such as *The Brady Bunch, Addam's Family, Beverley Hillbillies* and *Bewitched* have made the transition to features with varying degrees of success, but sitcom to movie hits have been more constant in the animated realm with *The Simpson's Movie* and *South Park: Bigger, Longer & Uncut*. Sitcom is a mainstay of TV and with its long running seasons – twenty-two episodes annually and many series, racing to get to 100 so as to get syndication.[4] There is no need to make a movie as it is there in your living room every night on reruns. Another reason for sitcoms failure to make it onscreen is its resistance to arc of character. *No learning, no hugging, no growing*, announced *Seinfeld* from the start. *Frasier* (Kelsey Grammer) must remain alone, stuck with his ageing father and his prissy brother. Liz Lemon (Tina Fey) must remain in awe to her boss Jack Donaghy (Alec Baldwin) in *30 Rock*.

These are people trapped in amber. Although there are some long running sitcoms that *do* develop a character arc (*The Cosby Show*, *Everybody Loves Raymond*), it is a basic principle of sitcom that characters do NOT escape, grow, change, learn or develop self-awareness. This is antithetical to the feature film, which takes the character on a journey and fundamentally changes them. This change may be towards marriage, coupling or another festival that signifies completion or the attainment of a goal, but it is completion. It is maturity, and from there it is not possible to go back.

The narrative cycle of sitcom allows for the moral tale and in many cases this is its function, to advise us how to behave and to define the boundaries of social acceptability. The feature film is not geared in this way; its boundaries are not networks, sponsors or advertisers but commercial concerns and MPAA ratings. Other TV genres, often involving cops or spies, are more adaptable to comedy and to feature films – *The Dukes of Hazzard, Starsky & Hutch, Get Smart,* and *21 Jump Street* have all fared well. In the case of the latter, *21 Jump Street* was originally a police procedural crime drama. They are narratives, based on a plot of the week, with ongoing developing issues within the characters' world.

Interview: Peter Baynham

The jump from writing sketch comedy to features is a big one and a common experience for the comedy writer. What follows is an interview with Peter Baynham, a UK writer (now LA-based) who began writing for satirical UK shows (*The Day Today*) and for Sasha Baron Cohen (*Brüno, Borat*) and is the writer of *Arthur Christmas*.

You came to movies out of writing for British TV. What was easy/hard about making the transition to longer form comic narratives?

---

[4]As opposed to British runs of six episodes that conclude in Series Two or Three.

I found my first attempt at a screenplay incredibly difficult after writing TV narratives. A screenplay, whatever kind of story you're telling, does tend to require some kind of change to the characters, or at least their circumstances. Shorter narratives such as sitcom require exactly the opposite: people want the same Basil Fawlty, Victor Meldrew or Captain Mainwaring week in, week out. That said, when characters like Alan Partridge or Borat made it to the big screen, it's not like they had some huge arc – they didn't particularly 'learn' anything. For many other reasons, movies are just *hard*. (Though not as hard as real jobs). You seem to struggle and argue about every part of the movie – whether the story, the plot or individual lines – from day one until the final cut. Also, with a movie, there tend to be a lot more voices and opinions all the way through the process, whether it's other writers, producers, executives, actors and test audiences. That's not always a bad thing, but when we made *I'm Alan Partridge*, it was just me, Armando Iannucci and Steve Coogan brainstorming and writing. The BBC didn't see the script – indeed, often didn't see *anything* until we delivered the filmed, finished, cut episodes! That said, I don't think the BBC works that way any more. Happy days … .

How closely do you work with Sacha Baron Cohen when writing and creating the characters and situations? Is it team writing or one-to-one?

I and the other writers work very closely with Sacha. We spend a huge amount of time discussing every aspect of the characters and their worlds. Sometimes it's team writing, sometimes it's one–to-one, depending on what's needed. Sometimes one person will go off and write up a first draft of a scene, and then everyone will descend on it. There's not a comma that doesn't get picked over, ripped apart, turned into a semi-colon, then a full stop, then cut entirely. Sacha is incredibly thorough and obsessive about getting it right, which I suppose we all are. It drives you nuts sometimes, but it's fun too. Sometimes.

How much of what happens in the mockumentaries is improvised? What's the strike rate when shooting off the cuff? How far can and do you go?

In movies like *Borat* and *Brüno*, a lot more material is pre-written (as are the story structures) than meets the eye. That said, Sacha is a remarkable improviser and that's a big part of what happens too. I don't think I could say what the strike rate is offhand, though hundreds and hundreds of hours were shot for both movies; that's just the nature of the thing. You're looking for the very best material, and even a three-hour movie of great stuff would be way too much for an audience to sit through. Also, given that these are movies with plots, sometimes material that might seem hilarious out of context may feel irrelevant or slow the story down, if so, it's out. We learnt this truth the hard way on *Borat*, where scenes I thought were the funniest things I'd ever seen got hardly a titter from test audiences, basically because they just didn't fit the wider movie. Or maybe because I just laugh at weird shit that nobody else does.

Is the work divided into gag writing, story-lining and plotting or is a more organic process?

It's more organic – if you imagine the organic vegetables at the supermarket – messier, dirtier and knobblier than their big, smooth, shiny GM counterparts. No, we do have plotting sessions, gag sessions etc., but not in any grand overarching, planned out way. Often what we focus on depends on what we feel is needed on a particular day. Or what we feel like doing. You sometimes put off the 'heavy lifting' of detailed plotting (which is still much easier than actual, literal heavy lifting) in favour of thinking up funny things to happen. But then, a story can be led by the scenes. On the *Borat* movie, we always knew we wanted him to visit a mega church; we brainstormed the scene for a long time before, relatively late on in the process, realizing it would be a perfect scene for his end-of-act-two low point. The same with a scene where Borat met some frat boys. We always wanted this scene to happen; but then, just ahead of filming, we decided to position it at a point where we wanted him to find out the horrible truth that Pamela Anderson (who he had decided to seek out and marry) *isn't* a virgin. We were confident a bunch of frat boys would know this and could be manipulated into imparting the information to Borat. You feel your way, I suppose.

Were you on set with Borat *and* Brüno? *If so, can you tell us about your involvement in the filming?*

I travelled around the country with both movies. I have spent time actually on set, but by the time Sacha sits down for his interviews, a huge amount of thought has already gone into what he's saying. So often the writers' purpose (and, more importantly, personal safety) is better served staying back at the crew hotel and honing the material for the following day's filming.

How did these lead to your working on more family friendly fare (Arthur Christmas)? Were you gun for hire or did people start requesting you?

I can't say that *Borat* led to *Arthur Christmas*! I actually had the idea for the latter before the former came out. I've been drawn to animation for a long time, and it was an idea that excited me, so I developed and pitched it. My agents at the time were actually pretty horrified that I wanted to follow *Borat* with a family animation. I think people like to pigeonhole you – even the ones supposedly working for you – and at the time animation was considered a backwater for writers, something that seems inexplicable to me in the era of Pixar.

How did you learn to write family and animated comedy? Who are your mentors (if any?) or did you simply learn as you go? Any tips?

I'm not sure I learnt anything different for animation and family comedy. Obviously there are jokes you can't do – though it's fun to try anyway sometimes – but yes, I think you learn as you go. In the end, whilst writing *Arthur Christmas* with Sarah Smith, we probably just learned to write *Arthur Christmas*. Which, once *Arthur Christmas* was finished, was a pretty useless skill. The only tip I think I could give, which I'd say for any genre, is to not try and second-guess what people want. It's a cliché to say this, but you personally have to like what you write.

Do you guide your career as a writer, or is there still an element of taking what's on offer?

I can't claim to guide my career, although there are ideas and projects I really want to do before I die or lose my mind. A movie takes a bloody long time to get from idea to screen, so in a lifetime, there isn't time to do that many. I have sometimes taken what's on offer. I've tried to make the right choices, not always successfully. Right now it's my priority to focus on my own ideas and push those. As for what the studios are looking for, it's hard to say. I'm sure certain genres are in vogue, but I've always hoped they will just respond positively to a particular idea. It's always depressing as a punter when an original idea for a movie comes out, is hugely successful, then is followed a couple of years later by a slew of uninspired imitations, presumably commissioned because that's what people were 'looking for'. Often these movies don't do anywhere near as well as the movie they copied, which would seem obvious.

Grimsby is a new departure for you and SBC, returning to England and a more parochial arena – what are your feelings about this and how is the new movie coming together?

The movie's coming together great, I think. The shooting seemed to go really well, it all seemed very funny. It's being edited right now, so we'll see. I loved shooting in the UK again. That said, although it starts in England, it's actually set around the world.

Who are your comic heroes and why (writers/directors/stars)?

Terry Gilliam – an incredible, passionate talent. John Cleese. David Nobbs (*The Fall and Rise of Reginald Perrin*). I once met him on a radio show and was speechless. Paul Abbott, who is obviously more than a comedy writer, but whose work has often made me laugh hugely. I heard him talking on *Desert Island Discs* and was blown away by how he has overcome so many obstacles to become what he is. I used to think my background was an unlikely one for a TV writer (left school at sixteen to join the Merchant Navy), and then I heard his story. Astonishing. Also the people I've been lucky enough to work with.

What advice would you give to aspirant comedy screenwriters?

This is advice to self as well: be original. Be truthful. Try to have heart or thought in there alongside the gags and set pieces; personally, as a fan, I don't like comedy movies that are just that – comedy movies. Often the movies I find funniest aren't comedies per se. An example (not a perfect example as it's TV) would be *Breaking Bad*, which could have my skin crawling – then laughing out loud, often from one scene to the next. Dramas that draw you in, have you believe in and genuinely feel for the characters and their situations can sometimes make you laugh more ('It's funny because it's true!'). So I would like to see comedies that strive for that truth and warmth. Oh, and if you have an idea you LOVE and would love to see, then write (or pitch) that, whatever people tell you the studios are 'looking for' this week.

Chapter 11

Action and Animated Comedy

Action

Mr. and Mrs. Smith. Beverly Hills Cop. Smokey and the Bandit. 48 Hrs. The Blues Brothers. Bad Boys. Night at the Museum. 21 Jump Street. How To Train Your Dragon. Kick Ass. Hot Fuzz. The Heat. Charlie's Angels. Spy Kids. Kung Fu Panda. Despicable Me. Small Soldiers. Toy Story. Austin Powers. Ghostbusters.

Many of today's blockbusters, both live action and animation, can be described as action comedies. Where there are quips, banter and comic set pieces, they will fall into this broad category. Prior to the 1980s there were action adventure movies that featured comedy but these were in the main madcap romps designed to lure audiences back to the big screen, such as *It's a Mad, Mad, Mad, Mad World* (Kramer 1963) or *Casino Royale* (Various 1967). There was *Every Which Way But Loose* (Fargo 1978) featuring Clint Eastwood and a chimp but the first of the modern action adventure franchises kicked off with *Raiders of the Lost Ark* (Spielberg 1981).

The precedent for having the comedy coming before the adventure is *The Blues Brothers* (Landis 1980) starring John Belushi and Dan Aykroyd as Jake and Elwood Blues, two characters they had developed on Saturday Night Live. This was a redemptive tale as they took on 'a mission from God' to save the Catholic orphanage in which they grew up from foreclosure. To do so, they had to reunite their R&B band and organize a performance to earn $5,000 to pay the tax assessor. Aykroyd, new to film screenwriting, took six months to deliver a lengthy script that Landis had to rewrite before production, and which began without a final budget.[1] On location in Chicago, Belushi's partying and

---

[1] In the 1998 documentary, *Stories Behind the Making of The Blues Brothers*, Aykroyd admits that he had never written a screenplay before, or even read one, and was unable to find a writing partner.

drug use caused long and costly delays, which, along with the car chases depicted onscreen, made the final film one of the most expensive comedies ever produced. It was, however, extremely profitable and is a cult favourite.

The template for action comedy is considered to be fellow SNL alumnus Eddie Murphy film debut in *48 Hrs* (Hill 1982) pairing Nick Nolte as a hard-nosed cop who reluctantly teams up with Murphy's wise-cracking criminal temporarily paroled to him in order to track down a killer. In *Beverly Hills Cop* (Brest 1984), Murphy plays a freewheeling Detroit cop pursuing a murder investigation who ends up dealing with the different culture of Beverly Hills. The former is an odd-couple buddy movie, the latter pure fish out of water. *48 Hrs* is seen as the first buddy *cop* movie, which lead to the *Beverly Hills Cop, Lethal Weapon*, *Bad Boys* (Will Smith and Martin Lawrence) and *Rush Hour* franchises.

They were hugely successful. Janet Maslin of *The New York Times* wrote '*Beverly Hills Cop* finds Eddie Murphy doing what he does best: playing the shrewdest, hippest, fastest-talking underdog in a rich man's world. Eddie Murphy knows exactly what he's doing, and he wins at every turn'. There was a strong James Bond influence in adopting more than the cursory throwaway gags. 'It was now OK to spend an hour wisecracking followed by a final half an hour shooting people in a totally non-comedic way. The comedy movie had officially been coopted, and this cross-pollination was to dominate the genre for another decade' (McCabe 2005).

Getting the balance right between the drama (the action) and the comedy is not easy. In *48 Hrs*, executives found the footage of the gunfight in the hotel to be too violent and, worried it would kill the film's humour, told Hill that he would never work for Paramount again. He did. (*Another 48 Hrs* 1990). In *Beverly Hills Cop*, Alex Foley's childhood friend Mikey Tandino (James Russo) is not only beaten up, but also shot in the back of the head. Although this gives good reason for Foley to pursue his killers, it unbalances the tone. As the genre has developed, a clearer demarcation has developed over where the comedy and drama ought to be. It is a fine balance. You need enough motivation and serious drama, but you skate perilously close to the comedy maxim of no one getting hurt for real. The level of cartoon action must be consistent. We know that Schwarzenegger can annihilate at will but the killing is always in the background. Close-up killing (of a minor character) assumes the gravitas of the old cowboy movies, as the dying gunman whispers his last wish for revenge.

Consequently, he put together a descriptive volume that explained the characters' origins and how the band members were recruited. His final draft was 324 pages. To soften the impact, Aykroyd made a joke of the thick script and had it bound with the cover of the Los Angeles Yellow Pages directory for when he turned it in to producer Robert K. Weiss (Zeman 2013).

Robert Zemeckis (a protégé of Spielberg) brought humour to the action adventure romp in *Romancing The Stone* (1984) before ramping up the science fiction genre with the *Back to the Future* trilogy (1985–90). These brought Boy's Own adventure movies to a new generation, but mainly it has always been about cops. The good cop, bad cop template allows for a straight transfer of the Laurel and Hardy or Lemmon and Matthau dynamic of opposing character traits thrown together. The modern action comedy is a higher budget version of the Abbot and Costello series or the Hope/Crosby *Road To...* movies.

Midnight Run (Brest 1988) is a slower-paced action film in which Robert De Niro stars as a bounty hunter and Charles Grodin as a mob accountant with a fear of flying. The comedy here is subtle and Grodin, as in *The Lonely Guy* (with Steve Martin, 1984) acts him off the screen. Sometimes there is a difficulty in defining whether the films are straight adventure (*Die Hard*) with a twist of humour, or based on a comic premise, as in the Owen Wilson, Ben Stiller reboot of *Starsky & Hutch* (Phillips 2004). As with *21 Jump Street* (Lord 2012), it was based on a long-running police procedural crime drama series, as was *Charlie's Angels* (McG 2000). It seems that most fictional cop TV series attempt to move the brand onto the big screen.

In order for a movie to qualify as action comedy, there must be crime, which means a kingpin criminal or criminal organization. The protagonist will be on the side of the law, after all this is a conservative genre, but will most often be a renegade, a reformed criminal or loose cannon. This is similar to the straight action movie, where, if militaristic, the chain of command is important. If the lead is a cop, he will be a detective; if in the military, he will be a sergeant, platoon commander or equivalent in one of the other armed forces. This is important for access to information. He cannot merely be a grunt – *Private Benjamin* is a rare exception, where Goldie Hawn still gets to lead her platoon into action. The action comedy character must be a player. He cannot be a desk jockey (unless unwillingly plucked from this into action), nor can he be in a high position of power, as this would deny him the opportunity of going into the field. Kelsey Grammer may command a submarine in *Down Periscope* (Ward 1996), but his assignment to the USS Stingray is a demotion. Other similar stories of such blowhards brought down are all based on the *Sgt Bilko* model of the crafty miscreant within the ranks, whose innate care for his men will triumph over avarice in the end. British military satires are less forgiving, implying that the corruption and incompetency begins at the very top.[2]

The detective or private investigator is the most suitable character type for crime, drama and comedy as he has access to all: the suspects, the man on

---

[2] See *Privates Progress* (1956) written and directed by the Boulting brothers.

the street, his fellow officers (for back-up or betrayal) and to the top brass, who control his operations. He is mobile but he can have his wings clipped, as so often happens. He is unlikely to die in the field – that is the fate of his buddy or an officer of inferior rank.

If the action is seen from the criminal side, this tips it into heist comedy (*Ocean's Eleven*, Soderberg 2001). There will often be a love interest, but this is a side plot to the main action, which takes place between buddy protagonists and thus is close to bromance.

The key to writing action comedy is to write a straight action movie and then layer the comedy on top. There are many tropes and clichés in the action/adventure comedy movie but they continue to work onscreen and are reinvented regularly. These include:

- The unlikely pairing of good and bad cop. These characters represent the unity of opposites but there is thin characterization because their main function is to solve the crime. Interpersonal relationship issues are added to create drama between them and their partner, their home relationships and those with their bosses. They are almost direct opposites and not complementary, so all they share is the job and have diametrically opposed ways of doing it, within the parameters of the law. The definition of what the law is, is flexible, and may include larceny, the mass destruction of public property (cars) and/or police brutality;

- They will not do things by the book, but as with military comedy this will prove that the book is ultimately right, because justice will be served in the end by due process. They ultimately kowtow to the concept of lawfulness;

- Their relationship mirrors that of the protagonists in romcoms. When they meet there is instant antagonism, the relationship is uneasy, leading to a full scale falling out and break-up. Once this is put into perspective by the trials of others, there is reconciliation. The homo-erotica is sometimes subtle, and sometimes overt, as in the French OSS-117 period spy movie spoofs (see *OSS: 117, Cairo Nest of Spies* or *Lost in Rio*);

- Unless it is a female or male-female pairing, women are reduced to love/sex interest or victim roles. They act as the subplot and on occasion (as in sitcom) the moral compass, e.g. when John McClane is trying to reconcile with his estranged wife Holly on Christmas Eve in *Die Hard*, (McTiernan 1988). With provenance in TV's *Cagney and Lacey*, the first screen action female pairing is *The Heat* (Feig 2013), starring Sandra Bullock and Melissa McCarthy as mismatched cops. Two women *not* paired as criminals is rare, the *Thelma & Louise* template, one exception being Bette Midler and Shelley Long as actresses *pretending* to be cops in *Outrageous Fortune* (Hiller 1987). Otherwise we have to go to Hong Kong, which has a tradition of female action stars (Michelle Yeoh, Cynthia Rothrock) or to Japan;

- Male-female pairings often appear in action comedy spy comedies. *Mr. and Mrs. Smith,* (Liman 2007)[3] is notable for being the film where Brad Pitt and Angelina Jolie met and fell in love. Mr and Mrs Spy live together but know nothing of each other's secret occupation. The only way we can buy into this ludicrous conceit is because spies are a construct. Like serial killers, spies are a blank canvas. The paradox here is that real spies are grey men or women, because a spy must be the least susceptible to suspicion. Their remit, to gather secret information, is unrelated to the top range marksmanship, advanced driving skills and superhuman physical strength attributed to that persuasive myth, the indomitable hero James Bond. So adaptable has the conceit of the spy become, that they can even be children, as in *Spy Kids* (Rodriguez 2001);

- Keeping the secret from your partner is also vital, as in 1991 French *Film La Totale!* Remade as *True Lies* (Cameron 1994). Harry Tasker (Arnold Schwarzenegger) leads a double life. At work he is a government agent with a license to kill, while at home he pretends to be a dull computer salesman. He is on the trail of stolen nuclear weapons when he discovers his wife is seeing another man because she needs some adventure in her life. Harry decides to give it to her;

- Action comedy can also cross over with the heist or 'one last job' movie, involving putting an elderly or retired team back together such as in *RED* (Schwentke 2010), which stands for Retired Extremely Dangerous. When his peaceful life is threatened by a high-tech assassin, former black-ops agent Frank Moses (Bruce Willis) reassembles his old team in a last ditch effort to survive and uncover his assailants;

- The nemesis will have a number of disposable henchmen; another trope developed from James Bond, in particular *Goldfinger* and *You Only Live Twice*, in which colour-coded boiler suits were introduced – later spoofed in the *Austin Powers* trilogy;

---

[3] Screenwriter Simon Kinberg came up with the idea for the film after listening to a couple of his friends undergoing marriage counselling. Kinberg noticed that the way they were describing it sounded 'aggressive and mercenary', and he 'thought it would make an interesting template for a relationship inside of an action film' (Murray n.d.).

- There will be a short timespan to solve the crime, most likely either 24 or 48 hours which must be consecutive. This is solely in order to introduce the *ticking clock* as real life police work tends to drag on. Most murders are domestic and solved quickly. Murder cases that are not solved within a matter of days are said to have gone cold. Disappearance depends on the importance of the victim. If it is a young, white girl, the interest will grow over time. If black, it is hardly there at all;

- At some point it will get personal. Despite there being big themes of police corruption, betrayal, truth and trust, there is often some familial connection to the nemesis, as in Sherlock Holmes and his brother Mycroft and its myriad variations;

- The stories are about law and justice. The main character needs to expose lies but it can only do so from outside the system. He is often stripped of his weaponry and authority because he needs intuition in order to solve the crime, thinking, as the cliché has it, as the criminal does. Again, in real life, criminals are indistinguishable from high-achieving businessmen, politicians and bankers;

- There will be the extended use of guns, other phallic weaponry and or martial arts;

- There will be extended action sequences that have no comedy;

- The movie will have a longer running time than the usual comedy as it mirrors the action/adventure movie. Often two hours;

- It is ideal for animation because physical laws are continually broken.

Animated comedy

Animation follows the laws of physics – unless it is funnier otherwise.
ART BABBITT, DISNEY ANIMATOR

Toy Story. Monsters Inc. The Incredibles. Team America: World Police. South Park: Bigger, Longer & Uncut. The Lego Movie. Frozen. Brave. Shrek. The Simpsons Movie. Kung Fu Panda. Who Framed Roger Rabbit. Chicken Run.

Snow White and the Seven Dwarves (Disney 1937) was the first full-length animated cartoon to be released, setting an industry standard and allowing Disney to dominate the market for decades until Pixar came along. Animated cartoons, from rostrum camera animation (Disney, Hanna Barbera) to stop-motion

Claymation (Aardman) to digital CGI (Pixar) are extremely expensive to produce – the lead-time for a feature being between two and four years. Stars are less expensive to hire than for live action and recognizable comic voices (Clooney, Murphy, Hanks) help sell the product for animated/CGI comedies. Since the perfection of CGI in the last decade (fur and hair were particularly difficult), animated comedy has become a market leader and today there are any number of little guys, unappreciated children and monsters that have made it to the big screen.

Disney's *Merrie Melodies* shorts (from *Steamboat Willie* in 1929) and competitor *Looney Tunes* were instant hits and the cartoon short became a staple of Saturday morning pictures. Single-frame rostrum camera animation was labour intensive and a series of laws – cartoon physics – came to be developed (see Appendix). DePatie-Frelang created the *Pink Panther* series and the first TV animated sitcoms were Hanna Barbera's *The Flintstones* (1960–6) and The *Jetsons* (1962/3). The first X-rated animated feature was *Fritz the Cat* (Bakshi 1972) based on a strip by counterculture artist Robert Crumb. Bakshi went on to make seven additional animated features including *The Lord of the Rings* (1978) and *Cool World* (1992).

Due to the labour involved in making a twenty-one minute sitcom episode, it was not until the 1990s that Matt Groening, known for his *Life In Hell* cartoons, developed a dysfunctional yellow family as shorts for the Tracy Ullman TV Show. Working with producer James L. Brooks, this became *The Simpsons*, which has now run for over twenty-five seasons. The success of this on Fox TV paved the way for Trey Parker and Matt Stone's *South Park* and Seth Macfarlane's *Family Guy*. The rise of the animated sitcom was achieved with corporate investment, big writing/production teams and little Asian fingers. Japan produces a great deal of animated Manga.

Toy Story (Lasseter 1995) was a game changer, the first CGI full-length animated cartoon made by Pixar and a huge worldwide hit, spawning sequels and vast merchandising opportunities. The concept, present in the treatment onwards, was the reversal that 'toys deeply want children to play with them'. This drives the whole character and narrative, one that has successfully been carried over into a trilogy. It is these kinds of questions that are at the heart of all animated comedy. In a sense they are childlike, or at least unfettered by adult reasoning. The tone that characterizes animation is one of wonder.

There are few animated comedy cartoons solely aimed at the adult market. The *South Park* movie is R-rated but comes with the Parker/Stone brand of approval: generally, apart from drama or action movies (*Persepolis*, *Sin City*) it is hard to get adults to see an animated movie. Ironically, *Family Guy/American Dad* and *South Park* have immense freedom in television sitcom terms (nudity, racism, sexism, anti-Semitism, homophobia, profanity and vomiting), doing and saying things that you could never get away with in live action, and it is *because* they are animated that it is seen as somehow safe. These shows bust more taboos than any movie mentioned in this book. As with pantomime, the writing of the animated feature has a natural home in childhood, but, as the children are accompanied by adults, the writers and producers will put jokes in for them as well. Another route is to mix live action with animation, as in *Who Framed Roger Rabbit?* or *The Mask*.

In story terms, animated features have roots in fairytale, folklore and horror, often with a reverse spin. *Shrek* and *Despicable Me* both take the forlorn monster who is looking for love or a friend. It is Frankenstein, King Kong or Beauty and the Beast. Writer and (co-)director of *Brave* (2012), Brenda Chapman considered it a fairy tale in the tradition of Hans Christian Anderson and the Brothers Grimm, and it is to these tales that the writer ought to look for inspiration.

Also, a decision must be made about super powers and magic. Flaws appear in fantasy when magic does not conform to set rules. *Toy Story* has talking toys and spaceman action figure Buzz Lightyear, but otherwise the toy world is an approximation of reality with the exception of the chase scenes. The shrinking device in *Despicable Me* does not, and the henchmen are pure invention. If a team, group or family has super powers (*The Incredibles*), – they must be unique to each person. Bob Parr (Mr Incredible) has super strength but limited invulnerability. His wife is Elastigirl. Sibling Violet has invisibility and the power to create a super shield and Dash has super speed. Their nemesis, Syndrome, intends to perfect the Omnidroid Monster (Dr Frankenstein again) and manipulate its controls to become a hero himself, and then sell his inventions so everyone will become equally 'super', thus making the term meaningless. The balance of who has or does not have super powers and the degree of them is important. The situation of equally matched opponents reduces many super hero movies to a boxing match – great if that is your thing, but it stalls in terms of narrative. It is brains or trickery that outdoes the villain, rather than sheer force. A lesson for the children.

In a 2003 comic book written by Jeph Loeb (*Superman/Batman*), Batman observed of Superman, 'In many ways, Clark is the most human of us all. Then ... he shoots fire from the skies and it is difficult not to think of him as a god. And how fortunate we all are that it does not occur to him.'

Siegel and Schuster's creation was based in part on Samson and Hercules[4] and is the template for the modern superhero (Batman does not have super-powers). *Action Comics No. 1* (which sold in August 2014 for over $3 million)

---

[4]Some have even suggested Moses or Jesus.

depicted a Superman whose powers were limited to lifting a car over his head, running 'faster than a speeding locomotive', leaping one eighth of a mile and having a dense body that could only be pierced by an artillery shell. It is the Superman myth that has invulnerability, the comic strip having been reinvented in the silver age by Alan Moore, and by John Byrne, with Superman surviving his death at the hands of Doomsday and with a further comic book re-boot in 2011. The concept of Kryptonite was not introduced until 1943 when radio serial actor Bud Collyer wanted to take some time off. There must be an Achilles heel. Superman's is his fondness for humanity; Batman's his pursuit of vigilante justice at all costs. Animated universes are only limited by the writers' imagination but must establish the physical laws of the creation. If you have flying cars, what are the traffic regulations? Does every vehicle fly or only selected ones? What limits your character physically and mentally? What is his or her moral code?

Here are my laws for animated character types.

1   Kids are smarter than any parent or grown-up, but not all talking animals;

2   Good shall always prevail, but tricksters are at the heart of all cartoons;

3   Cat/dog hierarchies are based on eugenics. The smaller and furrier a creature, the cuter it is. If large and dumb, it will prove not to be dangerous;

4   The lead character is not that smart and will need the plot explaining to him;

5   Heroes and heroines must be as Caucasian as possible, even if Asian, dark or red-haired. Bad guys cannot be fully black;

6   School playground rules apply. Big kids will terrorize little kids, but David defeats Goliath. You cannot rat them out, but victory will be achieved using mentor and magic;

7   Perseverance will win out. Small, individual and pitiable is good; corporate, greedy and pitiful is bad;

8   This is a world where parents are invisible because the lesson is you must learn to parent yourself;

9   The key to victory is within you (ugly duckling syndrome). Unlike in real life;

10 Bad guys are misunderstood and will relish the opportunity to be accepted by the end, in song.

For the cartoon laws of physics, please see Appendix Two.

Chapter 12

Double Acts: Buddy Movies, Bromance and the Road

Comedy teams grew out of burlesque and vaudeville. In 1910, Hank and Lank (Victor Potel and Augustus Carney) were a big success and produced a new short almost each week, matched in popularity only by *Mutt and Jeff*, a pair of animated characters developed from Bud Fisher's comic cartoon strip. Mack Sennett took the vaudeville team of Weber and Fields to the big screen and created big man and small man teams such as Mack Swain and Chester Conklin, naming them Ambrose and Walrus (McCabe 2005). Another, Billy Ruge was paired with bit-part actor Oliver Hardy as Plump and Runt (1916).

The buddy movie is a particular facet of American culture, and the male bonding traces back to the Mark Twain characters of Tom Sawyer and Huckleberry Finn. As observed by film historian David Thompson, 'You just wouldn't see three Englishmen behave the way American men do, who are truly happiest when they are together with other men.' Buddies became a popular feature of vaudeville, and when cinema came along they were ready to be reinvented for the screen.

The buddy movie begins with Laurel and Hardy, the ultimate comedy duo, whose adventures in the American Depression grew out of the one reeler and survived the transition to sound. They weren't a natural double act, being put together by producer Mack Sennett. Their exploits grew in popularity. Laurel and Hardy have differing names around the word – Dick und Doof in Germany, Flip I Flap in Poland and El Gordo y el Flaco in Spain – most of them meaning the skinny and the fat one. This template, of two men physically and psychologically at odds, established the norm – be they tall and short, fat and thin, dumb and dumber. They were the prototype for Abbot and Costello, Hope and Crosby, Lewis and Martin, Lemmon and Matthau, Aykroyd and Belushi, Wilder and Pryor, Martin and Candy, Myers and Carvey, Murphy and Nolte or Aykroyd, Gibson and Glover, Carrey and Bridges, and the interracial Chan and Tucker (*Rush Hour*) and Smith and Lee Jones (*Men in Black*).

The buddy movie is most often male, but there were popular male/female buddy movies in the screwball era with Grant and Hepburn (*Bringing Up Baby*), Grant and Russell (*His Girl Friday*), married couple Tracy and Hepburn (*Adam's Rib*), then later Hudson and Day (*Pillow Talk*) and the stand-up duo (Mike) Nichols and (Elaine) May. It wasn't until *Thelma & Louise* (Scott 1991) that a truly feminist movie was moulded and even then a man directed it, and they both died.

A recent feminine attempt to imitate the Eddie Murphy action-movie model is with Sandra Bullock and Melissa McCarthy in *The Heat* (Feig 2013), which came off the back of mega-hit *Bridesmaids*. The pair play off their physical attributes, McCarthy hefting weight and spitting cynical one liners, Bullock beautiful but married to the job – a reprise of her *Miss Congeniality* character.

The comedy action buddy movie sprang from where *The Blues Brothers* left off and featured another SNL alumnus, Eddie Murphy, already successful from his *In Concert* videos and *Trading Places*, who hit big with *Beverly Hills Cop* and *48 Hrs*. This in turn gave rise to the *Men in Black* franchise, *Starsky & Hutch*, *21 Jump St* and sequel.

Character

What Laurel and Hardy offered was reciprocal damage. Initially this was foisted on each other but later, a series of antagonists were introduced in the form of wives and their moustachioed foil, James Finlayson. Their comic tit-for-tat was sibling rivalry writ large and taken to the extremes of physical pain. The same can also be seen in *Dumb and Dumber*. Laurel and Hardy existed at a time and in a world where comic tomfoolery reigned supreme and their antics became increasingly cartoon-like. There was no problem in them playing their wives, or being hit so hard that their voices changed. They would bed down together and nothing was thought of it. The friendship was one of deep loathing, envy and mutual necessity, as with Vladimir and Estragon in Beckett's masterpiece, *Waiting for Godot*.

Hardy was the instigator, the one securing employment, ostensibly the sensible one. Laurel was inculcated in the scheme and here the comedy arose from his wish to help, to improve. Laurel, like Chaplin before him, was the idiot savant, a pure creative who would mechanize or industrialize the process of the work. Unfortunately this would have unforeseen circumstances (see *Busy Bodies*). This would set off a chain reaction and the escalating reciprocal damage would cause them both to be the recipient of further collateral damage. They would end up sitting in the rubble of their dreams and ambitions, having pushing the daily rock up the hill and, like Sisyphus, seen it come rolling back again. This was the comedy of a new, industrialized world and, like Chaplin or

Keaton, they were flummoxed by it, but the routine was set and the variations on it were endless. They later introduced clever wordplay, (Laurel being responsible for twenty-two of the movies) which showed off the balance of Laurel's surreal world view and Hardy's straight man rebuttals, creating catchphrases such as 'Why don't you do something to help me?' and 'Another fine mess you've gotten me into'.

A different pairing was the suave one and the coward, developed within The Marx Brothers and by Abbot and Costello. Lou and Bud employed cross-talk, a lightening quick series of exchanges and confusions best exemplified in the famous sketch 'Who's on First?' which they successfully carried over to their films. Bob Hope and Bing Crosby made a number of parodies during the War years, with the *Road To...* movies (see Road Movies) and perfected this trope, which was continued by Martin and Lewis.

The buddy movie is the double act, the feed and comic. With Laurel and Hardy you can see Laurel thinking about what he has been told, and taking it in inappropriate or different directions. The gag or laugh is short. The twist is made and the single comic moves on. The double act uses this as a basis for conflict, with the straight man questioning the veracity of the statement, taking it further. This forms the basis for a running gag (involving a series of callbacks) for a routine or a staged comic set piece.

The buddy act requires one foot in reality and the other in the comic realm. There is a mix of the fool inside and the fool outside. The job of the straight man – Dean Martin, Bing Crosby or Oliver Hardy – is to try to curtail the fool and to bring him into line. This is doomed to failure because the fool is his Id, a natural extension of himself. However, as the fool needs a base of reality as something to work from, the straight man has picked the part of him that will break the boundaries of convention.

In writing buddy comedy it must always seem that they could not exist independently of one another – ask not why they are together, but why are they not anywhere else?

What binds them are similar desires, simple ones such as money, the search for love or simply to get home. They have a rapport or shorthand that develops between them to exclude outsiders. This is because the nature of their friendship is an immature one, its codes, tropes and allegiances being those of the nine-year-old. They do have a moral view of the world but it is fluid and naïve. They are easily taken in by conmen and tricksters who play on their greed and sloth in order to trick them out of any riches they may accumulate. This extends to femmes fatales, who will also try to drive a stake between them. However, the bond is too great and, despite any play at longing or desire, they are in essence pre-pubescent.

Plot

Whilst buddy movie plots often consist of this teasing and testing (*Dumb and Dumber*), the male friendship will always survive such attempts unless a balance is achieved where both are partnered up and married off. In this scenario, the comedy is over for they have formed a mature relationship and outgrown the status of sibling children.

There is a lot of sitcom in this, with *The Odd Couple* (Saks 1968) being a prime example. Neil Simon's 1965 Broadway play was filmed with Jack Lemmon and Walter Matthau and later remade as an ABC Series (1970–5) starring Tony Randall and Jack Klugman. The 'two men in a domestic arrangement' idea was allegedly based on Simons' own divorce when he went to live with his agent. This is a *social* buddy movie, as they remain in one location, with enough personality differences to keep them at odds: one, fussy and house-proud, the other slovenly and devil may care. In the UK there are echoes of this in *The Likely Lads* (Clement/La Frenais), *Red Dwarf* (Grant/Naylor), *Men Behaving Badly* (Nye) and *Peep Show* (Bain/Armstrong). In the US there is *Frasier* and *Two and a Half Men*.

Lemmon and Matthau parlayed their double act into a roster of films including *The Fortune Cookie* (Wilder 1966), *The Front Page* (Wilder 1974),[5] *Buddy, Buddy* (Wilder 1981) based on Francois Veber's play *Le Contrat*, and then *Grumpy Old Men* (Petrie 1993) and its sequel *Grumpier Old Men*[6] (Deutch 1995). Despite both men having love interests (a love triangle making for greater conflict), the comedy was of mature adults with mature concerns and enmities. It was less them against the world, more them against one another. Sometimes it was slapstick, sometimes insult, although still incorporating the trope of reciprocal damage but adding more verbal interaction.

This aspect, of spite-ridden antagonists thrown together by order or circumstance, was to play out in the action-adventure buddy movies of Eddie Murphy, Mel Gibson et al. A more intimate and honest take is Alexander Payne's *Sideways* (2004) – a beautifully observed buddy movie set in the vineyards of southern California.

Bromance

Wedding Crashers. I Love You, Man. The Internship. This is the End. Ted. SuperBad. The Hangover.

---

[5] Based on Ben Hecht's *Hold The Front Page,* filmed as *His Girl Friday.*
[6] The latter being more a romantic comedy than a buddy movie.

The term 'bromance' was coined by Skateboard Magazine editor Dave Carnie to refer to the relationship of skaters who spend a great deal of time together (Elliott 2007).

Aristotle is the true prototype for bromance, who wrote in 330 BC 'It is those who desire the good of their friends for the friends' sake that are most truly friends, because each loves the other for what he is, and not for any incidental quality.'[7]

What were once called buddy movies have been rebranded as bromances. To draw a distinction between the two, the buddy movie tends to be more external and action based, whereas the bromance has a more intimate social setting with a degree of latent homosexuality. This is taken to its logical conclusion in *The Players* (*Les Infidèles*, Hazanavicius 2012), which examines male infidelity in all its forms.

It can be seen in the relationship between Ben Affleck and Matt Damon (*Good Will Hunting*), George Clooney and Brad Pitt (*Ocean's Eleven* and sequels) and Mike Myers and Dana Carvey (*Wayne's World*). The perfect buddy/bromance blend is *Butch Cassidy and The Sundance Kid* (Hill 1969), pairing Newman and *Redford* as the titular outlaws. It inspired the TV series *Alias Smith and Jones* and was spoofed in *Shanghai Noon*.

Wedding Crashers (Dubkin 2005) starring Vince Vaughan and Owen Wilson as fake siblings John and Jeremy illustrates the bromance motto of 'bros before hos'. Indeed, the Uncorked edition of the DVD extras provides an extensive list of male wedding-crasher bonding requirements and set out their relationship to women. A wedding party montage in Act One demonstrates that it is all about bedding them and no more. The emotional bond is entirely between the men and their fall out is the crisis of the movie. Its resolution is the usual trope of love and commitment over sex: Vaughan's character is spectacularly trumped by Isla Fisher's 'virgin' and, finding his soul mate in a woman rather than in his male best friend, he dumps Wilson for her. Likewise Wilson falls for his girl (thus breaking the rules), but eventually turns up at Vaughan's wedding to take this place as Best Man. The point here is that the men are after a carbon copy of themselves but with tits. The ending of the movie has all four heading off into the sunset and contemplating crashing a wedding together.

If the men here are chauvinist equals, *I Love You, Man* (Hamburg 2009) features a confident Alpha male and his protégé. It stars Paul Rudd and Jason Segel, following their pairings in Judd Apatow projects *Knocked Up* and *Forgetting Sarah Marshall*. The script, originally called *Let's Be Friends* by Larry Levin was sold a decade before but had been in turnaround. Director John

---

[7]Elder, J. (2008), 'A fine Bromance', *The Age*, 18 October 2008 (accessed 28 October 2014).

Hamburg (*Meet the Parents*, *Along Came Polly*) was approached but turned it down until he moved to LA and was himself looking for friends.

Real-estate man Peter Klaven (Paul Rudd) is about to wed fiancée Zooey but has no close friends and needs a Best Man (the symbolism is overt). He makes overtures at a number of men but when these fail, he comes across Sydney Fife (Jason Segel) at an open house where he is scamming free food and picking up divorcees. They bond quickly over a shared appreciation of rock group *Rush*, but Segel's Alpha Dog approach rubs many up the wrong way. Trust issues over borrowing money causes a rift, which is later resolved at the wedding.

The tropes of male friendship are examined, such as the den or playpen, the bonding over shared hobbies or references, the spurious advice offered, man-dating and the wingman approach. There is infatuation here and this is the core of the bromance which, in an urban metrosexual context, admits that we can fall 'a little bit in love with' a male friend who seems to have what we lack.

This is also evident in the UK Cornetto trilogy of movies starring Simon Pegg and Nick Frost, directed by Edgar Wright. These are bromances where the female characters are often overshadowed by the demands of male friendship. In *Shaun of the Dead*, Shaun's (Pegg) girlfriend Liz (Kate Ashfield) dumps him and he has to fight through the zombie hordes to get to the pub to win her back, in a uniquely unfussy British way. Their reuniting at the end still allows for his best mate (now zombified Nick Frost as Ed) to remain chained up so that they can still continue to have play-dates in the shed. The message is clear that ultimately, although men will compromise for a woman, the real relationship is with his buddy.

In *Hot Fuzz*, there is only the bromance, and in *World's End*, relationships with women are long over or non-existent. In the bromance, women intrude upon the space of the buddies, being portrayed as a stern mother character, bringing them back to reality, mocking their juvenilia. The audience, mainly male, identifies with the childish state these men are in. Why grow up? Why accept responsibility? It is the fear of puberty and inevitable maturity. Often the balance will be between the man with the job and the girl (at the cusp of undergoing maturation) being seen to be dragged back by his unemployed, lazy stoner buddy. Because they are adults, she will insist that he take on the new role or be discarded. *Ted* (Macfarlane 2012), starring Seth Macfarlane and Mark Wahlberg, has Mila Kunis exemplify this.[8]

His friend will try to keep him in the den or pit, delighted to have his buddy back. However, this state of infantilism is no longer enough for the protagonist, who has seen maturity and its benefits – pair bonding, sex and being taken

---

[8]'Shut up, Meg'.

seriously as a man – and has to ward off the desire to return to the infantile state, which was fun but had its limitations.

His bromance too may be a fossil friendship. He has grown out of it. He will continue to fail in life so long as he retains his immaturity. The goal for him is not to lose his buddy, but for him to put childish things into context. The dumping by girl or bromance brother (or both) instigates a soul-searching journey for the protagonist as he fights to have the best of both worlds. In these movies the girl is keeper of the moral high ground and she will set him a series for tests to see if he is able to attain it.

He will assume the mantle of these tasks and try to see his old buddy through her eyes. He will, instead of wallowing in filth, try to climb out of the sty. He will then assume the female part of the pairing and demand the same of his buddy. Resolutely a child, the buddy will refuse and this will lead to his losing the buddy also. Our hero is now faced by loneliness – the ultimate fear for a character in romantic comedy.

Realizing what he has lost will propel him onward to win back the girl. Once this is established, the marriage and his buddy bromance can continue, but on a more mature level. The plot here is the maturation of man at the hands of woman and is a relatively recent phenomenon.

Women in bromances

As the Laurel and Hardy films progressed and the wives were more fleshed out,[9] the arc of innocence changed, as can be seen in *Sons of the Desert*. 'Wives' became harridans to be avoided, placated or worshipped, a skewed version of womanhood that put the sexist onus on them as shrewish. The modern woman in the bromance has all the power in the relationship (if seen as something of a spoilsport); the sex play that she enjoys with the protagonist comes burdened by a relationship. That men wish to remain in an infantile state is perhaps a product of the consumerist culture of entitlement. The twenty-first-century urban man currently dresses in non-descript hooded tops, baggy oversized shorts, visible underwear, shoes lacking laces, sports and leisure wear, with comfort over elegance at all costs. Contrast this with Cary Grant, George Clooney or Clark Gable. The age of glamour and dressing to impress is over (for now). Our modern hero is happy with a videogame and a beer, his role model is Homer Simpson. Fashions will of course change, but right now, a culture of entitlement, immediate access to free porn, music, movies and games gives no reason for the male to climb out of the pit.

---

[9] They stopped playing their wives.

There is in Hollywood a roster of male comics who play versions of immature men, including Adam Sandler, Jack Black, Ben Stiller, Vince Vaughn, Robert Downey Jnr, Owen and Luke Wilson, Will Ferrell, Steve Carrell, Paul Rudd, Jason Segal, Seth Rogen and Jonah Hill, all of whom often feature in each other's movies. Worldwide Box office hits *The Hangover* and *Bridesmaids* featured none of them.

Road Movies

It Happened One Night. Due Date. Midnight Run. Planes, Trains and Automobiles. Smokey and The Bandit. Little Miss Sunshine. Road Trip. Flirting With Disaster. Thelma & Louise. O Brother, Where Art Thou? The Blues Brothers. Cannonball Run. The Adventures of Priscilla, Queen of the Desert. The Sure Thing. Bonnie and Clyde. Monte Carlo or Bust.

The road movie is another American invention. Although it is possible to do a road movie across Europe (*Monte Carlo or Bust*), the British Isles has the logistical problem that by teatime you will be at the coast. *Genevieve* (Cornelius 1953) was one exception that had Kenneth More, having completed the London to Brighton veteran car rally, make a bet with rival driver John Grigson as to which of their veteran cars could be the first to cross Westminster Bridge.

Europe has not only physical borders but also linguistic and cultural ones. The race and chase movies of the 1960s and 1970s did deal in part with these aspects (*Those Magnificent Men in their Flying Machines*, *It's a Mad, Mad, Mad, Mad World*), but they were more concerned with getting as many stars into a picture as they could to attract a television audience. In comedy terms, *The Cannonball Run* and *Smokey and The Bandit* cemented the road movie.

It Happened One Night was screwball comedy as road movie and the satire of Preston Sturges *Sullivan's Travels* looped back to Hollywood before heading off to the Deep South. Another template is *The Wizard of Oz* (1939). Dorothy's move out of the real world into the special one is spectacular and her journey involves a search for a grail, allies and tricksters – all features common to road movies. Its antecedents are Homer's *Odyssey* and the *Aeneid*, epic journeys in which the hero changes and grows over the time period of the story.

The New World of America, with its huge distances and minimal cultural/ language differences is ideal for this. Once automobile production took off after the Second World War, there was much increased mobility. Writer Jack Kerouac mythologized the freedom of the road in his novel *On the Road*, and to hitch Route 66 (which crosses the country from Chicago to California) became a beatnik grail. The Flower Power and Hippie movement was focused on California (in particular San Francisco) and there was a youth migration to that city. In movie terms it was *Bonnie and Clyde*, a Western, along with *Easy Rider* that popularized the idea of life on the road. A spate of dramatic movies such as *Duel, Two-lane Blacktop* and *Vanishing Point* showed the dark side of this freedom (1970s realism in reaction to the horrors of war) but the ability to up sticks and move hundreds of miles to another state is enshrined as part of the American way. It is the wagon train, frontier ethic that bites deep into the soul of every American.

No wonder that it has been treated comedically so often. The comedy comes in mismatched travellers and in the people they encounter on the road. First and foremost is the comedy pairing, brought together by apparent circum-stance, which often turns out to be contrived in order to land them in a foreign place, often without money, clothing or resources. It might be a pair of airline passengers stranded before Thanksgiving (*Planes, Trains and Automobiles*), a bounty hunter whose charge cannot fly (*Midnight Run*) or a man whose wife is due to give birth (*Due Date*) – in short, any reason to delay proceedings.

Being stranded miles from home is the next problem. The comic participant is often responsible for landing the other in this situation and thus antagonism is established. It is like being lashed to an idiot. The question here is of what you would do when taken out of your comfort zone? You are immediately thrown back on your basic human survival resources. Your needs become primal – food, clothing, shelter, money and, in this case, any form of transport. The importance and efficacy of the comic road movie depends entirely on how important it is to get home. There might be the promise of sex (*The Sure Thing*) or a relationship saved at the close (the birth of the child in *Due Date*). It might be a job or discovering your parenthood (*Flirting with Disaster*), a beauty pageant (*Little Miss Sunshine*), or simply enjoying your buddy's last days of freedom before he gets married (*Sideways*). It might be a family gathering or holiday celebration – one can never underestimate the pulling power of Christmas (*Home Alone*).

The goal is simple, but the true goal is to solve the underlying problem, which is an emotional one. Often the protagonist will be the serious one, the inner fool who is so buttoned up and concerned with the trivialities of life that he needs the outer fool, the comedian, to loosen him up. And so he will. There will be physical confrontations with plenty of antagonists; unfriendly locals, femmes fatales – offered as a conciliatory gift but actually a test of resolve, and agents of the law who may jail them momentarily or put out an APB, raising the stakes and making them wanted criminals.

During these events, the hero will come to see what has been missing in his life, freedom, hope and creativity, a mismatch in affections, bad decisions that must be reversed. He will be unable to do this until he has punched through the jovial devil-may-care attitude of his road partner. Others define us and this is the case here, as constant contact with strangers and changes in environment help to redefine the protagonist. This will be seen at the midpoint with a foreshadowing of the resolution. There is often a seeming betrayal by the comic of the protagonist.

Sometimes this is wilfull, sometimes accidental, but the result is the same, he must be pushed toward change. A symbolic death of the old life occurs – the shedding of clothes and adopting of a new costume, the loss of a valued accessory (a briefcase for example) and then the point at which they separate. The hero is alone, without resources, and must confront his own mortality. This too is symbolic for here it means letting go of the trappings of the old self in order that he may be reborn. The trickster companion will now reappear to save the day and provide the transport that will carry them homewards.

It is always better to travel than to arrive and the comedy set pieces keep coming with cameos and bizarre twists of fate. It is never in doubt that he will reach the destination, no matter what condition he finds himself in when the gets there. There is often a last minute dash and a ticking clock as the hero has adapted to the new environment and must conquer it to win the prize. The comedian's work is done and the comedy is over. He may achieve his reward from an earlier subplot.

Comic road movies can involve a group too, an ensemble piece that allows more characterization and flexibility. The distance is shorter, a necessity in that there is more complexity – *The Adventures of Priscilla, Queen of the Desert* or *Little Miss Sunshine* are examples of this. The road movie is an enduring and attractive subgenre. Getting out of town happens in many movies from *As Good As It Gets* to *Withnail and I*. Whilst neither are road movies per se, they explicate this desire for movement and a space to think, to recharge the batteries. The staging is often similar, based around leaving and hope, which is quickly replaced by adversity and challenge in circumstance and the road partner.

Act Two brings more pressure to bear. The goal of the journey has seemingly been abandoned and now it is down to base survival. Here the protagonist finds that his helpmeet is a trickster, and that he must face his own demons. The turning point comes as he negates the physical goal and sees the inner one clearly. External forces of antagonism will now come to bear upon him – the nemesis of Act Two, leading to a battle of wits and a long dark night of the soul. His road buddy will then come to the rescue (he has overcome his antagonism toward him and accepted the need to change), but still there is the race against time. There is always a happy ending to these movies – to go on such a journey and NOT return with the elixir would be too depressing and tonally wrong. The ending may be a change in character (*Midnight Run*), a birth (*Due Date*) or even a small ray of hope (*About Schmidt*), but they are sweet and upbeat. Even Miles, at the end of *Sideways,* finishes his journey by plucking up the courage to go and see the woman he loves.

Chapter 13
Christmas Comedy

Bad Santa. Home Alone. Gremlins. A Muppet Christmas Carol. National Lampoon's Christmas Vacation. Love Actually. Arthur Christmas. Scrooged. Serendipity. The Holiday. Ernest Saves Christmas. Elf. The Santa Claus. Trading Places. The Shop Around The Corner.

The holiday period, filled with life, laughter and joy, is an ideal situation for comedy. As a festival it falls under critic Michael Bakhtin's definition of carnival and is suitable for romantic endings. The conclusion of the year can act as bookend for a story, as in *Bridget Jones's Diary*, punctuate it as in *Bad Santa* or be at the centre as in romcom *The Holiday*. It is a time of wishes fulfilled, happy endings and new beginnings; the core of the movie does not even have to be the Christian festival, as all calendars mark midwinter as a time to celebrate a triumph over the ravages of nature.

Christmas is when our differences are swept away, a symbolic wiping of the slate. It is a time when we are supposed to be with our family in good cheer, willing to share and to give freely, which is why Charles Dickens' *A Christmas Carol* (*Scrooge*) is the perfect antithesis and why it has been remade so many times. It is also one reason why the Frank Capra classic *It's A Wonderful Life* works as such a tearjerker. Although unpopular at time of its release (the snow scenes were shot in August, using shredded paper) this trenchant take on suicide and remorse with its theme of 'I wish I had never been born' only found an audience through repeated showings at Christmastime on TV. This and the Bing Crosby musical *White Christmas*, are as much a part of the season as turkey, stuffing and bad jokes.[1] There is a huge pressure, not only to arrive in time and to bring suitable gifts, but

---

[1] The Germans watch a filmed one-hour play, *Dinner fur Ein* (*Dinner for One*). Written by a Brit, it is shown religiously each year on German television.

also to be with your loved ones and share your time generously. It is a time when children are (supposedly) rewarded for good behaviour and families pretend not to despise one another. A glow of conviviality hides the tensions, as in *Hannah and Her Sisters*, Woody Allen's chamber piece about human relationships.

There is the story of Saint Nicholas, which has resonance in all Western cultures, and its attendant mythology of the North Pole factory, elves and reindeer, the sleigh and the delivery of presents to each and every child in a single night. This has been mined for comedy in *Family Guy* and *Elf* alike. It is a time of willing suspension of disbelief. *Miracle on 34th Street* takes the idea that Santa might just be real and spins the whole in new ways. It is a time of magic – Narnia is set in a perpetual Christmastime – a suspension of work and a time devoted to pleasure.

The good-hearted comedy will focus on the lead up to Christmas; the developing romance, the rush to get home to be with loved ones, the present purchasing and outpourings of sentiment and love. Saccharin and syrupy, Christmas is an easy time to get the tear ducts going. All is motivated toward Christmas morning, the elixir being the gift and presence of the loved one. Santa must deliver all the presents in time for the children to wake and rush to the tree. It starts with anticipation and ends in reward and this trope cannot be altered, not matter how you warp the story.

Looking with a bad heart, behind this frontage the holidays are a time of great sadness and loneliness and many suicides and divorces occur at this time of year. Many do not have families or are estranged from them and/or their children. It is a time when the rifts between couples grow wide, rows loom, skeletons escape closets and there is murder, theft, sadness and loss. For some, the holiday period is to be endured and the New Year holds little promise. Both drama and comedy shy away from this and it is hard to find a Christmas story without a redemptive ending.

The Christmas period is a great framing device for comedy. In *Trading Places* (Landis 1983) Louis Winthorpe (Dan Aykroyd) is caught planting drugs in Valentine's (Eddie Murphy) desk at the firm's Christmas party in an attempt to get his life back. After a confrontation with Valentine, Winthorpe pulls out a gun and terrorizes the guests before fleeing. The contrast of the convivial Christmas party with a desperate and armed Winthorpe adds poignancy to a tense version of Twain's *The Prince and the Pauper*. *Die Hard* was an action movie that benefitted greatly from its Christmas Eve setting: it is, in a sense, setting an emotional ticking clock from the start, reducing the cinematic time frame to a few hours which is always dramatically effective.

One of the most popular Christmas films in modern memory is the John

Hughes-penned *Home Alone* (Columbus 1990),[2] in which eight-year-old Kevin McCallister is accidentally left in the parental home at when his family goes on vacation to Paris. As his parents desperately try to fly home, Kevin, once he has enjoyed his initial freedom, deals with a scary neighbour, 'Old Man' Marley and burglars (the 'Wet Bandits') Joe Pesci and Daniel Stern who have targeted the house. His mother Kate gets back to the US but is diverted to Pennsylvania, ultimately getting a ride with a travelling polka band led by John Candy. Kevin rigs the house with numerous booby traps. Harry and Marv break in, springing the traps and suffering various injuries. While the duo closes in on Kevin, he calls the police and escapes the house into a neighbouring vacant home. On Christmas Day, Kevin is disappointed to find that his family is still gone. He then hears Kate enter the house and call for him; they reconcile and are quickly joined by the rest of the McCallisters, who waited in Paris until they could get a direct flight to Chicago. Kevin keeps silent about his encounter with Harry and Marv, although Peter finds Harry's missing gold tooth.

The story covers the Christmas period up to the reunion on Christmas Day. There is a shape-shifting mentor figure in Old Man Marley and out-and-out comedy villains. The police, as in most children's comedies, are useless, being a threat rather than a calming influence. It was billed as a family film without the family, but its themes are universal: separation, a child forced to rely on his wits, reconciliation. Kevin has not misbehaved at the start and has no lesson to learn other than self-reliance. He is a victim of circumstance, but more a totem for others. He suggests that Marley reunite with his son, an echo of his own predicament. Kate is prevented from getting home; there is little as emotionally empathic as a mother returning to her son.

Christmas movies require heart, as does romantic comedy and a romance is often intertwined with it. Being a time for family, the nuclear family (or at least the desire to form such a bonding) is at the centre. Characters can explore their internal Scrooge and redemption is often on the cards. It is a time of magic and stardust and the comedy writer can be sentimental here. The opposite is true of comedies about other annual festivities, such as Prom Night or Spring Break.

---

[2] The $533 million *Home Alone* made worldwide was enough to earn it a place in *The Guinness Book of Records* for highest grossing comedy ever. See http://movie-gazette.com/1081 (accessed 13 December 2004)

Chapter 14
Sports Comedy

Sport is drama at its simplest and most compelling.

STUART VOYTILLA

Tin Cup. Heaven Can Wait. Happy Gilmore. Caddyshack. Space Jam. White Men Can't Jump. Bull Durham. Slap Shot. Kingpin. BASEketball. Dodgeball: A True Underdog Story. Whip it. The Bad News Bears.

The sports comedy is a particularly American phenomenon, focusing on winners and losers, taking part and playing the game. Anyone can relate to the simple dichotomy that one team has to win and one has to lose but, more than the thrill of competition, many of these movies are about being a team player. It is about how you play, rather than the result, which is why in some of the most notable examples of sports films, such as *Rocky* (Avildsen 1976), the protagonist loses the fight but wins on a personal level. Here, Stallone's character realizes that winning the Heavyweight Championship is unattainable so he instead goes the distance and wins self-respect.

In the sports comedy it is the team that fails, the one with comic flaws and infighting that is saved by a shape-shifting mentor figure that helps them to reign victorious in the end. It is the comedy of misfits, but they are losers up against real competition and opposition. There is no special dispensation for being weak.

Often the plots and themes are of maturation and acceptance.

We must invest in the journey and identify with the team of losers. It is them and us, and there are clear boundaries. The enemy or opposing team allows us comic distance. It may be about an obscure sport such as the Jamaican bobsleigh team in *Cool Runnings,* bowling in *Kingpin* or *Dodgeball*. The more unusual however, the more exposition will be needed to explain the rules, which can be done by employing a sports commentator or pair of pundits to offer a voiceover.

In order to create a sports comedy, first choose your sport. It is a given that the focus will be on the underdog. It can be as small as you like – Little League is fine. There will be a mentor, a fallen hero, a father figure or a veteran of the sport, who is now a coach or washed-up player (*Bad News Bears, Slap Shot*). The team, who must be rallied together, will consist of oddballs, each with a comic flaw. In previous eras these quirks might have been less than politically correct or examples of tokenism. The ultimate goal of the team, and by association also that of the lead character, is self-esteem (*Caddyshack*). It is easy to identify with this but the story needs a deep arc, taking the players to a level where it seems impossible that they will win out.

There will often be a romantic aspect, the girl being unable to fully commit to the man until he is a man. There will be rivalry, sometimes deep-seated, old wounds between the lead and the captain of the opposing team or between the mentor and his old rival. Unresolved issues are at the heart of the characters inability to progress, their physical inability to improve or to regain their game is a mirror of their mental status.

Cowardice and bravery is at the heart of the sports movie: even more so than the mechanics of playing the game. The league, team or match structure is useful as a peg on which to hang the comic sequences.

- The picking of players, roles and positions;
- Fitting of costumes or uniforms;
- Training montages;
- An injury or the weak dispatched;
- The playoffs, progress up the league ladder;
- The sight of the ultimate goal;
- Betrayal, desperation, last minute substitution;
- Success or failure.

There are parallels here with the military movie. In mythic terms, the story is the restoration of the king and the knight. The player is one who has to prove his mettle by stepping up to the plate and hitting the home run. Our hero may often begin in a shameful situation where he has experienced cowardice and has lost his mojo: it will not be until he takes a risk and learns to regain his bravery or finds it within himself that the team will be permitted to win. Indeed, he must initially fail. Only when there is no further to fall can a mentor lead him back toward the light. It is not merely his bravery either, but that of the team. Sports comedies are played out in public.

There is also an emphasis on class in the sports movie. The loser character is often faced by an opponent with the privilege that money and good breeding has to offer. This arrogant, self-important prig may be the captain of the opposing team or the owner of the club, but his intransigent views are put to the test by the gifted newcomer. An example is Adam Sandler[1] in *Happy Gilmore*, where the impetuous Gilmore transfers his ice hockey talents (he has a great slapshot style but he cannot skate) to golf. His violent temper and outbursts come to conflict with star shooter McGavin. Faced with a superior opponent whose unorthodox style is not banned by the authorities, McGavin resorts to cheating and here we have the maxim – cheats never prosper, another trope of the sports movie. The opponent is a sore loser who will be reduced to an infantile state, as with Judge Smails in *Caddyshack*.

There is also deception. The mentor figure often has to bend the rules in order for his team to win, but those rules are never broken, as this would mean cheating and would make them as culpable as their opponents. Bending the rules means holding off on information (such as the selling of the team in *Slap Shot*) and seeding problems, which the team will face when the going really gets tough.

In comedy terms, the slapstick element of players confronting one another plus Laurel and Hardy-like reciprocal violence is good for one sequence but may pale if there is little else. It is good to build up to the match, adding tension and then, as the match progresses (because after all this is now sport, not comedy) the laughs can come from counterpoint: pundits (*Dodgeball*), commentators, spectators, fans, rival managers, wives and girlfriends all offer amusing sideswipes.

In the US, there is a fanatical devotion to the national sports of football and baseball with enough of a built-in audience for them. In other countries, the relationship to the national sport is equally complex, for example the British and soccer (football).

Soccer movies

The Football Factory. Fever Pitch. Gregory's Girl. Purely Belter. Bend it like Beckham. Mike Bassett: England Manager. Grimsby. She's The Man.

Britain has a bizarre relationship with the beautiful game. Having created it, most of their movies work around the touchlines or the changing rooms This is partly because of perennially inclement weather, which makes it hard to film, but also

---

[1] Sandler has performed in three sports comedies to date. *The Waterboy* was based on his SNL characters of the excited southerner and Canteen Boy. Also *Happy Gilmore* and *The Longest Yard*, a remake of the 1974 Burt Reynolds vehicle. Critics were unconvinced that these could stretch to feature length narratives.

because its fans are partisan about allegiances and are obsessed by losing. The latter aspect makes redundant the US model of the small-town team whose players win out in the end and requires other solutions.

First, there is the *Roy of the Rovers* comic strip aspect of the talented young player who makes good. *There's Only One Jimmy Grimble* (Hay 1999) concerned a fan of Manchester City who comes into the possession of a pair of 'golden boots'. Further down the scale, *When Saturday Comes* (Giese 1996) has paternally troubled and drink-addled Jimmy Muir (Sean Bean) missing his chance to play for Newcastle United and getting a rare second chance. Staying with that team, *Purely Belter* (Herman 2000) tells of a pair of teenagers who will use any means to get season tickets for the Toon. The darker side of football, the hooligan aspect, is covered in many dramatic films beginning with Alan Clarke's relentless TV film *The Firm*. It has since been remade by Nick Love, who also made *The Football Factory* (Love 2004), both concerning hooligans trying to leave this world of violence. Many of these films are rites of passage, as a young man is mentored into joining the gang. Entry is granted but at great personal cost, as the protagonist submerges his identity into the thug element. There is the glamorization of violence, but its idea of manhood is a stunted one based on excess, challenge, drink and male bonding to the exclusion of all else. *Awaydays*, *ID* and *Green Street* all concern this topic and although there is comedy, this is not the focus.

British football films tend to favour juvenilia. *Fever Pitch* (Evans 1997) is a romantic comedy where Paul Ashworth's (Colin Firth) love of Arsenal FC threatens to destroy a new relationship. Sweeter still is Bill Forsyth's coming-of-age romantic comedy *Gregory's Girl* (1981) wherein gawky teenager John Gordon Sinclair falls for footie-playing local hottie Dorothy (Dee Hepburn) who takes Gregory's place. Hopelessly out of her league, he tries to date her but other local girls pass him around until he ends up with more suitable prospect, Susan (Clare Grogan), who confesses that it was all arranged by her friends, including Dorothy, 'It's just the way girls work. They help each other.'

Anglo-Asian hit *Bend it Like Beckham* (Chadha 2002) launched the careers of Kiera Knightley and director Gurinder Chadha. Jess, the eighteen-year-old daughter of a west London Sikh wants to play football but is forbidden. Her skills draw the attention of Jules Paxton (Knightley) who plays for a local women's team. They become best friends but both are attracted to coach, Joe. When they travel to Germany, the triangle collapses and her parents discover the deception and forbid her to continue. She continues to play for the team in secret and they head for the top of the league. Joe encourages her to apply for a scholarship in the US and ultimately, cultural and sexual prejudices, jealousies and parental boundaries are all resolved or mended.[2]

---

[2] It has recently been converted into a Musical.

Football mangers tend to come in for a lot of stick. Whilst *The Damned United* featured Michael Sheen as legendary manager Brian Clough, the mockumentary style *Mike Bassett: England Manager* (Barron 2001) began with the premise that the England manager had had a heart attack and the search was on for a replacement. Everyone turned it down. The UK has a poor track record with its managers, usually excoriating the present incumbent and retreating to the nostalgia of Alf Ramsey and his 'wingless wonders' of the 1966 World Cup Final. There is both intense press scrutiny into the private life of the manager and huge expectations of this post, which has been likened to being prime minister. The job is left to scraggy loud-mouthed patsy Mike Bassett, an underdog as per the US model. He hires inappropriate players, replaces the star with a veteran with a booze problem and becomes one of the most hated men in Britain. However, Bassett adopts some bizarre training methods and they go to Brazil. Brawling with the Scottish and Irish teams, bad goes to worse before they finally lose to Brazil in the semi-final. In keeping with a perverse British need to cherish its losers, Bassett is seen to have triumphed and is to continue in the role.

More recently, *The Hooligan Factory* (Nevern 2013) parodies the fan-as-hooligan genre, spoofing the male bonding, the marginalization of women, the undercover cops and the rampant desire to rise to the top of the firm. Football is troubled in Britain, as are its filmic tributes to the game, but each season there are fresh players and hopefully new strategies. Sasha Baron Cohen's *Grimsby* (Leterrier 2016) looks to be (in part) another plumbing of the murky depths of northern football fandom.

Sports comedies are dependent on a template of the underdog getting his chance to shine. The losing team model need not even be exclusively about sports. *The Internship* (Levy 2013) takes the Owen Wilson/Vince Vaughn partnership from *Wedding Crashers* lotharios to middle-aged obsolescence. Losing their jobs as wristwatch salesmen, they cheat their way onto a Google internship in Silicon Valley. As teams are formed, many of the sports tropes appear, with a bunch of nerd losers, a love interest (Rose Byrne), a snobby British nemesis (Max Minghella), pep talks, loss, winning, epiphany and even a game of Quidditch. This may not be the birth of a new subgenre of technological comedies, but it shows how a comedy template can be refitted for other purposes.

Chapter 15
Military Comedy

Tropic Thunder. Stripes. Operation Petticoat. Catch-22. Kelly's Heroes. Private Benjamin. Biloxi Blues. Hot Shots. Good Morning Vietnam. Sgt Bilko. Down Periscope. Small Soldiers. Major Payne. Private's Progress. Carry On Sergeant.

The military comedy too is almost exclusively an American form. Britain made several military comedies in the post-war period, such as *Privates on Parade, Private's Progress*, *Oh What a Lovely War* and *Carry On Sergeant*, but became demob happy once rationing had ceased. On British TV, the sitcom *Dad's Army* carried the torch from 1969 until the mid-1970s and is repeated on prime time TV to this day (a second version of the movie of the sitcom is due out in 2016), but this was about old soldiers who belonged to the Home Guard, a less military situation you could not hope to find. Old men playing at being soldiers they may have been, but it was a remarkably strong idea. In today's world the services have less relevance to life, and squaddie stories tend to blend comedy with horror as in *Dog Soldiers* (Marshall).[1]

Other than *Three Kings*, the Middle Eastern conflict has as yet spawned little comedy, barring elements in *Jarhead* that reflect *Catch-22* or *M*A*S*H*. Perhaps we are simply too close?[2]

The primary focus of the military comedy is patriotism, honour and duty. The military regime may be questioned but never overthrown. The satirical focus of *M*A*S*H* was the futility of war, not the organization or mechanics of the military institution. It was only in the last episode of the sitcom *Blackadder Goes Forth* that writers Richard Curtis and Ben Elton made a direct criticism of British

---

[1] Or play it straight and tragic with de-commissioned Gulf War veterans, as in *Dead Man's Shoes* (Meadows) or Nick Love's *Outlaw*. Neither were comedies by any stretch of the imagination.
[2] In the UK TV sitcom *Bluestone 42* concerns a bomb disposal squad located in Afghanistan, shot in South Africa.

foreign policy. *M*A*S*H* too – filmed around the time of the Vietnam War – was set during the Korean War.

The trickster hero

Into the rigid structure of the regulated, spotless military barracks comes the fool, the misfit – another fish out of water. He or she will immediately claim that they are there on false pretences or will in some other way be at odds with the prevailing forces of authority. Goldie Hawn, as *Private Benjamin*, is under the impression that she can leave the Army at any time having fallen prey to an Army recruitment pitch that promised beachfront properties and yachting. Hawkeye Pierce refuses to wear Army uniform. In *Good Morning Vietnam*, Adrian Cronauer arrives to work as a DJ in Saigon (Levinson 1987) for the Armed Forces Radio Services, only to find that his irreverent wit clashes with the prevailing guidelines on 'humour and music programming'. These raw recruits will arrive in the wrong state of dress, with a freewheeling, liberal attitude. This does not mean they aren't patriotic. They are advocates of individualism who happen not to do things by the book – and yet they will triumph, which proves that 'the book' is by no means perfect. However, without the book there is no drama and therefore no comedy.

In *Down Periscope* (David S. Ward 1996), Lt. Commander Thomas Dodge (Kelsey Grammer) is 'a capable yet unorthodox US Navy Officer about to be denied command of his own submarine for a third time because of his unconventional ways, including a notorious tattoo. Failure to secure a command will result in him being dropped from the command program and an assignment to a desk job.'[3] In order to prove himself, Vice Admiral Dean Winslow (Rip Torn) enables him to obtain command of a WWII-era diesel sub *USS Stingray*, SS-161 for a war game and orders him 'don't go by the book.'

Going against the grain of military command is easy, as it is so inflexible, something played for real in *Brüno* when the Austrian fashionista tries to join the US Army. In real life this disobedience would end in court martial and ultimately a dishonourable discharge. In times of war, desertion, disobeying a direct order or treasonous behaviour would result in your being shot. This ultimate threat is always somewhere in the back of our minds when we are watching military comedy, primarily because everyone has a gun, and yet because this *is* a comedy, we know it will never come to that.[4]

---

[3] Wikipedia, http://en.wikipedia.org/wiki/Down_Periscope (accessed 23 July 2014).
[4] Even when Brian and Stewie shoot themselves in the foot to get out of the Gulf in *Family Guy*.

The comic character in a military comedy will be out of his or her depth in a world of pain, discipline and punishment: Bill Murray in *Stripes*, Goldie Hawn in *Private Benjamin* or Robin Williams in *Good Morning Vietnam*. The misfit hero is often a trickster and con artist who has wiles and ruses to help him survive. The arc of this journey is how he will discover his hidden strengths and find out how to lead a team, having previously been a lone shark.

Initially he will do this by subversion. The king of these tactics is Sgt Bilko, created by Nat Hiken, portrayed by Phil Silvers on TV and Steve Martin in the movie, *Sgt Bilko* (2005). Bilko is at once part of the system and different from it. A sergeant, he rules the roost, but he is a trickster and con man. The chain of command cannot allow such renegades to exist in lowly places, as the grunts must always abdicate responsibility to the group. The system will tolerate some leeway higher up and many comedies of this kind portray generals, commanders and colonels as oafish, gullible charlatans or fools. They are rarely at the centre of the action: *Down Periscope* is an exception. The trickster hero is likely to be somewhere in the middle ranks, debased enough to suffer gruelling manual or physical punishment, but with enough respect from his platoon or company to enable him to fight the rigid levels a couple of layers above. Then there is the hard-nosed, inflexible Drill Sergeant, Sergeant Major or Lieutenant, a tailor-made role to illustrate the inflexible process of governing.

There is a learning process as they come to terms with the harsh new world. This usually means basic training and many of these films concern the six-week period of preparing to succeed as a conventional grunt. Laughs will be gained by their insolence or indolence in the face of authority. Imagine giving orders to Droopy or Stimpy the cat? These characters do not only defy authority, they negate it: by not caring, they render authority powerless to impose punishment. They often suffer and are seen to suffer from bullying, which will restore our sympathies to an otherwise spoiled and lackadaisical character (*Private Benjamin*, *Stripes*).

These clashes with authority will escalate into a series of collisions and conflicts. One point to note – the hero is rarely insubordinate to the higher ranks, because if an enlisted man were that rude to someone of that rank, he would be penalised so heavily that the comedy would evaporate. It is acceptable at the top of the food chain to create silly and inept characters. Although they wear the uniform and carry the power, they are physically weaker and older, dinosaurs that allow others to do the donkeywork. It will be the Drill Sergeant, who relies upon bullying one or more insubordinates to discipline the rest.

Once over the threshold they must now commit to the new world of the military. Escape routes have been tried and cut off and there is no way but forward. A fine example of this is Laurel and Hardy's short *Beau Hunks* (1931), in which Stan and

Olly join the Foreign Legion after Olly's sweetheart rejects him. Arriving at their Algerian barracks, they find that not only are all the other soldiers trying to forget their lost loves but that they are all the same woman – Olly's former flame.

They must descend into this world. Their hair is shorn thus removing their individuality. There is basic training and the mess hall and the shedding of skin in adopting a new uniform. There is testing where the trickster may be the butt of the Drill Sergeant's ire, but he may also become a mentor figure. The message being that the hero must abandon his individuality in order to fight for the platoon or company.

This hard-hearted character will push the hero to prove himself, and once this happens he will rally to his aid and express pride. The worst recruit will win the day. Often this happens in a war game exercise scenario (*Stripes*, *Private Benjamin*, *Beau Hunks and Periscope*) rather than in real battle as they are symbolic of the danger, but avoid the life or death conflict, which again would unbalance the comedy.

The trickster is not the leader and so the mentor character must be removed in order for him to take the position. If the mentor is also the antagonist then he must be tricked out of command or otherwise rendered immobile – leaving him to plan his revenge. The platoon itself will consist of less than fully rounded characters, more traits or walking catchphrases, as in *Dad's Army*. The band of merry men may consist of the following:

- The nerd or geek who will act as communication expert/radio operator. As in a heist movie, the specialist is always useful on the comic team;

- The physically inappropriate soldier. Usually portly, but he may also be gangly or myopic. Somehow this guy got though the medical but he is unable to undergo the rigorous testing. When he fails, as he will inevitably do, he may be sacrificed to put the heat under the hero's campaign of misrule;

- A soldier of a different race or sexuality. If they are subject to prejudice by the inflexible, intolerant military, this will create a strong need for justice among the ranks; this will be led by our hero;

- The dumb brute whose muscle can and will be used to aid the cause;

- The best friend. This character plays by the book and acts as wingman and advisor to our hero, constantly advising him that he is pushing it too far. The best friend is a link between the stony-faced military machine and our character who is a polar opposite. He kow-tows to the system in the hope that toeing the line will breed the promised promotions. He will be wrong in this. Once the trust is broken he will join our hero in his adventure.

In order to complete the task, the hero must use his skills and strength from his previous existence and for this there must be reward. This can be shore leave or promotion before the troops go into real battle, the final ordeal. This is where the group is further tested and it is now a life or death struggle. A real death, often of a minor character and sometimes off-screen illustrates the need for them to start playing by the rules. It raises the stakes, saying in effect that all that came before was mere preparation and now the hero must prove himself both as team leader and in the world of adult mature men. In *Kelly's Heroes* (Hutton 1970),[5] a group of WWII soldiers led by Clint Eastwood go AWOL to rob a bank behind enemy lines in France. Mistaken for the enemy, the group is strafed by American fighter planes. Forced to continue on foot, three of their number die in a skirmish around a minefield. This death urges them on, releasing the tension and laying the ground for twists, reversals and comedy further down the line.

At the end of a military comedy there will be a public recognition of the trickster and his squad in the form of graduation, parade or ceremony, just as there is a wedding in a romcom. Its purpose is to confirm that the hero has transformed himself to become an effective member of the new world. He has succeeded in both, overcoming the rigid rules and regulations but also keeping his individual creativity.

---

[5] Also a heist movie.

Chapter 16
Prison Comedies

A hundred and twenty five years ... Oh God, Oh God ... I'll be a
hundred and sixty one when I get out.
HARRY MONROE (RICHARD PRYOR), STIR CRAZY.

Take the Money and Run. Life. I love You, Philip Morris. Stir Crazy. The Longest
Yard. Porridge. Pardon Us. Doin' Time. Ernest Goes to Jail. Chicken Run.

Most comedy prison movies are based on other movies. *The Great Escape, The*
Birdman of Alcatraz, Papillion, Stalag 17, Midnight Express, Cool Hand Luke,
Scum, The Rock and *The Shawshank Redemption* are seminal works, establishing the tropes of the genre (there are around 300 prison movies), including
wrongful imprisonment, brutal guards, solitary confinement, awful rations,
corrupt gaolers and prison wardens, plans, riots and daring escapes. There are
neat reversals too, as in *The Italian Job* (1966), where the protagonist Charlie
Croker, has to break *into* the prison to see the crime boss Mr Bridger to get him
to fund a heist.

   Prison movies are about catharsis. Wrongful imprisonment or cruel and
unusual punishments have the effect on the viewer of 'there but for the Grace
of God go I', allowing us deep sympathy for a character who may be flawed
but above all is innocent of the crimes of which he is accused. Justice, both as
an abstract concept and a real one, reigns supreme and the ending of these
movies must reflect the world put to rights. In dramatic prison movies, there can
be tragedy for those who never escape or die trying (Randall P. McMurphy in
One Flew Over Cuckoo's Nest), but some crumb of solace must be offered: the
system will be brought down by the selfless actions of the hero, the warden is
arrested and an investigation will be launched into the legality and conditions of
the prison.

The comedy prison movie takes the tropes at face value but plays with them. Some narratives use a spell in prison as part of the narrative arc of the character. He may be imprisoned in Act Two and released by Act Three. For John Sullivan (*Sullivan's Travels*), it is catharsis. Having fallen from Hollywood heights to a labour camp, he faces six years' hard labour, enlivened only by the showing of a cartoon. Wrongful imprisonment is the norm. In *Stir Crazy*, down at heel writer Skip Donahue (Gene Wilder) and actor Harry Monroe (Richard Pryor) are heading for Hollywood, but in Arizona, to make ends meet, they perform a song and dance routine dressed as woodpeckers. During a break, bank robbers steal their costumes. They are arrested and a speedy trial ensures them 125 years. Their lawyer advises them to wait until they can appeal. The size of the penalty is ludicrous, and swift, erroneous justice (as in Sullivan's arrest) is par for the course, allowing us unquestioning sympathy. In *Shawshank*, there was always the question over whether Andy DuFreyne really had committed murder.

If the comedy character is not guilty of a major crime or a victim of mistaken identity, he may be a minor or habitual criminal – crimes that concern property rather than to the person. He can be a con man, burglar or drug taker, someone operating on the fringes of law and society, but violence, rape and murder go against the grain of the comic hero. He may be an old lag, like Fletcher in *Porridge* (Clement/La Frenais 1972) or *Let's Go to Prison* (2006), in which John Lyshitski is a car-stealing lost-cause repeat offender who has been in Rossmore State Penitentiary so many times he knows the staff and cons by their first names. He may be a coward, as in *Big Stan* (Rob Schneider), but most often he is an innocent abroad.

Romance, unless explored in same sex relationships (*I Love You, Philip Morris*) is likely to be curtailed to conjugal visits or hands pressed against the glass. Wives and girlfriends become distant idealized figures – either as angel, or if unfaithfulness is suspected, as demon. This is a male environment and women's prisons have only featured with any degree of comedy in the TV show *Orange is the new Black*.[1] The exploitative *Women in Prison* movies of the late 1930s onwards concern imprisoned women who are subjected to sexual and physical abuse, typically by sadistic male or female prison wardens and guards. The genre also features many films in which imprisoned women engage in lesbian sex. Some of the titles certainly imply comedy – *Love Camp 7*, *Isla*, *She*

---

[1] The series revolves around Piper Chapman, a bisexual woman living in New York City sentenced to fifteen months in a women's federal prison for transporting a suitcase full of drug money to her former girlfriend, Alex Vause an international drug smuggler mule. The offence occurred ten years prior and in that time Piper had moved on to a law-abiding life among New York's upper middle class. In prison, Piper is reunited with Alex (who named Piper in her trial, resulting in her arrest), and they re-examine their relationship and deal with their fellow inmates.

Wolf of the SS, *Bad Girls Dormitory*, *Chained Sinners – Medieval Fleshpots*, *Bikini Chain Gang* – but this is not intentional. Only Roger Corman's *Swamp Women* and Jean Claude La Marr's *Go for Broke* (2002) are intended to be comedies.

Movement in prison is restricted and timetabled. This has its advantages and disadvantages – you can focus in on characterful relationships and bucking the system but you are tied to the reality and drudgery of prison life. Prison is a state of inertia and incarceration, with its attendant ills of solitude, lack of basic human resources and the like, is a tough nut to crack. The inmates are waiting for release and all they can do is bide their time and work their way up the prison hierarchy to achieve nominal rewards. Solitary is limited in what can be achieved dramatically (fade in, flashback, fade out), so the cellmate is an important buddy or antagonist character.

Death Row is a questionable setting for a feature-length comedy as this location is for the terrorist or the mass murderer.

Character

The lead is an innocent in a corrupted world, one in which he is trapped until an agreed time of remission. His journey is to prove his innocence and is one of redemption. The prison officials and law represent a distant, unforgiving father. The hero may be in a state of arrested development where his juvenile antics have brought him to the prison and where he is now faced with unrelenting masculinity. He is going to have to grow up fast in order to fit with the regime. For him there will be physical and mental degradation.

He will need a mentor character to show him the ways and rules of this new world. This may come in the form of the cellmate, or a trickster character that knows the working of the system. For the protégé there are obvious benefits, but for the mentor? The hero needs some special talents which are going to be of use inside – and these must be made apparent to both the audience and to the ally in Act One. No one acts altruistically in prison; there is always a pay-off somewhere. In contrast to the heroes' innocence, all around is corruption and evil: his nemeses include the prison warder and the meanest guy on the block.

Whatever special talents the lead had on the outside are now removed. This is humanity at its most base, or most crazed. Whilst not strictly a comedy, *One Flew Over the Cuckoo's Nest* (Forman 1975) – is a prison satire in the *Catch-22* mode. Randall P. McMurphy is faking mental illness to get an easy ride, but the kicker comes when the other inmates tell him that they are there *voluntarily* and he is not. It is up to the venomous Nurse Ratchet to decide if McMurphy is sane or not – and, far from having a definite release date (as he would have had in a regular prison), he can be held indefinitely.

In more comedic terms, *Crazy People* (Bill 1990) has Dudley Moore, an advertising executive, having a nervous breakdown and being committed. Meanwhile his ads, which are truthful, become a huge hit and soon he and the inmates of the psychiatric hospital are designing successful advertising campaigns to the chagrin of the doctor in charge of the hospital. The hero will always be the sane one amidst the sea of lunacy and the tenet that often underpins the mental asylum movie is that the mad are saner than the rest of us – an outright lie. There are few comedies on this subject, perhaps because the comedian is exhibiting traits in his regular behaviour – speaking his mind, violating expectations, crossing thresholds – that could be construed as 'mad' already. The contrast with actual mental conditions as described in the DSM-IV is perhaps unsuited to comedy. In *Cuckoo's Nest*, the endearing traits of the patients, obsessions, inappropriate rage and the like have comic moments, but we cannot be seen to be laughing at the patients, as that is more akin to Victorian asylum visits. Psychotherapists, however, are fine for comedy, as in *What About Bob?* (Richard Dreyfus and Bill Murray) or *Analyze This* and *Analyze That* (Billy Crystal and Robert DeNiro)

The lead character must undergo a journey of redemption and maturity, with stages that mirror the military and sports comedies.

Plot

After arrest and sentencing, the crossing of the threshold is marked by physical change. The heroes' clothes are removed, his possessions taken (with perhaps the exception of a talisman), his hair cut and this individuality is taken away. Eating, sleeping and bathing are done together and all vestiges of privacy are removed. He will have to discard his civilian skin in order to survive. A plea will be made for clemency. 'I shouldn't be here' is a natural reaction, but the cry of innocence will be met with dark laughter because no one thinks that they are responsible for their crimes. The first night alone will be the hardest and surviving it gives more sympathy for the character.

Now come the tests. Instead of the basic training in a military movie or sports team montage, there is cruelty piled on cruelty. It is a kind of high school where the food is worse, the cliques more repellent and subversion only garners more punishment. There is no drill sergeant or coach here. There will be a direct attack on his manhood and here he will fail – this may be the point at which an ally is found. The hero has to accept the world for what it is before he is ready to change and the ally will help him to learn the system or to train physically and mentally for the challenges ahead. The B story is that of the warden (or the mentor struggling to get free) in which hidden agendas are revealed to our protagonist.

Abandoned by outside help, he experiences betrayal. A plan does not succeed because they are in a twilight world of stool pigeons and liars. There will be an attempted escape and harsh punishment brought down on the miscreant. In a war prison movie, this would involve their being shot (*The Great Escape, The Colditz Story*). An escape – if planned meticulously, guards bribed, routines checked, tools obtained, outside men ready – may fail and our hero is made culpable, so much so that he is sent either to solitary ('the hole') or to a worse institution – the classic inescapable prison (from which everyone escapes). In some prison movies that have comedy in them (but not at the forefront), the escape is only effective if it also fulfils the obligation that he requires to achieve maturity. Clooney's escape in *Out of Sight* was the beginning of a confrontation with his own nature, as it was with *O Brother, Where Art Thou?* (also Clooney).

Meanwhile, there is some redemption through sport out in the yard. Men trapped together will fall to their basest instincts. The bookish intellectual will be ignored or tortured unless his skills can be used in other ways, such as forgery, lookout or tattooing. Our hero, whose comic abilities of wit, fast thinking and talk are the skills which will enable him to talk his way out of a confrontation with the meanest mofo, is gearing up to find a solution. The people in the prison are not going to change so our hero must, and it is his redemption or rehabilitation which will allow him ultimately to go free. Here the A and B stories intertwine. If he has won the warden's confidence, he can use this as a bargaining chip with the populace. If he wins the confidence of the bad guy on the block, they can forge a team, again as in the military and sports comedy. This means giving up his individuality and working for the common good – in this case, escape.

He must learn that individual freedom, whilst his ultimate goal, is won with the help of others. Whilst requiring the physical ability to escape, he must also mature in this process. The betrayals and twists that lead us into the third act are playing out the father-son tussles and dynamics before our hero finally matures and stands up to the father figures. Once he has proven that he is their equal, they give way and the escape becomes of less importance – it is the redemption and the restoration of justice that is the goal. The triumph is here (he will be feted by all those who despised him before) and his elixir is his freedom.

There is also period prison comedy in the form of prisoner-of-war comedies. The premise of TV series *Hogan's Heroes* was that the POWs were using the camp as a base for their operations, spying and sabotaging the Nazis and helping other Allied POWs to escape. Their mastermind was Col. Robert Hogan, who owes a great debt to Phil Silvers (Sgt Bilko), his rogue team consisting of two Americans, a Brit and a Frenchman. The schemes were far-fetched (a phony Hitler visiting the camp), this being possible due to the incompetent commandant, Colonel Klink and his sergeant Schultz. Germans in authority were portrayed as inept, dim-witted and easily manipulated and German civilians as at least indifferent towards the German war effort – or even willing to help the Allies. Klink had a perfect record of no escapes, being assisted by Hogan to maintain the illusion that no one has ever escaped from Stalag 13. This was a sitcom, but POW camps have also featured in movies, most notably in Roberto Benigni's concentration camp comedy *Life is Beautiful*, in which a Jewish father convinces his son that the camp is a game. Its avoidance of crassness led to it winning the Best Actor Oscar for Benigni, but Jerry Lewis' take on similar fare – *The Day The Clown Cried* (1972) was never released. *The Colditz Story* and *The Great Escape*, whilst strictly dramas, had comic elements but there is mileage in a war that is far enough away to mock. There are other prisons and wars that have yet to receive a comic take, such as the Vietnam or Korean[2] wars. There are also fascinating and intermittently funny biopics of real criminals – *Bronson* and *Chopper* – in which the subject is a bad boy who will never be let out. For dramatic purposes they are given attractive and winning personalities to contrast with their violent ways. Getting the comedy right is hard in such a macho culture, but it can pay dividends.

---

[2] *Team America* had a section when celebrities were held by Kim Jong-Il.

Chapter 17

Crime, Caper, Mob and Heist Movies

You're only supposed to blow the bloody doors off!
CHARLIE CROKER (MICHAEL CAINE), *THE ITALIAN JOB*

Ruthless People. Fargo. A Simple Plan. Throw Momma From the Train. Dirty Rotten Scoundrels. Kind Hearts and Coronets. The Ladykillers. Butch Cassidy and The Sundance Kid. Thelma & Louise. The Big Lebowski. Raising Arizona.

Comedy and crime go together like peanut butter and jelly. Both concern transgressions and departures from the social norm, the outsider status and the promise of reward. Crime, detective and thriller are drama staples – you have a person who is about to commit, or has committed, a crime and a person who is trying to stop them or to find out whodunit. The stakes are high as are the penalties and, if the crime is serious enough, the penalty is the forfeit of your life. This degree of conflict is fuel for comedy, as we are engaged and thrilled by those who go beyond what is acceptable or appropriate within society.

There are certain crimes that are hard to convey in comedy. There are precious few in which rape is involved for example, and those that contain incest – although common in Shakespeare and among the crowned heads of Europe – are rare. Genocide too, is not a topic for comedy (as referenced in 'Satire') unless this takes an absurd science-fiction dimension concerning the annihilation of the human race as in *Mars Attacks* (Burton 1996). We must know that this is not really happening to allow the possibility for humour, so Alien vs Man comedies, of which there are many, can blow us up without consequence. *Dr Strangelove* (or *How I Learned to Stop Worrying and Love the Bomb*) (Kubrick 1964) also concerns the nuclear fate of man, but this is never seen, and the potential effect of mass destruction is discussed in the War room (where one must not fight).

Murder on a more human scale (if not a tautology) is also hard to do if this is the work of a serial killer. *Natural Born Killers* (Stone 1994) (see Transgression) has its comedic elements, but the black humour is that of Tarantino's *Pulp Fiction* and *Reservoir Dogs*. Stone intended the movie to be a satirical critique of the media in general.[1] *Man Bites Dog* is another black comedy that deals with killing on an everyday level, the satirical point being to reduce the act to the quotidian. To approach the act of murder without passion or motive is to us unspeakable, and this film shocks us out of complacency.

Terrorism as a subject for comedy is a tough one in a post 9/11 world. The *politics* of it were satirized in *Network* (Lumet 1976) and *Bananas* (Allen), but only *Four Lions* (Morris 2012) has dared to look at fundamentalism in a comic dimension. The taking of hostages and/or the random slaughter of innocent civilians have little comic mileage, but time moves on and attitudes change – maybe in twenty years?

The classic Ealing comedy *Kind Hearts and Coronets* (Hamer 1949) is murder as farce with a twist.[2] Although the conceit that murder for profit is a sound motive is one that suits the comic angle, murder is trivialized when tackled for comedic purposes. Whilst you may see struggle, binding and in rare cases, torture, the actual act of removing a life is usually accidental or happens off-screen, being too dramatic to fit the tone of comedy. Even the moment in *Pulp Fiction* where Vincent blows the head off a man in his car is a cut away.

In comic crime the victim is in some way deserving: a tyrant, monster or someone who cannot be reasoned with but who stands in the way of peace or financial gain. Murder must always be the last option, never the first. We must have sympathy for the murderer, so the first act must clearly portray the situation and character in such as light that he believes there is no other option. The murder may be long debated (internally or externally) or may happen early, in which case, the problem becomes the disposal of the body.

In *Weekend at Bernie's* (Kotcheff 1989) two young insurance executives discover their boss is dead but that he ordered their deaths to cover up his embezzlement. He had left orders *not* to kill them if he was alive so they attempt to convince people that he is. The innocent participants are therefore charged with perpetuating the lie. Getting rid of the body, as with

---

[1] Stone came to feel that the media was heavily involved in the outcome and had become an all-pervasive entity which marketed violence and suffering for the good of ratings. As such, he changed the tone of the movie from one of simple action to a satirical critique of the media in general.

[2] Louis Mazzini (Dennis Price) writes his memoirs while in prison awaiting his death by hanging. The film consists of flashback as he narrates the events leading to his imprisonment.

the gloppidda-gloppidda (cement) machine in *How to Murder Your Wife* (Quine 1965) – is a source of great comic invention. *Pulp Fiction* focuses on the clean-up operation, *Shallow Grave* (Boyle 1994) on the hiding of the body. The innocent, framed for murder, struggling to clear his name is a common trope.

The serious murder is darker in intent, as in *Throw Momma From The Train* (DeVito 1987) or *The War of The Roses* (DeVito 1989). The comic rule of 'never show the pain' is in evidence here, as the moment you do so you contextualize and humanize the act, allowing empathy, which is anathema to comedy. We must retain comic distance. All sorts of traps may be laid and avoided and a murder attempt brings the protagonist face-to-face with the completion of his task. Seemingly he has succeeded, and now must face the consequences and live with the rewards but also the guilt. It is this shame that throws the act into relief and now the anti-hero protagonist (or protagonists in these cases – both being as bad as each other) must express regret. Because there is a moral dimension to comedy (a resetting of society's moral compass), the need for remorse is paramount. 'He showed no regret for his crimes' is unconscionable to most; this is the true psychopath who kills out of curiosity. Once regret is expressed, often the murder is shown, by circumstance or chance, to have been bungled. The victim is alive and the guilt is expunged.

Moving down the scale, there is kidnapping, an ever-popular crime from *Swimming With Sharks* (Huang 1994) to *Ruthless People* (Zucker, Abrahams, Zucker 1986), in which millionaire Sam Stone (Danny DeVito again) intends to murder his hated wife to gain her $15 million fortune but is beaten to the punch when she gets kidnapped. Sam deliberately disobeys all of the kidnapper's demands, not paying the ransom and contacting both press and police – believing this will ensure her death.

Holding to ransom has specific tropes that must be followed and therefore can be twisted out of shape. First there is the plan and staking out the victim. Next comes the actual kidnap, the problem of trussing, binding and transferring the victim to a safe location. There is the delivery of the ransom note or message and accompanying demands. You must deal with the police and/or family of the victim, whilst you continue to live your normal life and keep the crime secret from others. There is feeding and looking after the victim and remaining anonymous. There is the drop and the exchange of the victim for money. There is getting away with it afterwards. There is stopping other partners in crime from squealing. Anything can and will go wrong. You may have to move the victim. The ransom demands may not be met and you may have to negotiate. There is the perpetual fear of discovery. All these allow for delicious black comedy and plenty of sympathy for the kidnapper.

Allied to this is the hostage situation, as in Dog *Day Afternoon* (Lumet 1975), which takes the dramatic route, but for laughs there is *The Ref* (Demme 1994),[3] in which Denis Leary plays an unfortunate cat burglar abandoned by his partner mid-heist, who is then forced to take an irritating Connecticut couple (Kevin Spacey[4] and Judy Davis) hostage. He finds that he has taken on more than he bargained for when the couple's blackmailing son and despicable in-laws step into the picture. Before long they're driving him nuts with their petty bickering and family problems. The only way for him to survive is to referee and resolve their differences, before the police intervene.

Both *Die Hard* (action) and *Misery* (thriller/horror) approach this situation from different angles. Comedically, it was most successful in *Nine to Five* (Higgins 1980), where Lily Tomlin, Jane Fonda and Dolly Parton capture their 'sexist, egotistical, lying, hypocritical bigot' boss (Dabney Coleman) in his home whilst they make some big changes in the workplace. Hiring a hitman to kill your boss is becoming the accepted norm, as in *Horrible Bosses* (Gordon 2011) where three disgruntled employees hire 'Mr Motherfucker' (Jamie Foxx) to commit their crimes for them in yet another version of *Strangers on a Train* (criss-cross).

Hitmen have been in vogue since Jules and Vincent in *Pulp Fiction;* Leon in *Leon* and John Cusack in *Grosse Point Blank* hit the screens and re-popularized the anonymous paid killer. The huge advantage to the hitman is that he is a blank. Since *The Day of the Jackal* (Zinnerman, 1973), the professional assassin or spy has been cloaked in anonymity, little more than a weapon for hire or of the state. James Bond was the first hitman to achieve such wide popularity and the role has changed greatly since Ian Fleming wrote the books. His Bond was closest to the current incumbent Daniel Craig, an unfeeling psychopath lacking the charm and élan of the playboy image of Connery or Moore. Here was a new character archetype to which you might append any characteristics, so we get Brad Pitt and Angelina Jolie in *Mr. and Mrs. Smith* as warring partners, or tagalong Cameron Diaz with Tom Cruise in *Knight and Day*[5] (Mangold 2010).

The rogue hitman (Bourne) is a cliché. Even *Bulworth* gets into the action, as Beatty hires a hitman to kill himself then decides against it ('do not deliver the package'). Having two hitmen, or even a conference of them allows for comic collisions and confusions and the territory has been mined before. *The Odd Job* (Medak 1978) starred *Monty Python's* Graham Chapman who, after being dumped by his wife, hires a hit man (David Jason) to kill him, but when his wife

---

[3]N.B. Also a Christmas movie.
[4]Spacey is again taken hostage in *Swimming With Sharks*.
[5]Formerly entitled *Wichita* and *Trouble Man*, the movie had a difficult birth. More than twelve writers contributed to the film, and the Writers Guild decided, due to this large number of contributors, to credit only Patrick O'Neill, who had put in effort on the early layout of the script.

returns he finds himself unable to cancel the contract. It was a remake of a TV portfolio comedy series, *6 Dates with Barker* (LWT/ITV), a showcase for the talents of British character actor Ronnie Barker. David Jason (who was to go on to appear with Barker in the sitcom *Open All Hours*) played the hitman in both.

There is also fraud, counterfeiting, theft and burglary. Money laundering and fraud is attractive because, well, who doesn't desire unlimited amounts of money? Burglary is the province of the minor criminal and opportunist. In comedy it is either something that affects the lead character as in *Home Alone* or it is something the protagonist(s) are forced to do in order to regain a McGuffin (e.g. *Sex Tape* 2014). The options here are manifold, the guard dogs, the forced entry or comic climbing of a building in order to do so, the search for the loot/safe/items and the danger of exposure. The alarm may have already been tripped, or the owners of the property may return unexpectedly, meaning that alternative plans (such as hiding) must be put into action. Being caught somewhere you shouldn't is a stock farce staple and, so long as we are in accord with the protagonists, it allows for delicious thrills.

The crimes of mugging and petty theft are unlikely to appeal to comedy viewers, although a back-story including these and a wrongful arrest or imprisonment is useful for character development. Introducing a character fresh out of prison always brings a frisson of excitement. Bad boys who need reforming are interesting characters and a single shot of a man leaving prison and crossing the threshold to his new life conjures questions such as, what was the nature of his crime? Has he reformed? Is he bent on revenge? Will he be drawn back into a life of crime? (Bad. No. Yes. Yes).

'One last job' is a staple of both drama and comedy. In drama, this will end tragically, with the participants dead or jailed indefinitely; in comedy, the big job is the life-changing one that will enable the participants to leave their criminal ways altogether as if they had been a mere lifestyle choice such as choosing a jacket or watch. The big job is almost always going to be the heist.

The heist or caper movie

The Italian Job. Ocean's Eleven. The Sting. The League of Gentlemen. Snatch. Three Kings. A Fish Called Wanda. Bottle Rocket. Lock, Stock and Two Smoking Barrels. Kelly's Heroes. Robot and Frank. The Great Train Robbery.

Heist movies feature a schematic three-act plot. First, there will be the gathering of the team and the preparations for the heist. There will be a mastermind who may or may not be known to the others, who will be chosen for their particular skills: these will include the con man, the safebreaker, the driver, the planner, the decoy, the athlete or muscle and the expert – although there will be variations depending on the target, be it a bank, casino, gallery or other stronghold.

An elaborate plan must be constructed in order to steal from a location that is seemingly impregnable: it is almost the inverse of the locked room mystery, a mainstay of early twentieth-century detective stories, which here forms part of the reveal.

Now You See Me (LeTerrier, 2013) is a caper in which a number of simultaneous heists are performed by four street magicians, masterminded by their sponsor, Michael Caine, star of one of the most famous caper movies ever made, *The Italian Job* (Collinson 1969). Location is paramount. Blueprints must be made, new technology developed to override elaborate alarm systems (*Mission Impossible*), decoys have to be set up, split-second timings checked and re-checked and getaway routes devised. Whilst all this is essential, none is more so than seeding the plot twists for the final act.

The second act will be the undertaking of the scam, either in full view of the people they are robbing or under cover of darkness. Things will more or less go according to plan but there will be nail-biting tense moments when all seems lost. Random events will occur, all of this intended to make us sympathize with the criminals (*Rififi*). It must be established that they are stealing from an arrogant rich man or uncaring institution and that the theft of the money or object is for noble ends – or at least that they are more deserving of it than the present owners. By now we are in accord and, as the forces of the law or private security close in, we are willing them to get away.

In the third act the plot unravels and the real twists (*The Sting*) become apparent. There may be betrayal and stool pigeons and the characters may turn on one another. Here the detective in charge comes to the fore and starts to figure it all out. A true cliffhanger ending arrived with *The Italian Job*, which left the outcome open-ended and has never been bettered. In earlier days the gang would have ended up in prison or dead, but it has become more common for them to get away with it so long as the mark or institution is sleazy or corrupt enough. The war heist movie, such as *Kelly's Heroes* (Nazi gold) or *Three Kings* (Saddam's gold) have a similar rag-tag military team execute the heist during wartime. Other period heists are worth considering. Exceptions to this template include Tarantino's *Reservoir Dogs,* which takes place in the aftermath of the heist and concentrates on ramifications, undercover cops, flashbacks, accusations and betrayals. *The Killing* (Kubrick 1956) and *Gambit* (Neame 1966) were also non-linear in this way.

In character terms, a charming charismatic lead conspirator is important, as with Danny Ocean (George Clooney) in *Ocean's Eleven*, or Charlie Croker (Michael Caine) in *The Italian Job*. He is the one with depth, although a subplot may feature a sidekick or mentor figure. He is also likely to be doing the job for hidden personal reasons (to get the girl back), which are his flaw. His nemesis is his flipside – what he would have become had he succeeded in life and been a white-collar rather than blue-collar criminal. At his lowest point he must come to terms both with this and with his true motivations. It is likely to be the cardinal traits of revenge or justice that carry him through, as well as a newfound loyalty to the team of misfits. Again there are elements of the military comedy here, in the team/training aspects and in trying to pull off an outrageous mission.

Heist comedies are ideal for an ensemble cast, containing larger than life roles for the main protagonists and for the love interest/femme fatale. The supporting roles are often one note, mere functions as listed above rather than imbued with any depth of characterization. This is because they cannot demand much screen time, as the caper movie is plot-heavy. It has to keep second-guessing us, allow time for character development and yet prevent the audience from working out how the heist might be pulled. The stakes are high and the writer must always be one step or twist ahead of the viewer, who must be made to wonder if and how they will get away with it, not whether it is right or not.

Mob comedy

Tina Vitale:
They shot him in the eyes.

Danny Rose:
Oh my God, he's blind?

Tina Vitale:
He's dead …

Danny Rose:
Of course, the bullets would go right through …
                                        BROADWAY DANNY ROSE

Married to the Mob. Prizzi's Honour. Mickey Blue Eyes. Bullets Over Broadway. Get Shorty.

Apart from *Some Like it Hot,* whose inciting incident concerned two musicians witnessing the St Valentine's Day Massacre in a parking garage, most comedy mob movies arrive post *The Godfather* (Coppola 1972). This genre defining

trilogy superseded the James Cagney school of Wisecracking Villains and introduced the family business, internecine wars, Machiavellian plotting, an operatic
scale and Italian Americans who were not besuited clichés, but dressed like
anyone else, except smarter. A new set of rules was devised from Mario Puzo's
book: family came first; the Sicilian code of Omerta, gory retribution and revenge
(vendetta!) was a dish served ice cold. The criminal family was glamorized,
wealthy, respected in the community (all of whom were required to pay the vig or
to 'wet his beak' from time to time), feared by enemies and loved by numerous
women – 'girlfriends for Fridays, wives for Saturdays', as Henry Hill noted in
Goodfellas (Scorsese 1990). The drama and seriousness of the Coppola and
Scorsese films was a red flag to parodists with *Mafia!* (Abrahams 1988) a.k.a
Jane Austen's Mafia! being the first to parody the genre. *Married to the Mob* and
Prizzi's Honour followed, but it was a TV series that changed the game.

HBO's *The Sopranos* (Chase 1999–2007) brought a sense of realism to the
heightened reality and glamorization of crime. Tony Soprano (James Gandolfini)
was a unique capo di capo. In therapy and lusting after his therapist, Jennifer
Melfi (Lorraine Bracco, who had played Henry Hill's wife in *Goodfellas*), he
was also in thrall to his wife Carmela (Edie Falco) and bound to his cousin and
protégé Christopher Moltisanti (Michael Imperioli).[6] Tony Soprano lived unglam-
orously in a Jersey suburb and shuffled around, a bear in a dressing gown, an
average American dad. The American mobster was thus humanized. He was
still no less dangerous – he would order a hit as and when required – but the
message was that these criminals are just like us. This comedic idea was too
good to waste and the mobster in therapy was explored in *Analyze This* (Ramis
1999) starring Robert de Niro and Billy Crystal and in the sequel, *Analyze That*
(Ramis 2003).

Bullets over Broadway (Allen 1994) saw Chazz Palminteri's gangster discover
hidden artistic depths as a playwright, and on a similar note, Chili Palmer (John
Travolta) in *Get Shorty* (Sonnenfeld 1995) has the gangster play the fish out of
water in Hollywood, writing, enforcing and teaching actors how to act – basically
a producer. The gangster in the real world is one way to go, but equally rich is
the reverse, the innocent civilian who unwittingly enters the mob, such as Hugh
Grant in *Mickey Blue Eyes* (Makin 1999) – a film that starred several actors who
would later go on to star in The Sopranos.

'Just when I thought I was out, they pull me back in', says Michael Corleone
(Al Pacino) in *The Godfather III*. This exemplifies the problem of leaving the
mob. *My Blue Heaven* (Ross 1990) starred Rick Moranis and Steve Martin,

---

[6] The story of *The Sopranos* was initially conceived as a feature film about 'a mobster in therapy having
problems with his mother'.

who played Henry Hill one month after *Goodfellas* came out. It was written by Nora Ephron (at the time married to Nicholas Pileggi) and concerned a gangster in a witness protection program, who struggles to conform to normal rules of behaviour.

What begins as drama ends as comedy. Joe Pesci, star of *Goodfellas* and *Casino*, moved on to appearing in *Home Alone* (1990) as a burglar, in *8 Heads In A Duffel Bag* (Schulman 1997) as a wise guy hired to transport eight human heads across the States to a crime boss and in *My Cousin Vinnie* (Lynn 1992) as a Brooklyn personal injury lawyer – which is as close to criminal as you can get.

Incompetent hitmen are bread and butter to the movies and British comedy movies have used them well. Colin Farrell's performance in *In Bruges*[7] (McDonagh 2008), and in the same director's *Seven Psychopaths* (2012) portrays the hitman as a few sandwiches short of a picnic. There are echoes of enforcer Kevin Kline in *A Fish Called Wanda* but the most potent ADHD hitman must be Ben Kingsley as Don Logan in *Sexy Beast* with Ray Winstone playing against type. An alpha force of nature (remember, he played Gandhi), he is all brute force and no finesse, equally enthralling and terrifying in a portrayal of an enforcer who will never take no for an answer unless you kill him.

---

[7] A wonderful movie whose character relationships echo those of British TV sitcom *Father Ted*.

Chapter 18
Transgression

Natural Born Killers. Three Kings. American Psycho. Happiness. Man Bites Dog. Bonnie and Clyde. Springbreakers. Life is Beautiful. South Park: Bigger, Longer & Uncut. To Be or Not To Be. Obvious Child.

What you can and cannot portray in comedy has always been subject to degrees of censorship, either by the Hays Production Code, the MPAA ratings that succeeded it or by libel and slander laws. Presently, the Internet is not policed except when pressure is brought to bear on a website that oversteps boundaries of taste, privacy or decency (pending). Overt crimes to the person or offensive racist views can be reported to authorities but there is no governing body covering its output. Each country/state/nation is struggling to define the boundaries in the new digital age and seeking to impose laws and taxation on this new media.

Meanwhile the Internet is producing comedy stars, such as US comic Bo Burnham, Issa Rae (*The Misadventures of Awkward Black Girl*) and UK Vlogger Dapper Laughs.[1]

Silent comedies were violent, but always within the dictates of comedic distance. This was comic pain, regardless of whether the performers were hurt or not, but there was no censorious body. It was the birth of the talkies that heralded issues. 'The presence of comedy was a problem for the administrators, making light of matters, which they deemed to be of great seriousness, with their apportionment of moral values. *The Red Headed Woman* (1932) made fun of a character played by Jean Harlow as she rose by having affairs: previously this would have been melodrama' (King 2002).

The spirited females of screwball comedy thrived only until the War years but 'going too far' brought disapproval. Mae West's sexual *double entendres*

---

[1] Who was given an ITV2 series, which was subsequently cancelled for being sexist.

were removed from her scripts. The script of her play *Diamond Lil* (1932) – later to become *She Done Him Wrong* – attracted the attention of James Wingate, head of the Studio Relations Committee, who advised her to avoid possible offensiveness by exaggerating the comedic elements.[2] Implication was the way to go. Innuendo in *His Girl Friday* (1940) and *Bringing Up Baby* (1938) (lots of jokes about bones) and *To Be or Not To Be* (1942) had to be carried across by implication as the Production Code Administration (PCA) curtailed all but the most simple of stories and actions.

These were interesting times. The cabaret of the Weimar Republic poked fun at the rise of Fascism, but the first major picture to tackle Nazism was Chaplin's *The Great Dictator* (1940), which lampooned Mussolini and Hitler, albeit safely from Hollywood as the US was neutral at that time. Critic Ronald Paulson states that 'Satire is that which arouses energy to action' (Paulson 1967) and that to satirize effectively, punishment may be possible. To get at your target there must be an aim to consequence – to show up those we condemn for what they really are, but if the subject is truly evil then it is not possible. This is to say, Hitler is beyond satire because pure evil is beyond punishment. Satire is involved with terror, which is a state of panic and ineffectiveness – not horror, which is the residue of evil. If a leader is demonized, satire ends and it becomes propaganda. *The Great Dictator* worked because the true horror of what was happening in Europe was as yet unknown – and the film works in that comic sphere of a degree of innocence.

Going further, Ernst Lubitsch's *To Be or Not To Be* (1942) attacked the brutality of the Gestapo and the Nazi policy of mass liquidation. Lubitsch was a German Jew and former slapstick clown who moved to the US in the 1920s and made romantic sitcoms. 'I was tired of the two established recognized recipes, drama with comedy relief and comedy with dramatic relief. I had made up my mind to make a picture with no attempt to relieve anybody from anything at any time' (Lubitsch 1942). It was set in German-occupation Poland where an eccentric Polish acting couple, headed by Jack Benny, has to stop vital information intended for the Polish Resistance falling into enemy hands.[3] 'Many people were offended because they weren't prepared to see the Nazis ridiculed rather than demonized and the film performed poorly at the box office' (McCabe 2005).

Mel Brooks remade it in 1983 to less effect. Where he did hit big was with *The Producers*, which was a movie, then a musical, then a remake of the movie. This was not a satire on Hitler, but on the ludicrousness of excess. Brooks was trying

---

[2]Maltby 1993: 55.
[3]Its star Carole Lombard died before its release on a flight back from a war bonds rally. Her line 'What can happen in a plane?' was cut from the movie.

to come up with the most offensive thing that mainly Jewish people would hate. It was 1968 and he was using provocation and shock tactics on a generation (or at least their parents) who had lived through WWII and the Holocaust. The latter remains taboo to this day. Jerry Lewis' *The Day The Clown Cried* (Lewis 1972) – famous for never being released – concerned a German clown, Helmut Doork, who ends up entertaining Jewish children in Auschwitz and leading them, Pied Piper fashion, into the gas chambers. Roberto Begnini's *Life is Beautiful* (1997) managed to find humanity in the camps. Begnini plays Guido, a Jewish-Italian bookshop owner who, imprisoned with his son in a concentration camp, tries to hide the true horror of what is happening by treating the whole thing as a game in which the boy has to win a thousand points to win a tank. The film won many prizes but rather than being a comedy per se, it is a tragicomic drama. In order to attack a difficult topic such as this the considerations are therefore –

- Tone;
- Target;
- Distance.

There has not been a comedy about the 9/11 World Trade Centre bombings or the 7/7 London bombings. Fundamentalism and terrorism has been mocked by Sasha Baron-Cohen in *Brüno* (Charles 2009), in his attempts to solve the Middle Eastern Crisis, in *Four Lions* (Morris 2011), where a cadre of home-grown British Muslims fail to cause an explosion at the London Marathon, and in *Team America: World Police* (2004) where puppet terrorists are ridiculed for their language (*'durka, durka'*) and radicalism. The real target is of course the American team, whose idea of executing foreign policy is wiping out most of Paris, the Middle East and North Korea.[4]

Puppetry or using animation establishes comic distance, which is why *The Simpsons*, *Family Guy* and *South Park all* get away with much more than live action. All three shows have been satirical, gross, offensive, racist, homophobic and sexist in varying measures but are rarely censured for it. If they are yellow, have grossly distorted chins or are comprised of cut-out paper, we are predisposed to accept this as a world in which all norms of behaviour are open to discussion. An ironic or sarcastic tone has a similar distancing effect.

Tone is established early in a movie and an uneven tone is a common criticism. If you use insult, embarrassment and humiliation, then softer moments

---

[4]Kim Jung Un was mocked in *The Interview* (2014) starring Seth Rogen and James Franco – a movie most notable for creating a brief furore when it was pulled from cinemas by parent company Sony after a hacking scandal.

or light comedy will seem out of place. Likewise, if the piece is a frothy romcom, then to suddenly add gross-out will throw it off key. Tone can be established by deciding on the target, which is to say how hard hitting you intend to be.

There are many targets for comedy and it is the acuity of hitting the one you choose that counts. It is too vague to attack consumer capitalism or bureaucracy, these must be personalized, analyzed and the inconsistencies pointed out. Movies such as *Thank You For Smoking* (Reitman 2005) (the tobacco lobby), *Wag the Dog* (Levinson 1997) (presidential re-election campaigns and spin) or *Brazil* (Gilliam 1985) (an Orwellian bureaucratic nightmare) all achieved this effectively. Nor does this have to be political. *It's Complicated* (Meyers 2009) took on middle-aged romances, *He's Just Not That Into You* (Kwapis 2009) faced up to home truths about dating, and *My Best Friend's Wedding* (Hogan 1997) and *Bridesmaids* (Feig 2011) both examined female jealousy.

With distance, there is little you can do but wait. The creation of comedy relies upon looking at events, people, systems, institutions or behaviours that are past their sell-by date, even if they are still current. We live in a society full of stupidity, jargon and incompetence and it is the job of the comedy writer to find a way of showing us the truth and lampooning it. You can have comedy about the Holocaust or rape or fundamentalism, but you must find a clever way – the comedic way – of dealing with the subject. Three examples of finding ways around potentially difficult subject matter are included here.

Heavily influenced by *Bonnie and Clyde*, road movies and mass media satire, *Natural Born Killers* (Stone 1994) – whilst being as ultraviolent *as A Clockwork Orange* (Kubrick 1971) – is shot in a frenetic style using b/w, animation, odd angles, colour schemes and enough parodies of TV sitcoms and commercials to make its comedic points. As *Bonnie and Clyde* examined the economy and social landscape of the 1930s, psychopaths Mickey and Mallory (Woody Harrelson and Juliette Lewis) seek to break the conventions that influence the masses, primarily the media – symbolically destroying it in the end, as represented by the killing of journalist Wayne Gale (Robert Downey Jnr).

Three Kings (Russell 1999) is an update of *Kelly's Heroes* (Clooney's character Archie Gates was originally intended for Clint Eastwood) in which, at the conclusion of the 1991 Iraqi War, a team of US Army soldiers find a map between the buttocks of an Iraqi soldier and go in pursuit of stolen gold bullion in Kuwait. Here, the Army and American attitudes toward foreigners and embedded journalists are all parodied, as the heist in the Gulf gets underway.[5]

---

[5]Former stand-up comic John Ridley had originally written the screenplay, then titled *Spoils of War*, as an experiment to see how fast he could write and sell a film. The writing took him seven days, and Warner Bros. bought the script eighteen days later. When the studio showed a list of their purchased scripts to Russell, the one-sentence description of *Spoils of War*, 'heist set in the Gulf War', appealed

American Psycho (Harron 2000) is a dark satirical comedy adapted from the 1991 book by Bret Easton Ellis, which lampoons the yuppie culture set in the stock markets of Manhattan. Patrick Bateman (Christian Bale) is a construct, an idea of a man rather than a real one, illustrated by his lack of back story, from his all-white apartment and addiction to clothes and facial products (in an early scene he peels off a clear mask) to the trappings of urbanized success. He kills a Wall Street rival because he has a more impressive business card and has a reservation at a better restaurant – an absurdly petty reason for murder.

'Like Jules in *Pulp Fiction*, Bateman has a habit of mixing his violent deeds with incongruous and earnest closely argued discussion of aspects of popular culture' (King 2002: 189), such as his love of bland '80s suit-wearing pop stars *Huey Lewis and the News* and his preference for post-Gabriel *Genesis* (most agree the earlier line-up was the real deal). Although he ostensibly works in 'Murders and Assassinations' (mergers and acquisitions) for a merchant bank, he spends his days drawing murderous doodles and using prostitutes for narcissistic and sadistic orgies.

As the killings accrue a detective (Willem Defoe) is dispatched to ask questions – but he is cowed and deferential to Bateman's superior status and it all comes to naught. A final bloodbath and rush to the office to cover his tracks is shown as a chimera and his supposed crimes go unpunished – being seen as a nightmare born of his own tormented mind and an elegant comment on consumerism and the American Dream of unlimited success and money. It is another update of Jekyll and Hyde which had already been made once as pure comedy in *The Nutty Professor* (Lewis and Murphy versions) and again as satire in *Fight Club* (Fincher 1999), with Edward Norton as the unnamed narrator and Brad Pitt as Tyler Duerden.

Comedy not only transgresses social norms in terms of violence and getting away with murder, but also in a more fluid approach to sexuality and gender.

Camp

The Adventures of Priscilla, Queen of the Desert. Hairspray. La Cage aux Folles (The Birdcage). The Rocky Horror Picture Show. Pink Flamingos. Adam and Steve. Serial Mom.

Camp is the frivolous, the kitsch and the sexually blurred. There is a tradition amongst European festivals for cross-dressing at carnival time, (Pantomime,

---

to him. Although Russell claimed he never read Ridley's script, so as not 'to pollute my own idea', he admits 'John gets credit where it's due. The germ of the idea that I took was his'.

Commedia dell'Arte), but in America this is limited to pockets of permitted displays of kitsch on parade floats at Gay Pride or Mardi Gras. US Sitcoms *Will and Grace* and *Frasier* adopted camp to great success (who would have thought that Frasier and Niles were really brothers?) but little makes it onto the big screen, perhaps because camp finds it hard to gain an audience larger than a cult following?

The word is of a French derivation, '*se camper*', to pose in an exaggerated fashion. It used to mean effeminate or homosexual, but has developed to cover a range of choices of behaviour. 'Camp is an aesthetic sensibility that regards something as appealing or humorous because of its ridiculousness to the viewer' (Babuscio 1993). Camp also includes that which is cheesy or *kitsch*, a usage first appearing in 1909 and attributed to being ostentatious, affected or theatrical.[6]

Two key components of camp are swish and drag. Swish includes sashaying and the use of limp wrists, falsetto voices, feminine pronouns and superlatives whereas drag is cross-dressing. Camp is not exclusively male; there are plenty of women who embody many of its precepts, such as Carmen Miranda or Bette Midler, as well as torch singers like Dusty Springfield, Kylie Minogue or Amy Winehouse. In cabaret, drag is well represented by Divine, Dame Edna Everage, Lily Savage, Ru Paul and the late Liberace, though officially 'not gay' he was as camp as a row of pink tents. TV shows that embody the camp ethic are the 1960s Adam West *Batman, the Addams Family, Dynasty* and *Dallas*. In *The Simpson's* episode 'Homer's Phobia', a gay character played by John Waters defines the meaning of the word 'camp' as *tragically ludicrous* or *ludicrously tragic*, which Homer misinterprets as 'when a clown dies.'

Filmmaker John Waters is the king (or queen) of camp with such cult master-pieces as *Pink Flamingos* (1972), *Female Trouble* (1974), *Desperate Living* (1977), *Polyester* (1981), *Hairspray* (1988), *Crybaby* (1990) and *Serial Mom* (1994). He is known for casting drag queens, non-actors and real life criminals, and for shooting all his movies in his hometown of Baltimore. The original *Hairspray* (1988) was adapted to become a long-running Broadway musical in 2002, then re-made as a hit comedy musical in 2007 starring John Travolta, Michelle Pfeiffer and Christopher Walken, and was a massive crossover hit grossing over $200 million worldwide.

Susan Sontag wrote extensively on camp in her essay 'Notes on Camp' in 1964,[7] creating fifty-eight theses and a literary sensation. She claims the essence of camp is its love of the unnatural: of artifice and exaggeration. Camp

---

[6]*Webster's New World Dictionary of the American Language*, 1976 edition, sense 6, [Slang, orig., homosexual jargon, Americanism] banality, mediocrity, artifice, ostentation, etc. so extreme as to amuse or have a perversely sophisticated appeal.
[7]Which was subsequently published in 1966 in a book.

is esoteric – something of a private code, a badge of identity even, among small urban cliques. I quote freely here from some of her observations.

> Camp taste draws on a mostly unacknowledged truth of taste: the most refined form of sexual attractiveness (as well as the most refined form of sexual pleasure) consists in going against the grain of one's sex. What is most beautiful in virile men is something feminine; what is most beautiful in feminine women is something masculine. (9)

> Camp sees everything in quotation marks. It's not a lamp, but a 'lamp'; not a woman, but a 'woman.' To perceive Camp in objects and persons is to understand Being-as-Playing-a-Role. It is the farthest extension, in sensibility, of the metaphor of life as theater. (10)

> One must distinguish between naïve and deliberate Camp. Pure Camp is always naïve. Camp which knows itself to be Camp ('camping') is usually less satisfying. (18)

> The whole point of Camp is to dethrone the serious. Camp is playful, anti-serious. More precisely, Camp involves a new, more complex relation to 'the serious.' One can be serious about the frivolous, frivolous about the serious. (41)

> Camp proposes a comic vision of the world but not a bitter or polemical comedy. If tragedy is an experience of hyper involvement, comedy is an experience of detachment. (44)

> The reason for the flourishing of the aristocratic posture among homosexuals also seems to parallel the Jewish case. For every sensibility is self-serving to the group that promotes it. Jewish liberalism is a gesture of self-legitimization. So is Camp taste, which definitely has something propagandistic about it. Needless to say, the propaganda operates in exactly the opposite direction. The Jews pinned their hopes for integrating into modern society on promoting the moral sense. Homosexuals have pinned their integration into society on promoting the aesthetic sense. Camp is a solvent of morality. It neutralizes moral indignation, sponsors playfulness. (52)

> The ultimate Camp statement: it's good because it's awful … (58)

France produces camp and farce in equal measure, none more so than in the work of playwright Jean Poiret, whose play was adapted by playwright Francois Veber for *La Cage aux Folles* (Molinaro, 1973). Veber also wrote the American version, *The Birdcage* (Nichols 1996) and *Le Placard* (*The Closet*), starring Daniel Auteuil as Francis Pignon, a man who pretends to be gay to keep his job. This has absurd consequences; one being that he is befriended by the office homophobe Felix Santini (Gerard Depardieu), under threat of disciplinary action for discrimination.

Because of its artifice, camp fits in well with comedy horror, when knowingly bad. This cannot include the monster/sci-fi movies of the 1950s, such as *Attack of the 50 Foot Woman*, *Them*! or *It came from Outer Space* as these low budget movies were made in all seriousness, but it does work with *Theater of Blood* (Hickox 1973) starring Vincent Price (always high camp), *Carry On Screaming* (Thomas 1966), the Hammer Horror movies and Amicus portmanteaus of the late 1960s and early 1970s, *The Little Shop of Horrors* (Oz 1986), Sam Raimi's *Evil Dead* movies and *Braindead* (Jackson 1992).

Ed Wood (Burton 1994) is a fine example of knowing camp, with star performances by Johnny Depp, Sarah Jessica Parker and Martin Landau (see Biopics in Subgenres).

Where camp leads to transgression is in its confrontation with gender expectations. Sexuality is a continuum but in understanding it we work in binary opposites. We expect certain behaviour and dress codes in men and women and when individuals do not confirm to this there is confusion, hatred or comedy, depending on the circumstances. The recent Amazon Prime series *Transparent* (written and created by Jill Soloway 2014) deals honestly and sensitively with transvestism as patriarch Jeffrey Tambor 'comes out'. Contrast this with the sketch in *Everything You Ever Wanted To Know About Sex* (Allen 1972) where Lou Jacobi is exposed on the street and ridiculed publicly.

Sexuality is not fixed however, and there are high-profile celebrities who challenge our expectations. David Beckham has an effeminate voice, Madonna the arms of a Stevedore. Lady Gaga is a homely girl from New York City but when she burst into the public consciousness she made great play of her bisexuality and did not quash rumours of her being a hermaphrodite.[8] There has been a growth in urban metro-sexuality and, whereas women can get away with wearing a boyfriend shirt (a form of transvestism) and boyfriend jeans are a fashion item, urban males are now sporting eyeliner, carrying man bags and are concerned with cosmetics, skin and hair products.

Clothes are loaded because they have connotative symbols, so whereas the pantomime dame transvestism of *Tootsie* and *Mrs Doubtfire* is easy to accept because they are seen as 'real men' (Williams character is a father, Hoffman's

---

[8]Which are obviously not true.

Dorothy only wants to work in his chosen profession),[9] it is still unacceptable for a male character to have much of the swish and drag about him unless he's going to come out soon. Women adopting male dress in movies (see 'Women') have a long history in music hall (Vesta Tilley, Ellie Shields) and in film. Julie Andrews in *Victor, Victoria* or Whoopi Goldberg in *The Associate* (Petrie 1996), who dresses as a man to get around the Wall St glass ceiling. This is evident to a lesser degree in Diane Keaton's performance as *Annie Hall.*

Its provenance lies in British Restoration comedy (or comedy of manners) in the period 1660–1710. Public stage performances had been banned for eighteen years and the re-opening of the theatres led to a renaissance in English drama. It was sexually explicit, and the audiences included aristocrats, servants and hangers on, as well as the middle classes. It also heralded the introduction of the first professional actresses and the first woman playwright, Aphra Behn. Seeing real women showing off their bodies was a shock and when they dressed as men it was termed a 'breeches role'. Out of some 375 plays produced on the London stage between 1660 and 1700, nearly a quarter contained roles for actresses in male clothes. Practically every Restoration actress appeared in trousers at some time, and breeches roles would even be inserted gratuitously in revivals of older plays.

So if the Europeans are comfortable with cross dressing and outward displays of camp behaviour, where does that leave America? 'Screaming' queens are still a minority taste. One movie that made a virtue of this, *The Adventures of Priscilla, Queen of the Desert* (Elliott 1994) featured two Aussies and a Brit and was a road movie comedy set in the Australian outback. The same idea was presented the following year in *To Wong Foo Thanks For Everything*, *Julie Newmar* (Kidron 1995), this time with Patrick Swayze, John Luguizamo and Wesley Snipes.

It was the 2007 version of *Hairspray* that broke through, and nowadays it is seen as something as a feather in the cap for big name stars to drag up. Kurt Russell in *Tango and Cash* (1989), Philip Seymour Hoffman as a drag queen in *Flawless* (Schumaker 1999) and Robert De Niro in a cameo in *Stardust* (Vaughn 2007). Transsexuals and transgender roles are now being offered, with Jared Leto playing a transgender woman (Rayon) in *Dallas Buyer's Club* (Vallee 2013) and winning the Best Supporting Actor Oscar for it. The above are not comedies, however, and issues of a broader spectrum of sexuality are not punching through to your multiplex romcom, with the exception of Kevin Smith's *Chasing Amy*, in which the titular girl is a lesbian or at least bisexual.

The *Borat* and *Brüno* mockumentaries might offer a reason. Played by a British

---

[9]Or indeed Curtis and Lemmon in *Some Like it Hot*. The motivation being not to get massacred.

Jewish comedian, they confront Americans on their own turf in two excruciating scenes exposing homophobia, racism and sexism: one in *Borat,* when he gets drunk with frat boys on a bus,[10] the second when Brüno goes cage fighting, but it is a set-up with his former gay lover, the resultant kiss being too much for the good ol' boys who are faced with ambi-sexual cowboys. *Brokeback Mountain* it wasn't. Does it take a foreigner to show us our hang-ups? Is comic distance only possible in this way? Comedy has to shine a light on societal issues and the braver the comic and writer, the closer to the truth we get.

---

[10] The boys claimed misrepresentation and tried to take it to court.

Chapter 19
Women In Comedy

Every man wants to protect me. I can't figure out what from.

MAE WEST.

A sense of power is central to the creation of humour.
The ability to joke about something simple is an underlying security of belief.

ERICA JONG.

Where The Boys Are. Romy and Michele's High School Reunion. The Banger Sisters. Outrageous Fortune. The Sweetest Thing. Thelma & Louise.

The role of women in writing and performing comedy has changed greatly over a century of cinema. From being billed as 'The Girl' in early silent films, women were either victims – chained to the railroad as metaphorical kitchen sink – or repressed into a nineteenth–century version of womanhood. The rise of Clara Bow as the 'It Girl' in the 1920s and prolific vaudevillian and playwright Mae West as the 'whore with a heart of gold' began to establish the individuality of women on screen.

Most comedy is male-orientated and performative. From an early age boys are encouraged to be extrovert and to display themselves, telling jokes and using humour as a weapon, whereas girls are expected to conform to ideals of dress, decorum and social placement, much of their comedy springing from behavioural observations and bitchiness, the latter being a corrective against other women who are not conforming to type. This chapter is devoted to the women who shattered the glass ceiling.

Mae West's most famous role was as Diamond Lil, in which men were sources of money or sex objects and the female was dominant.[1] If male-female relationships were a single narrative thread, it was an immensely popular one, and Mae West became the sex siren of her time. Her Diamond Lil character came to the movies in *She Done Him Wrong* (Sherman 1933), which also launched Cary Grant's career. She chose him as her leading man, telling a Paramount director that, 'If he can talk I'll take him' (McCann 1998). It was nominated for Best Picture at the Academy Awards and allegedly saved Paramount from bankruptcy. Her next, *I'm No Angel* (Ruggles 1933), was the most successful of her career and by 1935 she was the second highest-paid person in the US after William Randolph Hearst (West and Schlissel 1997). The Hays Production Code[2] stopped all that, heavily editing her screenplays and preventing her plays from being made into films. Mae West was a prime example of the unruly woman, a central figure in the medieval carnivalesque and one that was not to rise again in Hollywood for three decades.

Romantic comedy has always been targeted at the female audience. *Bringing Up Baby, The Lady Eve* and *His Girl Friday* provided roles for women who were a positive influence on their repressed male colleagues. They were portrayed as fast-talking characters that were the equal of their male counterparts in every way. This was rare. In Laurel and Hardy's *Sons of the Desert,* the pair tries to trick their wives so that they can sneak off to carouse at an all-male event. Women were seen as harridans, hausfraus or killjoys – whereas the men were freewheeling, childlike spirits who had to leave the domestic home to have any fun. Man was master of the house and assumed a dominant gender role. Many of the silent female stars are forgotten now as their role and function was (seemingly) to be tamed.

The unruly woman rose again as the Production Code dwindled. Ira Levin's *Stepford Wives* was a critical satire on the male approach to feminism, but the new emancipation of women did allow some female voices to be heard. Whilst still being expected to be 'sexy',[3] roles began to appear for the career woman

---

[1] Her most famous quote was. 'Is that a gun in your pocket or are you just glad to see me?' She was partnered with W.C. Fields in *My Little Chickadee* (1940), her last success before the Hays Code.

'Knowing she wasn't built like the skinny flapper starlets of the day, she used her sturdy curvy figure to create a raunchy persona that was as much a product of the naughty nineties as the roaring twenties" (McCabe 2005: 229) Her first play was called *Sex* (1926) and her second *Drag* (1927) which dealt with homosexuality. The police raided both and she was jailed for ten days on obscenity charges. *Drag* was banned. She co-authored her movie scripts, wrote most of her own dialogue and by the mid 1930s was the highest-earning woman in America.

[2] The Hays Code banned acts of gender impersonation that might blur boundaries.

[3] Jane Fonda became a star in sexy SF film *Barbarella* and was then roundly trounced for having political opinions over Vietnam, and was henceforth known as Hanoi Jane.

as go-getter and breadwinner. They were independent from men but their ambition was curtailed, being solely reduced to the entrapment of the male as husband and provider. These were East Coast urbanites. The nice-girl-next-door Doris Day and Shirley MacLaine roles began to give way to more freewheeling sexuality (*Bob and Carol and Ted and Alice*) and the acknowledgement that older women might have an appetite too (*The Graduate*).

Woody Allen gave voice to his women, Louise Lasser, Diane Keaton and Mia Farrow, but he was writing their words. The '80s brought forth stronger roles for Kathleen Turner, Sharon Stone, Meg Ryan, Bette Midler et al., but they were punished for the impudence of having a career by being portrayed as ballbusters and bunny-boilers.

It wasn't until *Thelma & Louise* (Scott 1991) that two women in a buddy/road movie achieved any real degree of freedom, but they went over a cliff. Writer Callie Khouri went on to write and direct the comedy drama *Divine Secrets of the Ya-Ya Sisterhood* in 2002.

Pretty Woman, starring Julia Roberts in a career-defining role, is a curate's egg of a comedy. Adapted from *Pygmalion* and *My Fair Lady*, this Cinderella/ tart with a heart of gold story concerns a brash, wilful woman who encounters a workaholic millionaire. It is redemptive but for whom? She saves him and he her, but the implication is that a woman has to be a beautiful prostitute in thigh-high boots to do this. Her entrance to refined LA society (Rodeo Drive, events, hotels) tempers her unruliness, but 'crucial to the film is the assumption that she maintain her original spirit' (King 2002). It is a film that seeks to have its cake and eat it.

Today's movie heroines owe homage to the iconic women of the past. As well as the above, Garbo, Colbert, Hepburn, Bacall, Monroe and Lucille Ball forged the way for women on screen. Gwyneth Paltrow, Jennifer Aniston, Renee Zellweger, Reece Witherspoon, Sandra Bullock and Cameron Diaz represent a modern kind of screen heroine: independent, self-reliant and with the ability to control their own finances, bodies and destiny. Being Hollywood they are also sculpted to perfection, creating an impossible ideal for any real woman to match, all this enhanced by armies of stylists and endless Photoshopping. There are few female role models who do not conform to the Hollywood fantasy model and women still become invisible beyond the age of forty.

In the UK, men often played women until the 1960s when the *Carry On* film stars Hattie Jacques, Barbara Windsor and Joan Sims brought degrees of feminine to the screen. They have since become clichés and the roles of Matron, harridan, spinster and sexpot was typecasting as old as Chaucer.

Others, such as Joyce Grenfell, played the silly-ass, or the great Margaret Rutherford, a fierce comic ogre. The age of permissiveness and the collapse of the British film industry resulted in soft porn movies and sex comedies and it wasn't until the 1980s that Julie Walters,[4] appearing in *Educating Rita* (1983), brought a re-emergence of the British unruly woman. She went on to star in *Personal Services* (1987) and *Billy Elliott* (2000). Her comic performances are mixed with gritty, bittersweet elements and she has become a national treasure. Emily Lloyd appeared briefly as an unruly girl in David Leland's' evocative period piece *Wish You Were Here* (Leland 1987), but sadly floundered.[5] Keira Knightley and Kate Beckinsale are two British actresses who have made the leap to Hollywood, but the former plays kooky, rather pliant roles (*Bend It Like Beckham*, *Love Actually*, *Seeking a Friend for the End of the World* and *Begin Again*) whereas the latter prefers actioners. Kate Winslet has appeared in comedy roles (*The Holiday*, *Carnage*) but is less of a comic actress than Oscar-winning writer/actress Emma Thompson, who brings a great comic sensibility to her roles in *Saving Mr Banks*, *Nanny McPhee, Love Actually* and the *Harry Potter* franchise.

Marianne Sagebrecht in *Rosalie Goes Shopping* (Adlon 1989) is one European character who disregards all social and legal restraints about money as she defrauds the world of US consumerism, but in European comedy there have been few as outrageous as their American counterparts, and some of these roles are taken by girls, such as Audrey Tautou in *Amelie* or Natalie Portman in *Leon* (Besson 1994).

The unruly comic male is less subversive as an unruly woman represents more of a challenge to the gender hierarchy. A man can indulge in drag – *Some Like It Hot, Tootsie, Mrs Doubtfire* – and still be considered a red-blooded male. Women dragging up – Julie Andrews in *Victor Victoria*, Gwyneth Paltrow in *Shakespeare in Love* (1998) or Amanda Bynes in *She's The Man* (2006) are more rare.

It is a cliché to say that women aren't funny and Marilyn Monroe, Whoopi Goldberg, Kathleen Turner, Lily Tomlin, Parker Posey, Christina Ricci, Lisa Kudrow, Kristen Wiig, Tina Fey, Isla Fischer, Amy Poelher, Diablo Cody or Elizabeth Banks would tend to disagree, to name but a few.

Part of the issue was stereotypical roles for women in comedy. The dumb blonde character was created by Judy Holliday in *Born Yesterday* (Cukor 1950), a form of idiot savant that was to be perfected by Marilyn Monroe in classic comedies such as *Gentlemen Prefer Blondes* (1953), *The Seven Year Itch* (1955) and her role as Sugar Cane in *Some Like It Hot* (Wilder 1959). Other roles in this vein are the nag, the gossip, the randy widow, the pecking housewife, the shrew, the good and the bad girl, many of which came from theatre. Traditionally, women writers have had to use pseudonyms (George

---

[4]Walters is a long-term collaborator of comic genius Victoria Wood.
[5]Due to ill health.

Eliot, the Bronte sisters) as it was seen as improper for a lady to be amusing. It took two women's movements to create the circumstances for women to be funny – the universal suffrage movement in the nineteenth century and feminism in the twentieth.

In movies, Bette Davis[6] portrayed unsympathetic and sardonic characters in *The Little Foxes* (1941) and *Now, Voyager* (1942), one of her best being *All About Eve* (Mankiewicz 1950), which explored female jealousy with real honesty. It won two Oscars for best director and screenplay and was based on a short story by Mary Orr called *The Wisdom of Eve*, published in a 1946 magazine. She was, however, not primarily a comic actress.

Gracie Allen became internationally famous as the foil and comedy partner of comedian/actor George Burns. They began in vaudeville, forming an act in 1922 and marrying in 1926. Burns had her feeding him the lines, but when her set-ups started getting more laughs than his punchlines, he flipped it round and made her the comic.

Gracie was the original 'ditz', acting zany and innocent – a kind of Stan Laurel – and her part was known in vaudeville as a 'Dumb Dora'[7] act. It was named after an early film of the same name that featured a scatterbrained female protagonist.

Their break in films came when Burns was offered $1,700 for them to shoot an eight-minute two reeler of their vaudeville act, *Lambchops* (Roth 1929). Subsequently they made a number of shorts and features together before moving to radio and long-running television series. Burns summed up the act by saying that all he had to do was ask 'Gracie, how's your brother? And soon he didn't even need to remember even that part as she talked for thirty-eight years'. Gracie was with him until her death in 1964. Burns was buried with her some thirty-two years later.

Lucille Ball was the star of her eponymous 1950's sitcom and had one of Hollywood's longest careers. She single-handedly created the studio sitcom and created four situation comedies starting with *I Love Lucy*. She had had a film career in the 1930s and 1940s as a contract player for RKO radio pictures, where she appeared in so many B pictures that she inherited the nickname the 'Queen of the B's' from Fay Wray.[8] She made a move to TV in the 1950s, and in 1962 was the first woman to run a TV studio (DesiLu Productions). *I Love Lucy* ended in 1957 after 180 episodes. Desilu and *I Love Lucy* pioneered a number of methods still in use in television production today, such as filming before a live studio audience with multiple cameras and distinct sets adjacent

---

[6] Her best-known quote was 'Fasten your seatbelts – it's going to be a bumpy night'.
[7] The Dumb Dora stereotype was developed by American cartoonist Chic Young,
[8] She appeared with the *Three Stooges*, *The Marx Brothers* and Fred Astaire and Ginger Rodgers.

to each other. During this time Ball taught a 32-week comedy workshop at the Brandeis-Bardin Institute. Desilu was also responsible for *Mission Impossible* and *Star Trek*.

Elaine May was originally half of double-act Nichols and May (Mike Nichols too went on to great success as a comedy director), then became a screenwriter, actress and director. She was twice Oscar-nominated for *The Heartbreak Kid* (1972) and *Primary Colors* (1998), and co-wrote *Heaven Can Wait* (1978) and the screenplay for *The Birdcage* (1994). Nichols and May created a new 'Age of Irony' for comedy, which included actors 'batting contemporary banalities back and forth' as a key part of their routine. Their style of comedy was picked up and further developed by other comics including Steve Martin, Bill Murray and David Letterman.[9] Lily Tomlin adds: 'The nuances of the characterizations and the cultured types that they were doing completely appealed to me. They were the first people I saw doing smart, hip character pieces. My brother and I used to keep their "Improvisations to Music" on the turntable twenty-four hours a day.'

Nancy Meyers is a hugely influential writer, producer and director of comedy movies. In 1980 she scripted *Private Benjamin*, which starred Goldie Hawn. It was a script everyone had turned down – the accepted wisdom being that a female lead with no male star was box office poison. Her next was *Irreconcilable Differences* (1984), before she turned to producing With *Baby Boom* (Shyer 1987), which she co-wrote. Both *Benjamin* and *Boom* were followed by short-lived TV series. With co-writer Shyer, she remade the 1950 movie *Father of the Bride*, then *I Love Trouble* (1994), a screwball-inspired comedy thriller. Her directorial debut was with the Lindsay Lohan remake *The Parent Trap* (1998).

Touchstone Pictures chairman Joe Roth asked her to rewrite a script *Head Games*, about a man who gains the power to hear everything women are thinking. This became *What Women Want* (2000) with Mel Gibson and Helen Hunt. Following her divorce, Meyers wrote and directed the post-divorce comedy *Something's Gotta Give* (2003), with Diane Keaton and Jack Nicholson, despite the studio thinking they were too old to be bankable romcom stars. Her next was *The Holiday* (2006), starring Cameron Diaz, Kate Winslet, Jude Law and Jack Black. *It's Complicated* (2009) starred Meryl Streep as a successful bakery owner and single mother of three who starts a secret affair with her ex-husband, played by Alec Baldwin. Meyers is a major player in Hollywood and her writing reflects the concerns of a much ignored demographic.

Leslie Dixon is another important comedy screenwriter and producer, known for *Hairspray* (starring John Travolta, Queen Latifah), *Overboard* (Kurt

Russell and Goldie Hawn) and *Outrageous Fortune* (Bette Midler, Shelley Long). *Mrs Doubtfire and Freaky Friday,* (Jamie Lee Curtis and Lindsey Lohan).[10] The Late Nora Ephron, not only a prolific screenwriter but also a novelist, playwright, producer, director and blogger, is best known for *When Harry Met Sally*, *Sleepless in Seattle* and *Silkwood*, all of which were Oscar-nominated. She was one of four sisters, two of whom (Delia and Amy) are also screenwriters and one (Hallie) is a crime writer and journalist. Her leap from journalism occurred when she helped her then husband Carl Bernstein to rewrite William Goldman's script for *All The President's Men,* as he and Woodward were not happy with it. The script was not used, but from it she was offered a chance to script a TV movie. She also *wrote My Blue Heaven* (Ross 1990), with Rick Moranis and Steve Martin, *Mixed Nuts*, another Steve Martin vehicle adapted from a French film, *Michael* (starring John Travolta) and *You've Got Mail* (with *Seattle* star Tom Hanks).

Current screenwriting women working in film and TV include Diablo Cody, Lena Dunham, Carrie Fisher, Tina Fey, Amy Poelher, Kirsten Wiig and Liz Meriwether.

When it comes to actresses, the A-list includes Jennifer Aniston *(Friends* TV series, *The Good Girl* (Arteta 2002), *Marley and Me, Along Came Polly*, *Horrible Bosses, We're the Millers*), Sandra Bullock (*Miss Congeniality, The Proposal, Heat*), Drew Barrymore (*Never Been Kissed, The Wedding Singer*, *Whip It, Charlie's Angels*), Cameron Diaz (*The Mask, There's Something About Mary, The Holiday, Bad Teacher*) Julia Roberts (*Pretty Woman, Notting Hill, The Runaway Bride, My Best Friend's Wedding*) and Reece Witherspoon (*Legally Blonde, Sweet Home Alabama*), with up and comers Isla Fisher (*Wedding Crashers, Confessions of a Shopaholic*), Tina Fey (*30 Rock* TV series, *Date Night*), Jane Lynch (*The 40-Year-Old Virgin, Role Models*), Jaime Pressley (*I Love You, Man*), Emma Stone (*Superbad, House Bunny*), Elizabeth Banks (*Zack and Miri Make a Porno*) and Melissa McCarthy (*Bridesmaids, The Heat*)

The above is proof enough to show the impact women have had on Hollywood, but is female comedy writing any different to the male? There are movies aimed at women, the romcom, some ensemble comedies (*It's Complicated*) and comedies that feature women in roles of self-empowerment and emancipation (*Working Girl, Nine to Five*), but Kristen Wiig and Paul Feig's *Bridesmaids* (2011) has not produced any more raunchy clones, save *Bachelorette* (Headland 2012). Feig directed buddy cop film *The Heat* with Sandra Bullock and Melissa McCarthy in 2013, Wiig appeared as a co-worker

---

[10]She also adapted the novel *The Dark Fields* by Alan Glynn to make *Limitless*.

in Ben Stiller's *Secret Life of Walter Mitty* and has contributed voice roles to animated comedies, but no firm feminist role has yet appeared.

When it comes to comedies featuring women in lead roles, the Bechdel test applies. This is named after American cartoonist Alison Bechdel, whose 1985 comic strip *Dykes to Watch Out For* demanded that a work of fiction – it was films originally, but it has spread to other media – must feature at least two *named* women, who must talk to each other about something other than a man. Most contemporary movies still fail this basic test of gender bias.

The issue is an industry that 'tends to think that a movie can't just be about women – it has to be about girl power, projecting a canned message of empowerment even if it leaves its characters dangling in the wind or humiliates them for laughs (Willmore 2014).

This is true of *Walk of Shame* (Brill 2014) and *The Other Woman* (Cassavetes 2014), comedies that profess to be about empowerment and female bonding, but reduce women to the good and bad girl, dumb, sexy or successful and controlling. *The Other Woman*, written by Melissa Stack, has Cameron Diaz discovering that her date is married and has a mistress, so when the women meet they decide to inflict sophomore revenge (the usual laxatives) before imposing financial ruin. Even with three female leads it fails the Bechdel test. As ever, they live alone in designer Soho apartments or immaculate Connecticut homes, and it is patriarch Don Johnson – Diaz's character's womanizing father – who gets the best lines.

Walk of Shame has Elizabeth Banks censured for having a one-night stand before attempting to turn things around and chide people for judging her. 'I'm a good girl', she says repeatedly. She delivers her big speech, noting, among other things, that she shouldn't have called what happened to her a 'walk of shame' and that a hook-up shouldn't 'automatically make me a pariah'. Up until then, the movie (written and directed by Steven Brill (*Little Nicky*)) highlights how everyone mistakes Meghan for a stripper, then a hooker, then a full-on crack whore. One night of casual sex has turned Meghan from good to working girl.

Getting more women behind the camera to write, direct and produce is the way things will improve. Elizabeth Banks produced *Pitch Perfect* and its sequel, Wiig co-wrote *Bridesmaids* and Cameron Diaz is producing the TV adaptation of *Bad Teacher* (2011) in which she starred. Lake Bell wrote, produced, directed and stars in *In A World* (2013) – a superb example of a sister who is doing it for herself.

Hollywood has always has been risk averse and conservative in its attitudes to women. *Obvious Child* (Robespierre 2014) starring stand-up comic Jenny Slate is a notable exception, an Indy hit, the writer director has denied that it is an abortion comedy but has noted that, unlike *Juno* and *Knocked Up*, it does not end in the delivery room. Stories concerning women who live without men tend to either focus on the moment of leaving them or follow the journey of self-discovery (*Eat, Pray, Love*) but more often return to love and security by the close of Act Three. Romcoms are changing again, fundamentally in some ways and major actresses are branching out into playing women who are less than perfect – Aniston in *We're The Millers*, Diaz in *Bad Teacher* – but it is the Indy scene where we are most likely to encounter fresh versions and visions of the feminine.

Chapter 20
Comedy Subgenres

This chapter is devoted to subgenres that, whilst less popular than broad family or romantic comedies still earn their place at the comedy table and have their firm fans. These might be the comedies of independent writer/directors such as Lake Bell's *In A World*, Todd Solondz's *Happiness* or the films of French playwright Francis Veber's work, or genres that fall in and out of vogue.

One such is the **comedy Western**, which each decade seems to produce a revisionist take, such as *Blazing Saddles* (Brooks 1974), *City Slickers* (Underwood 1991), *Wild, Wild West* (Sonnenfeld 1999) or *A Million Ways To Die In The West* (Macfarlane 2014). The Western was part of Hollywood cinema from its inception, with Annie Oakley and Buffalo Bill appearing in eponymous shorts in 1894, produced by William K. L. Dickson at the Edison Black Maria Studio.

Westerns underwent all four genre stages ending in parody and revisionism. *Butch Cassidy and The Sundance Kid* (Hill 1969) was a huge box office hit, bringing a buddy movie, a love triangle and a comedy to a genre that had previously been all about when men were men and women were scared. This was later used as the basis for the TV series *Alias Smith and Jones* (Various 1971–3)[1] with twin comic leads (Ben Murphy and Pete Duel).[2]

---

[1] *Alias Smith and Jones* began with a made-for-TV movie called *The Young Country*, about con artists in the Old West, produced, written and directed by Roy Huggins, who served as executive producer of *Alias Smith and Jones* and, under the pseudonym of John Thomas James, at least shared the writing credit on most episodes.

[2] In the early morning hours of 31 December 1971, series star Pete Duel died of a gunshot wound at the age of thirty-one. Upon learning of Duel's death, executive producer Jo Swerling, Jr. initially wanted to end the series but ABC refused. Swerling later stated: 'ABC said, "No way!" They said, "You have a contract to deliver this show to us, and you will continue to deliver the show as best you can on schedule or we will sue you." Universal didn't hesitate for a second to instruct us to stay in production. We were already a little bit behind the eight ball on airdates. So we contacted everybody, including Ben [Murphy], and told them to come back in. The entire company was reassembled and

TV had already had a long-running successful series set in the Old West with *Maverick* (Garner 1957–62), with James Garner[3] playing cardsharp Bret Maverick, joined by his brother Bart (Jack Kelly). By the mid-1970s, however, the genre had played itself out and it was a decade until Clint Eastwood's *Unforgiven* (Eastwood 1992), hit the screens in a revisionist take. It did not ignite a slew of imitations.

Issues of political correctness as regards the portrayal of Native Americans (or 'Red Indians') was a stumbling block – something now being addressed. In one Simpson's episode, Homer joins a Civil War reconstruction only to confront Abu in the Kwik-E-Mart and failing to understand what kind of Indian he is.

This and the other aspect of the Old West's history, slavery (referenced in *Blazing Saddles*), has come under closer scrutiny since the Oscar-winning drama *12 Years A Slave* (MacQueen 2013) and Quentin Tarantino's *Django Unchained* (Tarantino 2012), but there is a way to go. A slavery comedy is perhaps most likely to be made by black writers/actors and directors. *Cowboys & Aliens* (Favreau 2011) was a stab at blending Western with science fiction. The Western is always period, except when converted to science fiction (the original *Star Trek* was pitched as *Wagon Train in Space*), but as comedy seeks to comment upon society today, it feels like there is limited treasure to plunder, except in finding gold in other aspects of the period.

Fantasy comedy

Big. Groundhog Day. Splash. Click. Liar, Liar. Gremlins. Night at the Museum. Shrek. Being John Malkovich. It's A Wonderful Life.

Fantasy comedy uses magic, the supernatural and mythical figures for comic purposes. Fantasy conventions are turned on their heads with the princess being a klutz and the action hero being a cowardly fool – shades here of Bob Hope or Woody Allen. Although many action adventure and science fiction comedies play fast and loose with the laws of Physics, there are some comedies that take high concept and follow through.

---

back in production by one o'clock that day shooting scenes that did not involve Peter – only twelve hours after his death'. According to Swerling, the decision to continue production so soon after Duel's death was heavily criticized in the press at the time.
[3] After three series Garner left, and Roger Moore was added as brother Beau.

One such is the body-swap comedy, which was popularized in the 1980s but begins in 1882 with comic novel *Vice Versa: A Lesson to Fathers*, by Thomas Anstey Guthrie.[4] Set in the Victorian era, it concerns a businessman whose son fears his return to boarding school. Telling the boy that his schooldays are the best years of his life, a wish is granted employing a magic stone brought by an uncle from India whereby they exchange bodies. It was filmed as *Vice Versa* (Ustinov 1948) and remade in the 1980s (Gilbert 1988). Another take was *Freaky Friday* (Nelson 1976), which starred Jody Foster in a Disney vehicle where mother and daughter swap bodies: this too was remade in 2003 with Lindsay Lohan[5] and Jamie Lee Curtis.

The oriental mystical element is a staple too. The *Gremlins* (Dante 1984) were purchased from an antique shop in Chinatown (Mogwai being Cantonese for 'monster'). The warnings were clear as, like children, they must not be made wet, exposed to sunlight or fed after midnight. This is Pandora's Box for a modern age.

The body switch comedies of the 1980s were kicked off by Carl Reiner's *All of Me* (Reiner 1984), which was based on the novel *Me Two* by Edwin Davis. Starring Steve Martin and Lily Tomlin, Roger Cobb (Martin) is a disillusioned attorney called to the bedside of elderly millionairess Edwina Cutwater (Tomlin) to finalize her will. Having hired mystic Prahka Lasa, who has the secret of trans-ferring souls, she wishes to put hers into that of a beautiful young woman Terry Hoskins (Victoria Tennant).[6] Inevitably the transfer goes wrong and Roger ends up with Edwina's wilful soul controlling the right-hand side of his body.

In *Big* (Marshall 1988), a funfair fortune-telling machine grants the wish of twelve-year-old Josh Baskin (Tom Hanks) to be bigger, but wishes, dreams and desires have consequences. More body swap comedies followed, including *Like Father, Like Son* (Daniel 1987) with Dudley Moore and *18 Again* (Flaherty 1988) with George Burns.

Groundhog Day (Ramis 1993) combines romantic with fantasy comedy, even though writer Danny Rubin's original script lacked the love element. Weatherman Phil Connors is a misanthropic self-centred cynic (the reason why is not explained). As Rita (Andie McDowall) says to him at the halfway point, 'You don't love anybody'. He agrees, 'I don't even love myself', especially as he is caught in an endlessly repeating time loop of a single day that starts at 6am with the same song on the radio and features the same events. The beauty of this

---

[4] Under the pseudonym F. Anstey.

[5] Currently the 'unruly girl' du jour, Lohan has appeared in three 'twins' films to date – *I Know Who Killed Me*, *Freaky Friday* and *The Parent Trap*. She was also mooted to star in the good/bad girl *Carrie* remake.

[6] Ironically Martin did end up in her body as he married her.

conceit is that the magic is never explained. To spend time explaining how or why this occurred is irrelevant to the plot and characters and is wisely omitted.

Night at the Museum (Levy 2006), now a franchise, borrows from early horror *The House of Wax* (1959) and makes the exhibits real. Here, historical figures come back to life to haunt Ben Stiller – a conceit that has many possibilities. Another take on this is *Jumanji* (Johnston 1995) – a board game which, when certain incantations are muttered, *Beetlejuice*-style, throws you into the game. This kind of comedy fantasy uses some horror tropes, being a version of the Ouija board curse. The wish or curse is a metaphor for the hole in the lead character's life and a lesson for him to learn. So too do they share an arc of redemption. They often focus on a troubled individual, who requires an outside force to act as catalyst for them to change. The *sine qua non* of all comedy fantasies is *It's A Wonderful Life* (Capra 1946), based on the short story *The Greatest Gift* (Van Doren 1945). George Bailey (Jimmy Stewart) has given up on his dreams at the expense of others and is about to take his own life. The intervention of his guardian angel Clarence (Henry Travers) helps him to see what life would have been like without him. It is the inverse of *A Christmas Carol*, Charles Dickens' Christmas tale of Scrooge's miserliness and redemption, where ghosts, magic and the rule of three are used to convince the old man of his unscrupulous ways. The greatest version remains that played by Alistair Sim, one of Britain's finest comic actors. 'Be careful of what you wish for' is at the heart of most fantasy comedy movies, a message to the young, who at that time are most full of desires. It is a way of hinting at experience and that youth will give way toward age, without unduly scaring them to death.

Being John Malkovich (Jonze 1999) is a unique, career–defining start for Charlie Kaufman, whose bizarre portal into the mind of an actor is truly weird. An out of work puppeteer (John Cusack) gets a filing job on the tiny seventh-and-a-half floor, meets a femme fatale (Katherine Keener) and discovers a portal that leads into the mind of actor John Malkovich for fifteen minutes. Being as this is an American movie, hucksterism is at its heart and they start to sell tickets. Soon, his disgruntled wife (Cameron Diaz in her only dowdy role to date) gets in on the action – and tries to start a lesbian affair using it – and the real John Malkovich gets wind and wants a go. Then it gets weird. The idea of literally being inside someone's head was used in British comic *The Beano* in 'The Numskulls' (1962–), in which tiny technicians drive 'our man', and in the US sitcom *Herman's Head* (Fox 1991–4) with echoes of Jonathan Swift (Lilliput).[7] In movies, the device was also mined successfully in the final segment of Woody

---

[7] And more recently a Pixar movie, *Inside Out*.

Allen's *Everything You Always Wanted To Know About Sex *But Were Afraid to Ask* entitled 'What happens when you ejaculate?' featuring sperm preparing for a sexual encounter.

God and the devil

Michael. Heaven Can Wait. Oh, God. Bruce Almighty. Evan Almighty. Time Bandits. Religulous. Dogma. Little Nicky. The Devil Wears Prada. Bedazzled.

America is a puritanical, mainly Christian nation. Hollywood is well aware of this and, although its movies contain plenty of sex and violence, they fight shy of questioning their belief systems. *Dogma* (Kevin Smith) suffered terribly as a comedy because of this. Comedy struggles with philosophical conceits because the target is as nebulous as one of the heavenly clouds. Bringing it down to Earth, as in *Bruce Almighty* and its sequel *Evan Almighty*, is more manageable. The images of Heaven and Hell and their supposed inhabitants are limited to clouds, fire and brimstone, but makes for an uneasy subject beyond brief visits.[8] God is, if seen at all, portrayed as an old man with a white beard, as Morgan Freeman or as a bumbling bureaucrat as in Terry Gilliam's superb *Time Bandits* ('I may be God but I'm not entirely dim'). In animation there is almost total freedom and *The Simpsons*, *Family Guy* and *South Park* regularly make fun of our image of a creator and his only begotten son. Comedies about God tend to deal with fate and whether or not it is pre-ordained. Buying time for unfinished business and bargaining with the fates also means that the God stand-in can be the Grim Reaper, who makes appearances in *Scrooge*, *Monty Python's Meaning of Life* and Woody Allen's *Love and Death*. Ingmar Bergman's *Seventh Seal* had a man play chess with Death, a trope that was paid great homage in *Bill and Ted's Excellent Adventure*.

You cannot escape your fate but sometimes, as we learn in the movies, you can alter it by understanding your true nature and learning to become a better person because of it. A rich man cannot pass through the eye of a needle on Earth, but in Hollywood he buys the needle and has the gap widened by Mexican immigrants.

A screenplay about God or death will include an existential crisis point early on, one that will take the hero to an encounter with his maker or representative thereof. A challenge will be issued; either by man or God (whom man made in his own image) and the resultant quest is a comic Homeric odyssey. It takes a personality

---

[8]*A Matter of Life and Death* is one of the finest (Powell and Pressburger).

of great likeability to make this work, one that has the everyman values of a Jimmy Stewart character. Smart-mouthing God works with a character of supreme arrogance (Jim Carrey) or one with great humility. Angels work better on TV.

Devils are more fun – as witness British comic Peter Cook in *Bedazzled* (Donen 1968). In the usual Faustian Pact, he offers an unhappy man Stanley Moon (Dudley Moore) seven wishes in exchange for his soul. *Hellzapoppin!* was a 1941 musical version on a similar theme, and the devil often continues to make appearances in comedy. Faustian pacts include *The Devil and Max Devlin* (starring Bill Cosby and Elliot Gould), *Little Nicky* (Harvey Keitel) and Laurel and Hardy's *The Devil's Brother*. Redemption and forgiveness are sacrosanct in these tales and the devil will end up banished, as will his acolytes and cohorts, as with Nicholson in *The Witches of Eastwick*, George Burns in *Oh God, You Devil* and Dave Grohl in *Tenacious D and the Pick of Destiny*.

Comedy horror

Witches of Eastwick. Brain Dead. American Werewolf in London. Slither. Theatre of Blood. The Rocky Horror Picture Show. What We Do In The Shadows. Black Sheep.

> *Comedy and Horror are Siamese twin genres, joined at the nervous laugh.*
> ALFRED HITCHCOCK

Comedy and horror are regular bedfellows. Once the Universal horrors of the 1930s had established and popularized the genre, spoofs appeared from the same stable starring comedy double act Abbot and Costello, who encountered the lot. *Abbot and Costello Meet Frankenstein* (1948), *The Killer Boris Karloff* (1949), *The Invisible Man* (1951), *Doctor Jekyll and Mister Hyde* (1953) and *The Mummy* (1955) were knockabout farces, capitalizing on their vaudeville backgrounds and huge popularity.

An early combination of comedy and horror was in the medium of the comic book.

EC Comics was founded in 1944 by Maxwell Gaines. His son, William M. Gaines, inherited the company and founded *Mad* magazine. *Mad* presented dark tales in which the Crypt Keeper (*Tales from The Crypt*) mocks the living reader with puns and deadly jokes. Doctor Frederick Wertham MD felt this was poisoning the minds of children and published *Seduction of the Innocents* (1954), which, in a McCarthy climate of paranoia, snowballed. Outraged parent groups and (comic) book burnings led to a sub-committee hearing on the damage being done to youth. As a result, in an echo of the Hays Code, Gaines invited comic book publishers to create the *Comics Code Authority*, which was prohibitively censorious and killed off EC comics.

Concurrently with this, the 1950's SF horrors were patently daft, including *Attack of the Giant Leeches*, *Attack of the 50 Foot Woman*, *Zombies of the Stratosphere*, *Cat Women of the Moon* and *I Married a Monster from Outer Space*. *Ed Wood* (see Biopics) captured a flavour of the unintentional comedy of that time.

British director James Whale had already used dollops of mordant wit in *The Old Dark House* and *The Invisible Man* but allowed *Frankenstein* (1932) to be straight horror. *The Bride of Frankenstein*, the first sequel, turned horror into camp and racked up the comedy, including screaming queens of both genders.

Once we have configured the monster in horror, we are no longer terrified and a kind of grim fascination kicks in. We can accept and examine its terrible physical and mental scars with a quasi-medical objectivity and much subsequent enjoyment is to be had in sequels: *A Nightmare on Elm St*, *Friday the 13th* or the *Halloween* franchises where the bogeyman, instead of being nemesis, is now in effect the protagonist. It is his name and his face on the poster. We root for him as we did halfway through *Psycho* when Marion Crane was prematurely killed off, leaving no one but poor mummy's boy Norman Bates for us to care for. In this way, we are thrust into the position of the killer, amused at the plight of the victim, the more inventive the kill and the more deserving the recipient (slut, jock or nerd), the better.

These monsters – Freddy, Jason and Michael became popular in the 1980s when the home video revolution allowed anyone to get their hands on video-taped movies. It also spurned the 'Video Nasties' bill (Video Recordings Act) in the UK in 1982, which sent a lot of the schlock underground. As each subgenre of horror reaches its zenith, it falls open to parody. *Scary Movie* took as its starting point the moribund slasher subgenre, although Wes Craven's and Kevin Williamson's *Scream* (1997) had been there first.

Parody, if overdone, becomes susceptible to the law of diminishing returns, as with *Saturday the 14th*, *Repossessed, Pandemonium* and *Dracula: Dead and Loving It*. It works best when you are seeing for the first time the death of a particular format and are able to skewer its tired tropes – as with Mel Brook's *Young Frankenstein* (1974) which spoofed the 1931 Universal titular horror and its sequels. Brooks shot in black and white, using the same sets and sound stages, had a period score written specially and employed the filmic techniques of the era such as iris outs, wipes and fades to black. *Young Frankenstein* is played straight, with characters quite unaware that they are in a comedic situation, no matter how farcical.

Another subset of horror that has seen better days is the zombie or undead movie, of which *Warm Bodies* and *Zombie Land* are comic versions, along with a slew of minor variations such as *Wasting Away*, *Doghouse and Zombie Strippers*, all coming in the wake of the finest rom-zom-com of them all, *Shaun of the Dead*. Here, the joke was a subtle inversion in that it was the protagonist who is a zombie, living a suburban drone-like existence, avoiding commitment, hating his McJob, ignoring his girlfriend, in the words of Beckett, 'Living and partly living'. So when real zombies[9] stumble along he cannot configure them. This was Pegg and Frost's first outing as bromance brothers, but the horror setting was a useful one for male bonding and splattered brains. Zombies, lumbering or speedy, are a handy metaphor for the dying days of capitalist consumerism (*Dawn of the Dead*), militarism (*Day of the Dead*), the Bush administration (*Land of the Dead*) and any number of social concerns, the better ones involving a satirical edge.

Another way to go is splat-stick, essentially slapstick involving blood, gore and intestines. Throw enough of these at the screen and we move beyond the stage of revulsion and disgust to laughter. It is *Grand Guignol*, the ballet in blood. David Cronenburg said, 'We all need periodic releases from the tyranny of good taste'. This kind of comic horror deals with the abject, a fascination with bodily waste, that which is part of us, at once alive and now dead. Because we cannot believe our eyes, there is a cognitive failure at this sheer excess leading to shock and the release of laughter. If this were real life, we would be traumatized, but fiction allows the laughter reflex to shut it down. This is the province of the gore hound – the fan who is excited by pushing and testing his boundaries for excess – and best examples include Peter Jackson's *Braindead* (1992), *Slither* (Gunn 2006) and *Tokyo Gore Police* (Nishimura 2008).

An American Werewolf in London (Landis 1981) is perhaps the perfect blend of comedy and horror wherein a miserable hiking trip leads young American backpackers David Kessler and Jack Goodman to a Yorkshire pub full of rural characters. Duly warned of howling beasts, they do not keep to the path, Jack is slaughtered and David is bitten. On his recovery, David begins to have bizarre nightmares and undergoes nocturnal, carnivorous wanderings as he starts to mutate. Written as cold synopsis, this is straight horror. The comedy comes in the use of music to lighten the mood (a non-verbal nod to the audience), and in the reappearance of Jack, his decomposing best friend. Griffin Dunne's sarcastic deadpan lifts the whole ship afloat. Even dead he remains jocular and the mismatch creates the humour, that and the gallows humour of the victims who appear to helpfully suggest ways that David might kill himself. There is also some broad comedy when David awakens in London Zoo, in his naked post-lupine state, and has to make his way back to Alex's apartment, protecting his

---

[9]Their presence gracefully unexplained, as with its predecessor, the daddy of all Indy horror movies, George Romero's *Night of the Living Dead* (1968).

modesty with a red balloon. It is a great practical examination of what might happen if you were to become a werewolf.

There are others who have successfully crossbred horror and comedy, including Douglas Hickox's *Theatre of Blood* (1972), Joe Dante (*Gremlins*, 1984) and Sam Raimi with the *Evil Dead* series. The key is to write a straight horror and to subvert it. *Tucker and Dale vs. Evil* (Craig 2010) takes the rural backwoods horror and gives it a spin. Here it is the halfwit hillbillies who are the innocent victims of circumstance. When they try to help a girl drowning in a swimming hole, they are taken for monsters and no matter what they do the bodies keep piling up. In *Behind the Mask: The Rise of Leslie Vernon* (Glossermann 2006), the slasher tropes are slyly taken apart and before she knows it, the journalist sent to investigate and interview your friendly neighbourhood serial killer is herself embroiled in the plan. You need to know and love your horror. Those movie spoofs that disrespect the genre miss the point: the teenage girls want to have sex, outside and in danger. They all need to do the stupid thing so that the audience can feel superior and know what the stupid thing is – because they are not so very far away from being children who have no conception of common sense. Horror is a restorative, as is comedy. It is checking the pulse of the teen (or superannuated teen) to see if he or she is learning the lessons. Adding comedy only takes a soupçon or a twist. The deadpan comptrollers in *Cabin in the Woods* (Goddard 2012), the knowingness of *Piranha 3D* (Aja 2010) or the games with death in the *Final Destination* series are superior efforts.

More recently, the vampire/twilight/werewolf myths have been superbly spoofed in *What We Do In The Shadows* (Clement 2014), a Kiwi take on four vampires who flat-share, a cult film in the making.

Independent and auteur comedy

It is hard to define the truly independent comedy. If it is one that is financed and produced outside the Hollywood studio system, then these are few, as the economies of production and distribution necessitate some connection to or contribution from the majors. As the horror movie brats of the late 1960s and early 1970s (Romero and Hooper) self-produced their output, in comedy terms there is only John Waters who made a self-financed series of low-budget camp comedies using his hometown of Baltimore and a cast of regulars (*Woman Trouble*, *Pink Flamingos*). He has of late been subsumed into the studio system (*Hairspray*); his outrageous campness and obscenity neutered via the musical form, his status now revered as National Institution.

Some countries (UK, Eire, France) have government/lottery/broadcaster funding, which is drawn upon by producers and investors, but the output is minimal and the releases scattershot. Only the UK's Working Title could be called a studio.

Is it the work of an auteur with a unique style? A product that appeals to a different sensibility than Hollywood or one that transgresses NC-17 boundaries by being dark, sexual or profane? Is it Kevin Smith's *Clerks* or the camp violence of Quentin Tarantino? Is it Spike Jonze and Charlie Kaufman's *Being John Malkovich* or Todd Solondz's comedy drama *Happiness*? Are the Coen brothers true Indies?[10] They have been in bed with Miramax, as has Tarantino. And what *is* an auteur? The debate is ongoing, but a body of self-penned work featuring the artist as performer might form a ground rule (except for directors). There may also be an individual style that breeds an adjectival form (Capra/Chaplin/Burton-esque) or a team of regular players.

The first true independent was Charlie Chaplin, who with D. W. Griffith, Mary Pickford and Douglas Fairbanks founded United Artists[11] in 1919 in a reaction to the restrictive practices of the producers on wages and creative decisions, which were later to lead to the studio system. UA struggled in its early years but by the 1930s only Chaplin was rich enough to produce the pictures he wanted.

Putting aside Chaplin and the silent comedians, it was Preston Sturges who pioneered the conceit of the writer-director by selling his screenplay of *The Great McGinty* to Paramount Pictures for one dollar on the condition that he could direct. He subsequently won the Oscar for writing the best screenplay, paving the way for Capra, Wilder et al.

In France, physical clown Jacques Tati framed his silent comedies in the 1950s with the use of diegetic sound and continued to thrive as his Monsieur Hulot character over five films.

The only true independent of comedy might be Woody Allen, who has been making films outside of the studio system (although United Artists were his distributor in the 1970s) for much of his adult life. It was a fortuitous confluence of events that made this possible, smart management from Rollins Joffe and a Hollywood system that was collapsing but also experimental and offering opportunities to artists. His deal with Orion allowed him to continue to cheaply

---

[10] They began with Sam Raimi on his Independent comedy/horror *Evil Dead*, then financed their first movie *Blood Simple* (1984) with donations from friends and family. Since then, their body of work has included broad comedies such as *Raising Arizona*, *The Hudsucker Proxy* (a toast to screwball), *Intolerable Cruelty* (an anti-romcom), *O Brother, Where Art Thou?* (a nod to Preston Sturges' *Sullivan's Travels*), *Fargo* and epic stoner comedy *The Big Lebowski*.
[11] It is now wholly owned by MGM.

produce his films, one a year for many years, a contract that was renewed until poor box office led to its termination. Since then he has gone cap in hand to European funders and partnerships, but has continued to make mostly comedies. He has had a late flowering, a return to form that started with *Midnight in Paris* and has continued with *Blue Jasmine* (winning an Oscar for Kate Blanchet).[12]

His fellow writer on Sid Caesar's *Your Show of Shows*, Mel Brooks always worked for the studios and has a team writing for him. Kevin Smith began as an independent with *Clerks,* but later work was studio funded (*Chasing Amy* and *Jay and Silent Bob*). His recent *Red State* struggled because he let it be known that he makes fair demands of distributors.

British character comedian Sacha Baron Cohen has created four comic monsters to date, *Ali G Indahouse*, *Borat*, *Brüno* and Prince Al Hadeen (*The Dictator*). He too has a team of writers, but his public profile indicates that he will not be able to fool the public and continue to make mockumentaries of such calibre. Compatriot Steve Coogan has his own production company *Baby Cow*, but his efforts to break Hollywood have so far been uneven. He parlayed his character Alan Partridge into *Alpha Papa,* but his screen successes are sporadic, playing factory records supremo Tony Wilson in *24 Hour Party People* being one of his best.

We turn to Spain for a true auteur in the form of Pedro Almodovar, whose body of comedic work is undeniable (see Worldwide Comedy).

Back in the US, there is a case for the following as being auteurs with a significant body of work: John Hughes, Jerry Lewis, James L. Brooks, Albert Brooks, the Reiners, the Zucker and Farrelly brothers (and Jim Abrahams), Judd Apatow and Tina Fey, Nora Ephron and, soon, Lena Dunham.

In order to become a comedy writer/director, the writing will be your jumping off point and your audition. Unless you are privately or crowd funded to the tune of several million dollars, the accepted route is to sell scripts and move on from there. Movies are made three times, first in the writing, then in the directing, and then in the edit. The scope of this book is based in the first, but it is good to understand the nature of the writer's role in Hollywood, which might be summed up in the words 'bend over'.

If a producer is in at the start and stays right to the end of a film, the writer is most often dispensed with on the first day (or long before) of principal photography. This is why you are paid a tranche of your salary on that day. Writers are sometimes required for on-set rewrites, but this is rare. Once the final shooting script is delivered and locked, your job is over.

---

[12] A recent report (Jan 2015) has stated he may return to TV.

The work of the director, however, is only just beginning. The script is the blueprint for all that will follow. A movie is made in the planning and pre-production stages. Casting, storyboards, locations and a microscopic examination and analysis of the script and each and every scene are all vital to prepare for the task ahead. Once a director gets on set, it is twenty-hour days every day, answering all the questions put to you by cast and crew.[13] Footage must be obtained before the light goes, the horse wrangler has to leave, and the best (or usable) performances are coaxed out of actors still learning lines in their trailers. If you are made of strong stuff, are addicted to coffee and bakery products and have no interest in sleeping then perhaps you too can be a director.

Currently the Hollywood system is 25 per cent down on comedy production, much of its focus being on blockbusting fantasy/SF/action movies with little to no dialogue that will play worldwide (and in particular the emergent Chinese market). There is a massive focus on box set TV drama for streaming and download. Small, dedicated sketch comedy websites have been subsumed by YouTube, which is increasingly seen as *the* market to break a career in performing. The writer is as invisible as ever, but if he is inventive, he will find a way to get to market. Most writers require a producer and are dependent on him for their livelihood (it is show-business, not show-show), but we live in an online world where true independence is not only possible but also quite desirable – the problem as ever being to monetize this.

Biopic comedy

Ed Wood. Man on the Moon. Butch Cassidy and The Sundance Kid. Lenny. The Naked Civil Servant. Good Morning Vietnam. Chaplin. The Life and Death of Peter Sellers. A Liar's Autobiography.

Comedy films about comedians and performers are a small subset, some comic – the work of writers Scott Alexander and Larry Karaszewski, *Ed Wood* (Burton 1994) and *Man on the Moon* (Forman 1999) – some mixing comedy and drama – *Chaplin* (Attenborough 1992) with Robert Downey Jnr or *Funny Girl* (Wyler 1968), the story of Fanny Brice, starring Barbara Streisand. Some are tragic, such as *Lenny* (Fosse 1973), starring Dustin Hoffman.

The 'tears of a clown' is an enduring trope, from Grimaldi onwards. Joseph Grimaldi 'was comedy's first superstar. Born in London on 18 December 1778, Grimaldi went on to become the greatest English clown of his day. ... however,

---

[13] Billy Wilder said, 'You give up when the legs go'.

not for nothing did he adopt the catchphrase "I make you laugh all night but I am Grim-all-day"' (Dessau 2011) He performed for over thirty years at great physical cost, his body so battered and broken that he had to retire at forty-nine and be carried to the pub after that, dying destitute at fifty-eight.

Another comedians tale tells of a man who goes to see a psychiatrist in Hamburg in 1950, explaining to him that the woes of the world are getting him down. The psychiatrist tells him that the world famous clown Grock is in town that night and he should go to see him to cheer himself up. 'I can't', says the man. 'Don't you *see*? I *am* Grock!' (Dessau 2011).

Comedians and comedy actors flock to express on film the difficulties of the profession. The story has a familiar arc – born-in-a-trunk, the absent or abusive parent, the hard childhood, the early years of struggle, the love that got away, sacrifices and betrayal, the ruthless rise to the top, coming adrift, facing the self, redemption and triumph or ultimate tragedy.

As mentioned earlier, life does not have a plot. A biopic must by its nature be selective, choosing those elements of the history and those characters that work for the story, fashioning them into a narrative with a dramatic arc. Sometimes, a broad canvas is used, as with *Chaplin* or *The Life and Death of Peter Sellers,* sometimes a specific crisis point is chosen on which to hang the story (the last eight or so years of Tony Hancock's life were the subject of a BBC 'Screen One' television film called *Hancock* (1991), starring Alfred Molina).

In order to write a biopic that is comedic or about a comedian (or double act) there must first be a wide enough recognition of the particular star or stars; either the name must be known to millions or there must be notoriety (*The Fatty Arbuckle Story* is yet to be made). There has to be a notable event or performance that can form the apex of the story, be that suicide or triumph. By its nature, events and characters are compressed, and it is much more about what is left out than what is put in. Trying to retrospectively form meaning and direction into a life is a challenge to any writer, and it is even harder to please the fans and family. It is a job best undertaken to commission.

Ensemble comedy

Parenthood. Grown Ups. American Pie. Clerks. Hannah and her Sisters. Manhattan. Pulp Fiction. A Fish Called Wanda. This is the End. Best in Show. The Royal Tenenbaums. Anchorman.

In ensemble comedy the focus is not on a single character and his goals or desires, but on a group of characters with multiple plots and subplots that intertwine and resolve themselves thematically by the end of the movie. These movies will show us a number of different perspectives on a particular world. This may be a team, and there is crossover here with military, sports and heist comedies, or they are a group of people with similar objectives as in *Animal House*, *M*A*S*H* or *American Pie*. Usually a leader will become apparent, or if not there must be a protagonist with whom we identify. In *Parenthood*, this is Steve Martin; in *Grown Ups*, Adam Sandler.

In a dramatic ensemble piece, there may be the opportunity for an individual to perform a comic cameo, most notably Tom Cruise's pick-up artist and inspirational speaker Frank Mackey in *Magnolia* or corpulent agent Les Grossman in *Tropic Thunder*. In Woody Allen's chamber piece period in the 1980s (*Hannah, Crimes and Misdemeanors, Husbands and Wives*) there was ample opportunity for this, if it was not the Woodman himself.

The term 'ensemble' can describe a world, an issue or a number of characters coming together in one place, often for an event such as the funeral for a friend in *The Big Chill*. For the purposes of narrative cohesion, there will be a communal event, theme or social issue and the most successful of ensemble comedies gather all of these together. There will be a connection between the characters, either by blood or marriage, circumstance or coincidence.

Ensemble comedy is hard to manage, as the writer must juggle several balls in the air at any one time. The more characters you have, the more exposition is required and the danger is that they become ciphers if there is no time to flesh them out. In a sense, they are representations of attitudes and opinions, as in a bad play. We are, however, exploring a world, for example that of minimum-wage store clerks in *Clerks*, the dysfunctional family in *The Royal Tenenbaums*, television ethics or the lack of them in *Network* or *Broadcast News. Grown Ups* and *Parenthood* both involve family vacations.

The Cannonball Run and *It's a Mad, Mad, Mad, Mad World* were unified by event, that of a race, and heist movies are similarly motivated to bring together a number of offbeat characters. With an event there is a built-in time period – the race or heist must end, and often there is a narrator to bookend the story. The tone here can vary, with some plots being quite dramatic – as is that of the protagonists in a romance.

A Fish Called Wanda (Crichton 1988) is an ensemble comedy starring John Cleese, Jamie Lee Curtis, Kevin Kline and Michael Palin; it is also a robbery/heist black comedy and a romance. Based around one event – theft.

Bridesmaids is about marriage, and we are introduced to the competing maids of honour and bridesmaids with echoes of *My Best Friend's Wedding* and *Wedding Crashers*.

Place can help to nail down the parameters of the story, as in *Meatballs*, which brings people together for summer camp, or *Caddyshack,* which is set in and around a golf club. In this sports ensemble comedy 'the emphasis is more on the ensemble than the sports. There are no training sequences, the stakes aren't particularly high and the hero does not unify a team' (Petri 2003).

There is suspense and surprise. Suspense is important. Will Archie Leach get away with it? Will Kristen Wiig lose her best friend in *Bridesmaids?* In plotting terms a comic cliffhanger can be suspended by moving on to another storyline, but again, too many characters and we will lose sight of the themes and individuals. By shying away from the depth of characterization required in the protagonist, it is easier to parcel these out to the minor characters, thus thinning the comedic effect. A strong lead is advised, one who is in a strong dilemma or relationship conflict that contrasts with the others.

Chapter 21

Worldwide Comedy

On YouTube[1] and Vimeo, it is possible to upload comedy product in the form of sketches and short films to full-length features from anywhere that has the Internet. Using DV cameras, reasonable sound, lighting, editing software and creditable performances, you can, in effect, create a movie in your bedroom and distribute it internationally. Only language is a barrier but auto translation and subtitling is fast becoming a reality. What counts is your ability to amuse an audience. Much of this is in the amateur vein and, at time of writing, most clips that go viral are snippets of real life: pranks, pets and the chance capturing of events. They are however, quick hits and as such are disposable. There is no narrative arc and it takes a writer to create drama. The internet is a good place to hone the skills of comedy sketch writing on sites such as *Funny or Die*, *College Humor*, *Channel Bee* or the Brazilian absurdist/satirist comedy troupe *Porta dos Fundos* (Back Door). The comedy sketch can also act as a trailer for longer form comedy: the comedy writer/director's best shop window is to place his trailer online to encourage crowd sourcing and other funding.

However, the focus of this book is on the movie. In this chapter I have selected the countries with a strong tradition of comedy or who are producing emerging comedy talent. I will comment on the styles of comedy that seems to do well in terms of their respective markets.

The English-speaking world

Fred Karno,[2] responsible for the custard pie in the face gag, was a theatre

---

[1] YouTube and Facebook have surpassed MySpace and other early online delivery systems and are brand leaders. So long as they do not allow themselves to be swamped by advertising, it seems they will continue, at least for a while.
[2] Frederick John Westcott (26 March 1866–18 September 1941).

impresario whose comedy troupe, *Fred Karno's Army*, included Charlie Chaplin and his understudy Stan Laurel. Musical comedy was the mainspring of early cinema and Will Hay, George Formby and Gracie Fields were huge movie stars of the 1930s. Formby and Fields came to notice in *Looking on the Bright Side* (1932). Both had strong regional accents and became national figures under the stewardship of Ealing Studios[3] founder Basil Dean. Dean's successor Michael Balcon[4] made 'a conscious effort to project an image of Britain and the British character' (King 2002)' producing propaganda war movies *Went the Day Well* (1942) and *Undercover* (1943), and later the famous and hugely respected Ealing Comedies, which employed social comment and an ensemble cast in portraying post-war Britain.

Passport to Pimlico (Cornelius 1949) played with post-war ideas of independence, and subsequent comedies explored subjects such as rationing (*Whiskey Galore* 1949) or the mistrust of big business and technology (*The Man in the White Suit* (1951). The films lasted a decade (1947–57), the latter being dark murderous fantasies such as *Kind Hearts and Coronets* (1949), *The Lavender Hill Mob* (1951) and *The Ladykillers* (1955). Director Charles Crichton was so well thought of that he was later used by actor/comedian John Cleese to direct *A Fish Called Wanda* (1988).

Ealing was '… a world that is essentially quaint, cosy, whimsical and backward-looking … that enshrines what are seen as quintessentially English qualities: a stubborn individuality that is heroic to the point of eccentricity' (Richards 1997), aspects that continue to appear in its current movie output.

A different vision of Britain was shown in *The Happiest Days Of Your Life* (Launder 1950), which introduced the particular British comic arena of the public school. Prep school had already been mocked in print in Richmal Crompton's *Just William* stories and the *Jennings* books, but it was artist Ronald Searle's drawings of unruly schoolgirls[5] that caught the eye of producer Sidney Guilliat. He and director Frank Launder (with writer Val Valentine) created the *St Trinians* quartet, *The Belles of St Trinians* (Launder 1954), *Blue Murder*, *Pure Hell* and *Train Robbery*,[6] depicting an England that had probably never existed. The St Trinians girls were a prepubescent rabble and the films were 'a template for the paradoxically quaint but subversive style of British Comedy that worked its way into the *Doctor* and *Carry On* franchises' (Nathan 2005). The school is crooked from the top down, from headmistress Miss Fritton (a cross-dressing Alistair Sim), who would overlook criminality if it served the school, to the staff, a

---

[3]Ealing was the first dedicated sound studio in Europe.
[4]Balcon took over Ealing Studios from 1938 onwards.
[5]They first appeared in 1941 in the satirical magazines *Punch* and *Lilliput*
[6]There was a lame sequel *Wildcats* in 1980.

dissolute drunken bunch of wrecks, ex-cons and lesbians. The sixth form was a criminal cadre interested in bootleg gin and illegal gambling, aided and abetted by Flash Harry (George Cole) the epitome of the wartime spiv.

Public schools featured again in *School for Scoundrels* (Hamer 1960), although this was more a grown-up affair, more radically in *If* (Anderson 1970) and then in the 1980s with Monty Python's *The Meaning of Life* (Jones 1983) and Michael Frayn's farce *Clockwise* (Morahan 1986), both featuring John Cleese as a harassed headmaster.

The public school movie returned with the 2000s reboot of the *St Trinian's* franchise but despite its appeal to a younger demographic, the series had lost its radical edge. Still with school, *The Inbetweeners* sitcom (three series, 2008–10) distilled the comic elements of sixth-form pupils – the liar, the lovelorn, the idiot and the prude – into four characters, Jay, Simon, Neil and Will, who shared one simple desire: to get laid. This was realized in *The Inbetweeners Movie* (Palmer 2011), which took them out of the school environment to a holiday in Crete and set a record for the most successful opening weekend achieved by a comedy film in the UK, only surpassed by its sequel *The Inbetweeners 2* (Morris 2014).

Comic George Formby had created a template for the 'little man' who wins through against the odds, later perfected by Norman Wisdom as his Gump character in *Trouble in Store* (Carstairs 1953). This persona, an extension of Chaplin's tramp figure continued through the decades with Tony Hancock and Mr Bean. Early Formby and Fields films *No Limits* (1935) and *Keep Your Seats Please* (1936), appealed to the eccentric outsider and the small-scale community and were aimed at a domestic audience, as well as a colonial and postcolonial one.

The US dominated the global market in the 1910s and 1920s and their distribution companies kept a tight rein on the product. It was hard to compete with their production values and reach, but the Ealing comedies were successful in America, as were the later Monty Python films, as well as the Richard Curtis/ Working Title romcom revival films, including *Four Weddings and A Funeral* and *Notting Hill*, the latter recouping $116 million on a $42 million budget.

Britain too has a noble satirical tradition and this is reflected in its films. Notable successes were a trio of satirical films made by the Boulting Brothers. *Left Right and Centre* (Gilliat 1959) imagined politicians from either side of the fence falling in love. *Private's Progress* was a darkly comic look at conniving tricksters within the military, and its successor *I'm All Right Jack*, took the main cast and put them in trade and the commercial sector. This satire not only attacked the powerful bosses and corporations, but also the emergent trade unions, with Peter Sellers in one of his finest roles as Fred Kite, the working-class shop steward who was as blinkered as his capitalist bosses. Innocent toff

Henry Windrush[7] (Ian Carmichael) was sent to work and work he did, falling foul of a time-and-motion studies man and causing an industrial relations crisis.

Political/social satire continued with *The Rise and Rise of Michael Rimmer* (Billington 1970). Penned by John Cleese, Graham Chapman, the director and Peter Cook, who starred in a prescient satire of media spin. Peter Cook was criticized for his performance,[8] which concerned a mysterious man (a blank canvas about whom we know little)[9] who enters an advertising agency as a time and motion man, resulting in his becoming the boss. From here he commandeers opinion polls, tweaks them and goes into politics, where muckspreading, murder and Machiavellian twists lead to his becoming prime minister and then president, whereupon he cons the British public into voting against democracy. A Kennedy-like assassination attempt fails and the film ends on a freeze frame of his success. We get the government we deserve.[10]

Britain has its high and low culture. Thirty-one *Carry On* ensemble comedies were produced cheaply at Bray and Pinewood, starring a reparatory company of comic actors. It began with *Carry On Sergeant* and soon moved from spoofing the professions (*Nurse*, *Doctor*) to broader parodies of film genres (*Cowboy*, *Screaming*, *Cleopatra*). These were hugely popular seaside postcard/end of the pier entertainments and this, along with the James Bond franchise, kept the British movie industry afloat.[11]

Television sitcom was hugely popular. *Hancock's Half Hour* had viewing figures of a third of the population (more during its radio days) in the 1950s and 1960s. During the 1970s many of these sitcoms were parlayed into spin-off movies, most of them involving the device of transposing the cast from rainy Britain to the emergent package holiday market of Spain.[12] *Steptoe and Son*, *Till Death Do Us Part*, *Please Sir*, *Porridge*, *Are You Being Served?*, *Dad's Army*, *The Likely Lads*, *Rising Damp* and *Love Thy Neighbour* all made it to the big screen, with a trio of *On The Buses* films (1971–3), the first of which (amazingly) took more at the box office than *Diamonds Are Forever*.

---

[7] Ironically named after the ocean liner that brought West Indian immigrants to England in 1948.

[8] William Cook in *The Guardian*, available at http://www.theguardian.com/film/2007/jun/30/television.comedy (accessed 30 June 2007)

[9] Cook based the role on David Frost. He admitted not being a good actor, but he suited the part.

[10] French political philosopher Alexis de Tocqueville (1805–59) said, 'In democracy we get the government we deserve'.

[11] An attempt was made to replicate the *Carry Ons* with a sitcom spin-off, the 'Up' series (*Up Pompeii, Up the Chastity Belt* and *Up The Front*) with stellar British writers, but the 1970s were hard times for distributors the Rank organization – they made more from Rank Xerox machines than from the cinema chains – and for films in general. As audiences turned to colour TV, cinemas were closed, changed function to bingo halls, were divided into three screens or used for soft porn.

[12] This has proven to be a winning formula as *Kevin & Perry Go Large* (Bye 2000) and *The Inbetweeners Movie* (Palmer 2011) both replicated this formula in Iberia.

Despite the fact that the lack of narrative arc in sitcom does not transpose to the big screen (three acts instead of two), this is a trend which has continued. Comedies *Bean* and *Mrs Brown's Boys D'Movie* both succeeded at the box office. Perhaps the most successful character comedian is Sacha Baron Cohen, who created Ali G, which was adapted into *Ali G Indahouse* (MyLod 2002) before he and his writers turned to the mockumentary format for *Borat*, *Brüno* and *The Dictator*.

In Scotland, writer director Bill Forsyth produced a winning series of wistful romances, *Gregory's Girl* (1981), *Local Hero* (1983) and *Comfort and Joy* (1984), whose scripts were less about performative comedy and more about character.[13]

George Harrison and Dennis O'Brien's Handmade Films company rescued *Monty Python's Life of Brian*, who had their funding cut once EMI saw the script.[14] They also made *the Meaning of Life* and a great deal of smaller British fare, using the ex-Pythons where they could – Michael Palin in *Personal Services* and *A Private Function*, Graham Chapman in *YellowBeard* and Eric Idle in *Nuns on the Run*. It was John Cleese who achieved most post-Python success with *A Fish Called Wanda* in 1988.

Aside from the huge box office of Bollywood, the immigrant Asian community was also beginning to make comedy[15] with *Bhaji on the Beach* (1993) followed by *East is East* (1999) and *Bend it like Beckham* (2002), featuring actress Keira Knightley. In the 1990s, writer Richard Curtis, in conjunction with *Working Title* films (Eric Fellner and Tim Bevan),[16] launched a series of British romcoms,[17] creating an image of heritage Britain and pumping up the tourist industry. A series of successful films followed. *Sliding Doors* and *Jack and Sarah* rode the wave, but the middle classes are rarely portrayed in British cinema: its focus is exclusively up toward the gentry or down toward the cheery working man. A new strain of working-class films too appeared. Simon Beaufoy's *The Full Monty* (Cattaneo 1997) arrived at a time of national mourning over the death of Princes Diana. Its tale of chirpy northerners dealing with the post-industrial collapse of the mining industry by taking to stripping caught the hearts and minds of the general public.

This and the equally heart warming *Billy Elliot* (2000) later became long-running musicals. *The Full Monty* created a boilerplate for the underdog. Find a

---

[13] Character in extremis also forms the semi-improvised work of social realist film director Mike Leigh, whose *Nuts in May* and *Abigail's Party* are comedies of manners in the lower middle classes

[14] Referenced both in *Michael Palin's 1969–79 Diaries* and in Robert Sellers' *Very Naughty Boys*.

[15] BBC Radio, then TV series *Goodness Gracious Me* launched many careers.

[16] Who also produced the Coen brothers' *Fargo*.

[17] Curtis also wrote the script for *Bridget Jones's Diary* from the book by ex-girlfriend Helen Fielding.

dispossessed group of people, give them a hobby and an unrealistic goal and see them triumph against the forces of oppression. *Brassed Off*, *Kinky Boots* and *Calendar Girls* all succeeded by using this template and chirpy period working-class people can be seen in British films to this day, witness *Made in Dagenham* and *Pride*.

Out of 1990s TV sitcom *Spaced* came the writer/director team of Simon Pegg and Edgar Wright who made the Cornetto trilogy, a trio of genre spoofs including *Shaun of the Dead* (the first rom-zom-com), *Hot Fuzz* (an action movie) and *World's End* (sci-fi).

Since its inception under Major's government in 1994, Lottery funding has been a double-edged sword. On the one hand it has revitalized the British film industry; on the other, it produced public-funding duds produced by committee. More recently the Harry Potter and James Bond reboot franchises has meant busy studios at Pinewood, Elstree, Cardiff and Shepperton.

There are seemingly three options for British comedy: gritty northern, posh southern or gangster/hooligan (the films of Guy Ritchie, Matthew Vaughn and Nick Love). The issue with British comedy is twofold; first, the backward nature of its culture. Nostalgia is a feature of the British film industry, which excels in period pieces, making up the majority of funded features. Britain is a country with a lot of history and this seeps into the native writer.

There is a perceived golden age, always thirty–fifty years ago, where manners, common sense and policing by consent existed, immigration was not an issue and one 'knew one's place'. This runs deep. As much as we want to hear new voices, much of the comedy struggles to find an audience, especially in the multiplexes against Hollywood or Bollywood fare. The writer begins in TV and the leap from there is often across the pond (see Baynham interview).[18]

The second issue is class. ITV Period Drama *Downton Abbey* with its Edwardian view of upstairs and downstairs cultures of indentured servants and glass-chinned nobility has found a huge following. The posh are humanized (the rich have their problems too) and the servant's are poor-but-humble: it's a soap that begs the question, why is this so popular in a devolved twenty-first-century multicultural Britain?

I Give It a Year (Mazer 2013) is an anti-romcom about a couple that meet, fall in love and marry in haste. Before the ink is dry on the certificate there are doubts. The British do cynicism and satire better than anyone. They love to laugh at themselves and the defining British trait is not taking themselves seriously. This infuses the comedy like words in a stick of rock. There is the perverse element to the British culture of tear it down and ruin it so no one else

---

[18] Damon Beesley/Ian Morris, 'All British Sitcoms are about class', *Robert Elms Show*, 31 July 2014.

can have it, a kind of hooligan chic. There is the fight for the underdog because he's *our* underdog trope, the tall poppy syndrome of levelling anyone who gets above their station, which is contrasted with a blind reverence for pomp and ceremony. The British love celebrity, fame and fortune, but will not put in the concomitant work to achieve it. There is a paradoxical culture of wanting something for nothing and also one of entitlement. There is a love of a good bargain. The British character is continually at war with itself and it is a wonder that more films have not been made out of Jekyll and Hyde.

The paradox in writing a British comedy is that it must centre on the individual (or ensemble cast of quirky types), but in order to sell it must have universality. It cannot be parochial, but peculiarity, cynicism and invention are what attract an audience. It is a small country with big ideas but often backward-looking as it strides forwards. This is perhaps why *Mr Bean* was such a huge international hit. It reverted to silent comedy and the little man for its comedy heart.

Ireland

The Irish film industry has grown in recent years thanks partly to the promotion of the sector by *Bord Scannán Nah Éireann* (Irish Film Board) and the introduction of heavy tax breaks. There are now over 6,000 people employed there. Previously, only filmmakers Neil Jordan and Jim Sheridan were well known, but now there are over a dozen directors and writers with growing international reputations. Ireland has an influence disproportionate to its small size, one that it has always enjoyed in the fields of literature and theatre. Whilst the making and showing of films was subject to censorship by the Catholic Church (most notably the banning of *Life of Brian*), the Irish Film Censor's Office now makes virtually no cuts or bans and allows the individual to choose.

The Irish have a native wit, producing a list of comedy writers as long as your arm, including George Bernard Shaw, Oscar Wilde and Flann O'Brien and numerous contemporaries. There is light and dark here, from the punishing satire of Jonathan Swift to the playful surrealism of Spike Milligan, and this is reflected in its comedy film output. On the lighter side (but often with a dash of doom) there is *The Commitments* (Parker, 1991), *The Van* (Frears 1996) and *Mrs Brown's Boys D'Movie* (Kellet 2014) which earned £4.3 million in the UK and Ireland in its opening weekend, breaking records in Ireland for the highest box-office gross on the opening day of an Irish-made film.

In terms of black comedy, playwright/screenwriter/Director Martin McDonagh wrote and directed the hitman comedy *In Bruges* (2008) starring Brendan Gleeson and Colin Farrell, and executively produced his brother John's movie, *The Guard* (2011), with Gleeson and Don Cheadle. John Michael McDonagh has since used comic performers Dylan Moran and Chris O Dowd in his drama *Calvary* (2014). These films tend to feature flawed conflicted men, in thrall to earthly pleasures but struggling to retain some kind of dignity and to rediscover a relationship with God, if not the church – about which they are deeply cynical. This is often played out in the relationship between two men, antagonists who at once despise and need one another. The template for this might be Samuel Beckett's *Waiting for Godot*, his bleakly comic absurdist masterpiece.

Canada

Canada suffers from little brother syndrome being located right next to the United States, yet having none of the kudos and being the butt of the jokes (although many centre on how *nice* they are). A lot of American product in film and TV is shot there but the native film industry focuses less on comedy, more on drama, horror and SF, with *Jesus of Montreal* and Vincenzo Natali's *Cube* being breakout hits. Canada has produced a hugely disproportionate number of comedians and comedy actors including Mike Myers, Leslie Nielson, Jim Carrey, Dan Aykroyd, Thomas Chong, Michael J. Fox, Eugene Levy, John Candy, Seth Rogen, Catherine O'Hara, Rick Moranis, Martin Short, Matthew Perry, Michael Cera, Rachel McAdams and Ellen Page, not to mention 'The Shat' – William Shatner.

Canadian comedy starts with gross-out movies, *Meatballs* (1979) with Bill Murray and *Porky's* (1981), then goes quiet for a decade before *Les Boys* (1997) – which led to a series of hugely successful Quebecois ice hockey comedies. Sketch group, *The Kids in the Hall* made a movie called *Brain Candy* in 1996. *Canadian Bacon* (Moore, 1995) is mockumentary and a rare fictional work from Michael Moore. It is not technically Canadian, but it features John Candy who is. The storyline concerns a president who attacks Canada to improve ratings, an idea that pops up again in *Wag the Dog* (Levinson 1997), where he has a spin-doctor fake a war to avoid a sex scandal. All-out war with the US would have to wait two years for *South Park: Bigger, Longer & Uncut* (Parker 1999).

Animation is popular in Canada, producing the *Care Bear movies* and a thriving artistic community that produce shorts and images for music videos, but as for break-out movies it seems to be one a year. In 2007 it was *Juno* (Reitman 2007), starring Michael Sera and Ellen Page, covering the sticky subject of teen pregnancy.

One Week (McGowan 2008) concerned a young man diagnosed with cancer who heads west across Canada on a motorcycle, a tale told with wry humour and deadpan delivery. *Gunless* (Phillips 2010) is a comedy about an American Wild West outlaw who finds himself befuddled by Canadian civility north of the 49th. *Suck* (Stefaniuk 2011) is about a rock band that rocket in popularity after one of them (Jessica Pare) gets turned into a vampire. It is black horror comedy and a music Industry satire. Echoes here of Canadian horror *Ginger Snaps* (Fawcett 2000), which created the female werewolf (or vixen). Two death-obsessed sisters, outcasts in their suburban neighbourhood, have to deal with the tragic consequences when one is bitten by a werewolf. It's a movie with comic touches in the vein of *An American Werewolf in London*. *Starbuck* (Scott 2011) is about a shiftless man (Patrick Huard) whose donated sperm resulted in hundreds of disparate, now adult children. Despite wanting to avoid the publicity of being outed, he becomes curious about their lives. *The Art of the Steal* (Sobol 2013) tells of Crunch Calhoun (Kurt Russell), a third-rate motorcycle daredevil and semi-reformed art thief, who agrees to get back into the con game and pull off one final, lucrative art theft with his untrustworthy brother, Nicky (Matt Dillon). It is a random bunch of comedies, and there is no discernable thread, save perhaps of what *can* get made and on what budget. Being so close to California is clearly too tempting for most.

New Zealand

No such problems for the former British colony, who have a line in quirky comedy horrors. Peter Jackson is their progenitor, starting out with a trilogy of splat-stick comedies. *Bad Taste* (1987) was a splatter comedy, on which everyone worked for free and at weekends. It concerned aliens that come to earth with the intention of turning humans into food and was completed with an injection of money from the New Zealand Film Commission. His next was *Meet the Feebles* (1989), a musical comedy in the Muppets style, made with help from enthusiastic Japanese investors and described by Jackson as alienating, very black, very satirical, very savage. *Braindead* (1992) (released in North America as *Dead Alive*) is a landmark in splat-stick, reversing the zombie trope by having the comic hero underdog trying to keep them all inside his mother's house rather than keeping them out. It is a broad comedy with infected monkeys, *Psycho*-like touches, Lynchian uncles and a blood-smattered weed trimmer used to dispatch the living dead.

His style influenced a strain of horror comedy, starting with *Black Sheep* (King 2006) and more recently *Housebound* (Johnstone 2014) and *I Survived a Zombie Holocaust* (Pigden 2014). Two other comedies of note are *Goodbye Pork Pie* (Murphy 1980), the first New Zealand movie to go to Cannes. It was a low-budget hit about young tearaway Gerry, who steals a yellow Mini from a Kaitaia rental company. Heading south, he meets John (who wants his wife back) and a hitchhiker named Shirl. Soon they are driving to Invercargill to find her with the cops in hot pursuit. Eluding the police with hair-raising driving, verve and trickery, it's not long before they are hailed as folk heroes. *Boy* (Waititi 2010) is a coming-of-age comedy drama financed by the New Zealand Film Commission and was the highest grossing New Zealand film at the box office. Waititi's latest, *What We Do In The Shadows* (2014), co-directed and written by *Flight of the Conchords* star Jamaine Clements, is a cult horror comedy shot in mockumentary style.

Australia

Aussie or 'Ocker' comedy begins in the home country of the UK with *The Adventures of Barry McKenzie* (Beresford 1972). McKenzie was a fictional character created by Aussie comedian Barry Humphries and suggested by British comic genius Peter Cook. The character featured in a comic strip in British satirical magazine *Private Eye*. His (sexual) adventures as a fish out of water in London were compiled into a book *The Wonderful World of Barry McKenzie* that ironically, was banned in Australia for indecency, but was then filmed. It might lay claim to being the first gross-out movie.

The Aussie character, physically tough, crude and rude but essentially naïve, was then parlayed into a huge hit in *Crocodile Dundee* (Faiman 1986) starring Paul Hogan, which placed a similar idea of sending the naïve fish out of water (Dundee was a backwoodsman) to New York. It was based on a true story, that of Rodney Ansell, and was a worldwide success. It spawned two lesser sequels, the latter taking Dundee to LA. No matter, the concept of the Australian was on the map.

Baz Luhrmann's *Strictly Ballroom* (1992) was the first of his Red Curtain trilogy.[19] Scott Hastings is a champion ballroom dancer but to the chagrin of the Australian ballroom dance community, he believes in dancing his own steps. Fran is a novice dancer and an ugly duckling that audaciously asks to be Scott's partner after his unorthodox style causes his regular partner to dance out of his life. Together, these misfits try to win the Australian Pan Pacific Championships and show the Ballroom Confederation that they are wrong and that there are new steps. It was based on a 1984 stage play created in part by Luhrmann, who later agreed to convert the medium to film so long as he could direct. This too was a huge worldwide hit, and the ugly duckling theme continued into the long-running UK TV celebrity dance competition *Strictly Come Dancing*.[20]

Muriel's Wedding (Hogan 1994) concerns another ugly duckling, Muriel Heslop (Toni Colette), who finds her life in Porpoise Spit dull and spends her days alone in her room listening to Abba music and dreaming of her wedding

---

[19] They have a theatre motif. The others are *Romeo and Juliet* and *Moulin Rouge*.
[20] A reboot of *Come Dancing*, which ran for fifty years.

day. Muriel had never had a date and was in thrall to her abusive father who was a corrupt politician (is there any other kind?). When she steals some money to go on a tropical vacation, she meets a wacky friend Rhonda (Rachel Griffiths), changes her name to Mariel and follows her dream to Sydney. Although it is a comedy about the desire to get married, it deals with serious issues such as self-esteem and disappointment. Writer/director P. J. Hogan went on to direct *My Best Friend's Wedding* (1997) in the US.

Chris Noonan's 1995 part-animated comedy drama *Babe* was an adaptation of Dick King Smith's 1983 novel *The Sheep Pig*, the story of a pig who wants to be a sheepdog. It won a Golden Globe and produced a sequel *Babe: Pig in the City*. It is a tale of anthropomorphism with none of the darkness of *Watership Down* or *Animal Farm*.

Way out there is the drag queen road movie, *The Adventures of Priscilla, Queen of the Desert* (Elliot 1994). Another high concept is *The Man Who Sued God* (Joffe 2001), starring honorary Australian Billy Connolly as advocate Steve Myers, who is disillusioned with the lies and deception he experiences in court and decides to quit. He invests in a yacht and goes off sailing only to wake up to find his yacht has been struck by lightning. The insurance company declines his claim on the grounds that it was an 'Act of God'. Steve files a claim against God, naming the Pope and the local Bishop as representatives of God, and thereby the respondents. It was a No. 1 box office hit.

Robert Sitch is an important Australian writer/director who started out in TV comedy and has produced several top Aussie movies, including *The Castle* (1997), *The Panel* (1998), *The Dish* (2000) and more recently, *Any Questions for Ben?* (2012).

The Castle is the definitive Aussie comedy. An Aussie *Simpsons* variant, it tells the story of one family's struggle to keep their home from being compulsorily acquired by the Government to make way for a local airport extension. Many of its lines have seeped into Aussie culture, including 'straight to the pool room', 'tell him he's dreaming' and 'how's the serenity?'. While many Australians find it a boorish, clichéd red-necked portrayal of their culture, the narrative never slips into churlish belligerence or negative stereotypes. *The Dish* is a historical comedy based on the moon landings as seen from the Aussie perspective. Based on actual events, NASA used a communications dish based in Parkes, New South Wales to communicate with Neil, Buzz and Michael Collins when they landed on the moon. The ensemble cast is led by Sam Neill, accompanied by US import Patrick Warburton and locals Kevin Harrington, Roy Billing and Billie Brown. In *Any Questions For Ben?*, Ben (Josh Lawson) is a twenty-something up and coming marketing guru invited to his old school to speak at a careers event, also attended by Alex (Rachael Taylor), an old classmate. This rekindles a mutual attraction between them and is also a life-changing event for Ben.

Australian comedy has outlived its brash stereotypes (although they can still be seen on TV) and produces world-class comedies as well as actors. There is a place for romcom here, but there is a clear market too for considered high–concept ideas.

Other territories

France

Since Antoine Lumiere created the first cinematograph in Paris on 28 December 1895, cinema has belonged to France. *L'Arrivee d'un train en gare de la Ciotat* (1895) is considered to be the birth of cinematography: its early years (1896–1902) were dominated by four firms, the Lumiere and Pathe brothers, Gaumont and Georges Melies. The Lumiere brothers created the cinema's first visual gag, The *Waterer Watered* (*L'Arroseur Arrose* 1895). It is about 45 seconds long, in which boy steps on a hose, the gardener looks at the hose, is soaked and then chases and smacks the boy. A happy tale of child abuse. It was Melies who invented many of the techniques of film grammar and pioneered the visual gag. 'The filmmaker experimented with techniques in the then-new film media creating techniques to trick viewers' (Carroll 1996). Melies used many of these in his first SF film *A Trip to the Moon*.

The work of pioneering comedian Max Linder (Gabriel-Maximilian Leuville) – the first true movie star and a huge influence on Chaplin, was not rediscovered until the 1960s. Press focused more on the double suicide pact he had with his wife. He was a great star in the pre-War years, suffered gas poisoning in 1914. From 1905 he worked with Pathe films as an extra, making over 400 films. His big break came when rival comedian Andre Deed (1884–1938) left for Italy. Linder's first appearances as Max Linder were *The Skaters Debut* (1907) and *The Legend of Punching* (1905).

Deed was a French actor who created an Italian character – Cretinetti – who was popular in countless one-reel comedies in a clowning style that harked back to Pierrot. He was known as Boireau in France and Foolshead in the UK and US. He worked with Melies and Pathe and became the first director comedian of surreal situations that descended into mayhem. Linder's persona was well developed, a dapper would be gent impeccably turned out with an eye for the ladies and the good life, but the elegance was a foil to slapstick events. It was a huge influence on Chaplin, who is said to have referred admiringly to Linder as 'the professor' (McCabe 2005) and on Mack Sennett.

France was a world leader in comedy in 1900–14. Paris has the highest density of cinemas in the world.[21] It is the third biggest film market after the US and India, and in terms of revenue after the US and Japan. It is the most successful film industry in Europe. In 2010, it produced 261 films. US films account for 47 per cent of the share, and domestic films for 40 per cent.[22]

Jean Durand had a troupe *Les Pouics*, who greatly influenced the Keystone Kops (Sennett). When sound arrived, French cinema turned to the avant-garde theatre and music hall for ideas. Rene Clair made *An Italian Straw Hat* (1927), some of whose farcical tangling on either side of a wall influences Terry Gilliam's *Brazil*, and *A nous la libertee (Freedom for Us*, 1931), a satire on the machine age, was an inspiration for Chaplin's *Modern Times*. In 1929, Maurice Chevalier made *The Love Parade*, a musical comedy about the marital difficulties of Queen Louise of Sylvania directed by Ernest Lubitsch. In *Le Million* (*The Million*, 1931) a lottery ticket goes missing in a caper, and successfully bridges the comedy styles of the silent and sound eras. (McCabe: 247). In the 1930s, Marcel Pagnol created *The Baker's Wife* (*La Femme du Boulanger*, 1938) with early French comedy star Raimu.

Post-war auteur Jacques Tati created a visual style that harked back to Max Linder – his heyday being the 1950s, in which he made *Jour de Fete, M. Hulot's Holiday* and *Playtime*, all considered classics. Another notable hit was *The Great Stroll* (1966), starring British character actor Terry Thomas. Written and directed by Gerard Oury, *La Grand Vadrouille*[23] is a comedy about two ordinary Frenchman helping the crew of a RAF bomber shot down over Paris to make their way through German-occupied France to escape arrest, and was the most successful film in France for over forty years, with over 17 million cinema admissions

A new social comedy emerged in the late 1970s with an emphasis on the battle of the sexes. Huge crossover hit *La Cage aux Folles* (*Birds of a Feather*, 1978) derived from a Francis Veber play and was directed by Edouard Molinaro. Veber began to direct and much of his work has been remade in Hollywood: Mike Nichols' *The Birdcage* (1996) is one. Billy Wilder adapted another for his last films *Buddy, Buddy* (1982). Others include *The Man With One Red Shoe,* starring Tom Hanks (1985), *Three Fugitives* (1989), *My Father The Hero* (Gerard Depardieu is a Veber regular) and *Le Placard* (*The Closet*, 2001). Most notorious is *Le Diner les Cons* (1998) remade as *Dinner for Schmucks* by Jay Roach starring Paul Rudd and Steve Carrell (2010).

Jean-Marie Poire's *Les Visiteurs* (1993) was also a big hit (13.6 million ticket sales in France) he later went on to make *Le Pere Noel est une ordure (Santa Claus Stinks* 1982), which was remade as *Mixed Nuts* with Steve Martin.

---

[21] Wikipedia, *20 Questions about Studying in France*, (accessed 12 July 2014).
[22] Wikipedia, *All Cinema of France* (various sources).
[23] It was released in the US under the clumsy title *Don't Look Now, We're Being Shot At.*

Jean-Pierre Jeunet made *Delicatessen* (1990), a quirky visual hit, and later *Amelie* (2001), which introduced the world to Audrey Tautou and to some wonderful French whimsy. A charming confection of a film, it has many sight and sound gags and callbacks, which echo Linder and Tati.

Patrice Leconte is another auteur, creating *Monsieur Hire* (1989), the *Hairdresser's Husband* (1990) and *Tango* (1998), a black comic road movie where three men go in search of a wife that one of them must murder.[24]

Oscar-winning actor Jean DuJardin and writer/director Michel Havanavicius are a more recent comic force, beginning in 2006 with *OSS 117: Cairo, Nest of Spies* (2006) and its sequel *OSS-117 Lost in Rio* (2007), in which they mastered the James Bond spy spoof: both are pitch-perfect period pieces, puncturing the fragile balloon of male chauvinism. They then went on to win Oscars for *The Artist* in 2011, a comedy about the end of the silent film era. Their most recent collaboration, *Les Infidèles* (*The Players* 2012) is a portmanteau piece with multiple directors. It examines male infidelity in all its forms, some as vignettes or sketches, others longer, excoriating examinations of male lies and self-delusion. The main story features DuJardin and Gilles Lellouche, as two unfaithful husbands seeking priapic thrills in Las Vegas and concluding by taking the bromance to its logical conclusion (see Buddy Movies). If you cannot be French (or at least French-Canadian) you can only look on with awe at a country that fully supports its film makers, created *Cahiers du Cinema* and auteur theory, and which hosts Cannes each summer – insisting that all of Hollywood comes to them, rather than the other way round.

Spain

In a country lacking a clear comedic tradition (except for Miguel de Cervantes' *Don Quixote*), Spanish comedy begins with surrealist Luis Bunuel, who was hugely influential in the 1970s with *The Discreet Charm of the Bourgeoisie* (Bunuel 1972), in which three couples meet for a meal they never eat. There is also *Bienvenido Mr. Marshall* (Berlanga/Bardem 1952), a satire about an American visit to a small Spanish town, but under Franco, Bardem was arrested several times and they were unable to make any international impact.

Pedro Almodovar Caballero has taken Spanish cinema to the world, along with making stars out of his regular cast such as Carmen Maura, Antonia Banderas, Victoria Abril and Penelope Cruz. Originally condemned for addressing a younger audience [the *pasota*], he produces his own work and transgresses sexual and gender boundaries with gay abandon. He came to notice in his break-out movie *Pepi, Luci, Bom y otras chicas del montón* (1980) that looked at the new Spanish

---

[24]McCabe 2005: 250.

punk scene and depicted sex, rape and drugs. *What Have I Done To Deserve This?* (1984) and *The Law of Desire* (1987) introduced the comic talents of Carmen Maura. *Women On The Verge Of A Nervous Breakdown* (1988) was his big international breakthrough and was followed by *Tie Me Up, Tie Me Down (Atame!,* 1989) and *High Heels (Tacones lejanos,* 1991), *Todo sobre mi madre (All About My Mother,* 1999) and *Talk to Her (Habla con Ella,* 2002). He returned to comedy in *Volver* in 2006, and again in *I'm So Excited* (2013), which he described as a light comedy set entirely on a plane bound for Mexico, piloted by two bisexual pilots and several gay stewards (it was funded entirely on pre-sales). Of late, Almodovar has moved from comedy to drama and even psychological horror, as in his version of *Les Yeux sans Visages, The Skin I Live In* (2011). Almodovar appears to be following the Woody Allen model of 'early funny pictures', a spate of dramas and then a return to comedy.

He is also a member of the *Escuela de Madrid* (Madrid School of Comedy), others being Juan Jose Bigas Luna, who caused interest with *Jamon Jamon* (1992) and *The Tit and the Moon* (1994). There is also *Airbag* (Ulloa 1997) in which the main character loses his engagement ring on his stag night in a prostitute's vagina – a homegrown hit. Another wild man of Spanish cinema is Alex de la Iglesia, who made sci-fi comedy *Accion Mutante (Mutant Action,* 1993) and satire *Dying for Laughter (Muertos de risa,* 1999), about a double act who despise one another. Another cult favourite is *Day of the Beast* (1995) in which a Basque priest tries to raise enough evil to summon Satan and prevent the birth of the beast on Christmas Day. He has been likened to Guillermo del Toro and early Peter Jackson. There is more comedy horror to be found in the third part of Jaume Balaguero and Paco Plaza's REC series, *REC III Genesis* (2013) which concerns a plague infested wedding – echoes here of Sam Raimi's *Evil Dead* series.

Like Spanish art, its comedy is colourful but with a heavy use of black and a big dollop of surrealism (Dali, Picasso and Goya). Rather like Ireland (and with similar financial problems), there is the shaking off of old beliefs and a liberating sense of anything goes. No taboo is too great for Almodovar and his acolytes. The writer might consider, however, that once all the toys are out of the pram, where is there to go?

Mexico

One of the best known Mexican coming–of-age road movies is *Y Tu Mamá También* (Cuaron 2001) about two teenagers on a road trip with a woman in her late 20s, which took $2.2 million in its first weekend, making it the highest box office opening in Mexican cinema history. Bigger still is the debut of writer-director Gary 'Gaz' Alazraki, *Nosotros los Nobles (We Are The Nobles* 2013) which has raked in nearly $8.5 million and concerns three spoiled Mexicans who are cut off from their family fortune and forced to do the unthinkable: get a job. There are ploys and double bluffs and some fine twists.

Other films originating in Mexico are *The Sisterhood of The Travelling Pants* (Kwapis 2005), *Bandidas* (Espen Sandberg 2006), an action crime comedy with Salma Hayek and Penelope Cruz, and *Instructions Not Included* (Derbez 2013). Here, Valentin is Acapulco's resident playboy until a former fling leaves a baby on his doorstep and takes off. Leaving Mexico for Los Angeles to find the baby's mother, Valentin ends up finding a new home for himself and his newfound daughter. He raises her for six years, whilst establishing himself as one of Hollywood's top stuntmen, but their offbeat family is threatened when the child's mother shows up out of the blue.

From Prada to Nada (Gracia 2011) is a Latino spin on Austen's *Sense and Sensibility*. *The Perfect Game* (Dear 2009) is a sport comedy based on the true story of a group of poor kids from Monterrey, Mexico who shocked the world by winning thirteen games in a row and the Little League World Series in the only perfect game ever pitched in the Championship. They encountered many adversities including nearly being deported and bigotry that wouldn't allow them into certain restaurants or travel on certain buses. It is a tale in the tradition of *Hoosiers* (1986) and *Coach Carter* (2005). Another sports comedy is *Rudo Y Cursi* (Cuaron 2008), which concerns rival siblings in professional soccer. Mexican comedy cinema is in rude health, allowing many comedy genres to enter production.

Brazil

The Brazilian comedy scene is influenced by British sketch troupe Monty Python's Flying Circus (see Sketch Comedy), the leading exponent being the comedy collective *Porta dos Fundos* (Back Door). Its creator, Fábio Porchat, is one of Brazil's most prolific comedians, who, rising to fame on Brazilian television, wanted to take comedy to the next level but realized that the medium of traditional media and television channels would be too restrictive. Brazilian TV does not do political correctness – there is still 'blacking up' – and Globo, one of the main broadcasters, has made it clear that any new comedy would be restricted by strict censoring rules. Brazil's stringent anti-satire laws have resulted in government takedown requests and it is illegal to broadcast political satire during election campaigns.[25] *Porta dos Fundos* tread a fine line between the political and tasteless. In one sketch, *Pobre* (Poor), they poke fun at rich tourists who

---

[25] There is still evidence of pressure being brought to bear on this issue in the US and UK.

like to visit favelas and see how poor people live. 'They love it when you wave at them, but make the heart sign with your hands – they love that the most.'

In August 2012, *Porta dos Fundos* launched their own YouTube channel funded from an online T-shirt shop whose products feature their most famous sketches. *Na Lata* (On The Can), a spoof of named Coke cans, which has had over 15 million views and now has English subtitles. There are also Pythonesque religious sketches such as a polite Jesus working as a carpenter. As well as starring in Brazilian sitcom *A Grande Família* (*The Big Family*), Porchat appears in the film comedies *O Concurso* (Vasconcelos 2013) about people taking exams to enter the Brazilian civil service and *Vai Que Dar Certo* (*Things Will Turn Out Fine*) (Farias 2013).

Other Brazilian comedies which have not as yet achieved mainstream success include the family-orientated *Até que a Sorte nos Separe* (*Till Luck Do Us Part*) (Santucci 2012), the high-octane Minha *Mãe é uma Peça* (*My Mother Is A Character*) (Pellenz 2013), starring Paulo Gustavo in drag, and *Mato Sem Cachorro* (*The Dognapper*) (Amorim 2013), a romantic comedy with Leandra Leal and Bruno Gagliasso, moving beyond soap heartthrob to play a bearded geek. All four were made in 2013, indicating a developing market for homegrown Brazilian comedy.

Asia

Eat, Drink, Man, Woman. Mr Vampire. Shaolin Noon. Tokyo Gore Police. Save The Green Planet! Kung Fu Hustle. Dead Sushi.

Comedy has an active tradition in China, Hong Kong and Taiwan, which has been bolstered by Hong Kong popular filmmaking and shared elements of a common cultural heritage. The film industry is big on parody, Kung Fu and comedies of urban life. There are subgenres not found in the West, such as prodigal son comedies, gambling comedies, vampire comedies, and comedies based around the lunar New Year. The Kung Fu and police thrillers of the 1980s provide the entry point to this varied culture. *Laughing Times* (Woo 1981) was written and directed by John Woo, starring the Chinese Charlie Chaplin Dean Shek, and produced by Shek, Karl Maka and Raymond Wong. Maka's Cinema City studios repackaged the martial arts comedy for a new generation; including the *Aces Go Places* series of slapstick spy spoofs. The studio was reputed to operate a joke quota of a specific number of gags per minute.

Outside Hong Kong, Jackie Chan is the most famous of the action-comedy filmmakers. The successor to Bruce Lee (he was a stuntman on Lee's movies) and working in a similar vein to Buster Keaton and Harold Lloyd for his stunt comedy, he had a minor role in *The Cannonball Run* (1981). He was so impressed by outtakes shown during the credits – something almost *de rigeur* in movies today – that he adopted the conceit for all his subsequent movies.

Chan broke through with fast food comedy *Wheels On Meals* (1984) and his *Police Story* movies, and since the 2000s his career has swung between Hong Kong and Hollywood, his first blockbuster success being cop buddy-action comedy *Rush Hour* (1998) in which he co-starred with Chris Tucker, grossing $130 million in the US alone. He also starred with Owen Wilson in *Shaolin Noon* (2000), which spawned a sequel, *Shaolin Knights* (2003). By now he was tiring of Hollywood pigeonholing and so started his own film production company JCE Movies Limited, whose films have more dramatic scenes and include *New Police Story* (2004) and *The Myth* (2005). He has taken on many action and dramatic roles and his 100th movie, *1911* was released in 2011. He was co-director, executive producer and star. At Cannes in 2012 he announced his retirement from action movies.

Stephen Chow is equally famous in Hong Kong (he uses no fewer than eight names) beginning with gambling comedy spoof *All For The Winner* (1990). He took on Bond parodies with *From Beijing with Love* (1994) and was a chef in *The God of Cookery* (1996). He has appeared in urban fantasies, historical fantasies (monkey/joker/king) such as *A Chinese Odyssey* (1995) and as a lawyer in several legal comedies. He even appeared in the African comedy *The Gods Must Be Crazy*. His style includes toilet humour and a mangled nonsense language called *molaitau*, which translates as 'the gibberish of the underdog'. He achieved more mainstream success with *Shaolin Soccer* (2001) and *Kung Fu Hustle* (2004), the latter enhancing not only his reputation but injecting hope into the Hong Kong film industry.

Lunar or New Year movies (screened during the Chinese New Year) have, since the 1990s become a big part of the Asian film calendar. Many components appeared in Ang Lee's *Eat, Drink, Man, Woman*, such as clashing families, conflict over food, generational and gender misunderstandings. They can be formulaic or involve a degree of social critique and usually have a happy ending in which couples reunite and address the screen audience directly to wish them good luck. Raymond Wong of Cinema City studios is a major producer and acted in the *All's Well That Ends Well* series and in *Big Rich Family* (1994).

Gender and controversial sexual issues were confronted in Ang Lee's *The Wedding Banquet* (1993) concerning a gay couple, and Peter Chan Ho-Sun's *He's A Woman, She's A Man* (1994) about a woman who becomes a man to break into showbusiness (shades of a reverse *Tootsie*) and ends up as the focus of both halves of one couple. It spawned a sequel and started a trend for comedy dramas based on gender and relationship complications.

Taiwanese art-house director Edward Yang also made political drama and black comedy *A Confucian Confusion* (1994), which was a call for nouveau riche Asian countries to reconsider their traditional ways. An ensemble piece, all the characters are connected by blood, friendship or sexual chemistry.

Japanese comedy is a different plate of sushi, offering a blackly comic ultra-violence of *Clockwork Orange* levels in *Ichi the Killer* (Miike 2001) and the recent *R100* (Matsumoto 2014), in which a man joins a bondage fetish club from which he cannot leave for a year. The Japanese/Taiwanese/Korean horror revival of the early 2000s with *Ringu (The Ring)* spawned a lot of bizarre and extreme comedy horror, the market leader being the ballet of blood that is *Tokyo Gore Police* (Nishimura 2012), which, apart from doing what it says on the can and aside from the gore and terror, offers moments of pure satire in television ads that purport to help young teens to commit suicide.

More overt comedy horrors include *Vampire Girl vs Frankenstein Girl* (Nishimura 2009), *Alien vs Ninja* (Chiba 2008) and the films of Noboru Iguchi, the master of extreme comedy and gore, whose output puts him somewhere between John Waters and Roger Corman and includes *Machine Girl* (2008), *RoboGeisha* (2009), *Zombie Ass: The Toilet of the Dead* (2011), *Dead Sushi* (2012), *Gothic Lolita Battle Bear*[26] (2013) and the sequence 'F is for Fart' in the portmanteau horror *ABCs of Death* (various)

Japan is a polite, rigid and insular society, which for centuries was isolated in its language and customs and was uncontaminated by any other country. This constriction, combined with a massive expansion in media, technology and electronics after the Second World War has led to a huge conflict of cultures. On the one hand the extreme geisha culture of obeisance and respect for forefathers, learning and wisdom; on the other, Manga, gothic Lolita schoolgirls and images of sex with octopi and other multi-tentacled Kraken-like creatures. *Tetsuo Body Hammer* (Tsukamoto 1992), whilst not a comedy in any sense, is an introduction to the total enmeshing of man and machine, a Japanese *Metropolis*. Where creative types can break free in film, television and Manga media, they go somewhat overboard but in a playful brightly-coloured comic book way so there is always a comic distance. The splat-stick and gore is pure *Grand Guignol*. Iguchi is not concerned with the violence and his philosophy is that movies ought to be pure spectacle, filled with images that will entertain confuse and shock. 'I was influenced by the ghost houses or freak shows at Japanese play lands. I was easily scared but loved those facilities since I was a little child. I always think a movie should [be] like that, as an entertaining tool. My policy of making movies is to surprise and entertain the people at the same time' (Bartlett 2014). Iguchi's

---

[26] A *Tokusatsu* film – meaning it includes special effects.

innovation was that even though 'very bloody films already existed, what was new about [our movies] was that we merged the gore with a funny action film, and we took it further from there in our later films'. He began in adult films, where he met long-time collaborator Yoshihiro Nishimura, who made *Tokyo Gore Police.*

South Korea too has a huge output of movies, especially romcoms, which reflects its emergent economic strength. It has a growing youth culture and, although it also has a pure language and unique culture, unlike Japan the movies have a more conventional feel to them. *Save the Green Planet!* (2003) is a knockabout romp, but Korea is producing stars and comedies at a rate of knots. The master of revenge movies Chan-Wook Park (*Old Boy, The Vengeance Trilogy*) made *I'm A Cyborg But That's OK* (2006).

Attack The Gas Station (*Juyuso Seubgyuksageun*, 1999) is crime comedy directed by Sang-Jin Kim and is considered one of the best South Korean comedies. Four anarchistic youths decide to rob a gas station but the manager has been robbed before and has hidden the money. They decide to take over the gas station disguised as workers and keep it open. In order to do so they have to take the workers hostage. *Sex is Zero* (*Saekjeuk Shigong*, 2012) is one of the highest-grossing Korean comedies ever by director Je-gyun Yun. A twenty-eight-year-old college student has finished his mandatory army service, but is socially awkward around others. He encounters an army buddy and is persuaded to join a fitness club. He falls in love with charming freshman student Eun-hyo Lee (Ji-won Ha), but is given the cold shoulder, as she fancies someone else – nods here to *American Pie*. This sex comedy has plenty of dirty jokes and inappropriate situations and spawned a sequel in 2007. *Going By The Book* (*Bareuge Salja*, 2007) is an action comedy directed by Hee-chan Ra. Jung Do-man (Jae-yeong Jeong) is a low-ranking traffic cop whose tendency to do things 'by the book' gets him in trouble, as when he pulls over his new boss, the newly instated police chief and issues him with a traffic ticket. Annoyed by the fine, the police chief has bigger problems; the town of Sampo has been hit by a string of bank robberies: to reassure the public he decides to carry out a realistic drill, which will demonstrate the police force's capability. Do-man is chosen to act out the part of the bank robber, but with his usual fastidious attention to detail he sets out to commit the perfect crime.

All of the movies listed here indicate one thing, that a good story sells, and that a really good story can be resold to Hollywood. There are common themes in all countries – little guys who want to be noticed, guys who commit crimes or who want to get laid, romantic comedies of all sexualities and persuasions, over the top concepts that will attract an audience. A compelling character or characters are at the heart of this and this is why we go to the movies – to dream and fantasize, to identify, to yearn, to say 'there but for the grace of God go I'. A hundred years of cinema and we are all still turning out comedies at a rate of knots.

Conclusion

There is nothing new under the sun. This oft quoted maxim is bullshit, because we have technology and are living, in the West, in the new industrial revolutionary period that is the information/Technology Age. It is as radical as was steam, steel and mechanization. We obtain news, information and much of our daily contact from our phones. Contact with anyone in the world (given battery, broadband and Wi-Fi) is instantaneous. These new delivery systems have permitted anyone to tell their story online but because of this, we filter constantly, so how are we to gain attention?

With good story telling.

Relationships are fractured and the idea of marriage is under close examination. No longer born out of fiscal necessity or to ensure longevity, we *choose* to wed or not, and yet romantic comedy continues, asking new questions of sex, love and procreation. Childhood is changing, with a questionable fear of terrorism or paedophiles that has the young trapped inside watching screens and becoming obese, and yet they can access information in seconds.[1] We still have our norms, our proverbs and our paradigms. How might they be twisted and updated? What new Grimm's or Anderson's fairy tales can we now conceive?

Politically there is trouble in the East, but there has always been trouble in the East and much of it we started. Left – and right-wing politics are losing value as concepts, and the central ground belongs to the same rich, entitled landowners and industrialists. There is satire to be found not just here but among the fundamentalists and terrorists, just as the feminists and unionists were mocked.

Employment can no longer be taken for granted. Aside from in the professions, a job for life cannot be guaranteed and the concept of a career – an ascending ladder of promotion in one field, is no certainty. Writing is a series of jobs if you are lucky.

We have portfolio careers, often wearing many hats. Our food, leisure and lifestyles are all in flux. It is an exciting time and one that bears comic

---

[1] Except for that damn buffering wheel.

examination. The writer ought to take nothing for granted, always questioning and examining, sometimes in anger and sometimes in awe. And that is where the comedy will come.

The comedy film is a perennial that will last as long as cinema. People will always want to laugh at themselves, at institutions and at society. So long as there is strife and idiocy in this world, there will be comedians and comedy writers to poke fun at them and the way we deal with them. It is a question of form.

Some Like It Hot (Wilder 1959) 'broke several fundamental rules of screen comedy[2] but went on to be enshrined by the American Film Institute as the Best Comedy of All Time' (Errigo 2004). Wilder shot the movie in black and white (it was kinder on the male make-up and enhanced the period setting) and it has never dated. Nor has *When Harry Met Sally*, except in its fashion choices. Some comedy genres veer toward redundancy but are then miraculously reborn. There are subgenres that seem to offer little at present, but as soon as a critic announces the death of one style, it mutates and reboots,[3] fit for purpose for a new generation.

Romantic Comedy is a much-maligned genre, vulnerable when it goes for mawkish sentimentality and brave in its insistence on the supremacy of love. The anti-romcom, the bromance and more feminized and feminist takes on the genre have not led to its demise; instead they have questioned its values, the state of marriage, the blending of race, gender and sexuality and asked pertinent questions of urban romance. Hooking up, marriage, divorce and remarriage, youth and old age are all targets for comedy. Where there is an audience there will be money to produce movies.

Can comedy go too far? There is no limit to gross-out or the embarrassment of cringe comedy, only in whether it appeals or not. Social taboos of rape (*Man Bites Dog*), paedophilia and incest (*Happiness*) have been broached on screen, as has religion (*Dogma*), politics (*Wag the Dog*), foreign policy (*Team America: World Police* and terrorism (*Four Lions*). Most were not huge hits,[4] but found an audience. It is the job of comedy to offend and confront issues, redundant behaviours and attitudes – to tear down and ridicule. The worst a comedy can be is safe or reliable. It thrives on surprise and unpredictability, on new views of the world, on new relationships.

And these, on evidence, just keep on coming.

---

[2]The story springs from a gristly mass murder, the script was only half-written when shooting commenced and the picture runs two hours, to cite three big no-nos.

[3]Cannibal cowboys anyone?

[4]*Team America: World Police* (2004) cost $32 million, and earned $50 million.

beer

Miller 'High Life' Pilsner (Milwaukee, WI) *draft*   5
Tiger Lager (Singapore)   6
Great Divide 'Titan' India Pale Ale (Denver, CO)   7
Bell's 'Smitten' Golden Rye Ale (Comstock, MI)   8

wine

sparkling	glass	bottle
Chenin Blanc, Taille aux Loups, 'Brut Tradition,' Loire, FR	14	54

white		carafe
Grechetto, Palazzone, 'Vignarco,' Umbria, IT, '14	9	36

red		
Graciano, 'Viña Zorzal,'Navarra, SP, '13	12	48

sake

	glass	bottle
Momofuku Nama Honjozo (Akita, JP)	9	44
Momokawa Junmai Nigori (Forest Grove, OR)	10	52

slushie

Spicy Lychee*   6/12
Mulled Cider   4/7

non-alcoholic

San Pellegrino Grapefruit   5
Diet Coke   3
Mexican Coke   4

*contains alcohol

Dinner – April 6, 2016

daily

Beef Tartare* - brown butter, herbs, rice crackers	15
Mayan Prawns – Sichuan pepper, garlic chili oil, lettuce	14

buns

Shrimp – spicy mayo, pickled red onion, iceberg	13
Shiitake – hoisin, scallion, cucumber	11
Chicken Meatball – jalapeño, iceberg, paprika mayo	12
Brisket – horseradish, pickled red onion, cucumber	13

spring

Pea Shoots – Fuji apple, sesame, kimchi vinaigrette	7
Spicy Cucumber – scallion, togarashi, almonds	7
Sugar Snap Peas – horseradish, pickled carrot, Hozon	12

small plates

Soy Sauce Egg	3
Kimchi/Pickles	4/6
Rice Cakes – chicken, egg, bonito	13
Smoked Chicken Wings – garlic, Thai chili, scallion	14

bowls

Momofuku Ramen – pork belly, pork shoulder, poached egg*	16
Pork Shank Ramen – cilantro, chili, scallion	17
Hozon Ramen – scallion, chickpea, kale	16
Ginger Scallion Noodles – pickled shiitakes, cucumber, nori	14
Chilled Spicy Noodles – Sichuan sausage, Thai basil, cashews	14

Momofuku Cookbook, Lucky Peach Issue 18: Versus and subscriptions sold here.
Please let us know if you have any food allergies.
*Consuming raw or undercooked meats, poultry, seafood, or eggs may increase
your risk of food borne illness.

Appendix One

The Hays Code enumerated a number of key points known as the 'Don'ts' and 'Be Carefuls'.

It is resolved that those things which are included in the following list shall not appear in pictures produced by the members of this Association, irrespective of the manner in which they are treated:

- Pointed profanity – by either title or lip – this includes the words 'God', 'Lord', 'Jesus', 'Christ' (unless they be used reverently in connection with proper religious ceremonies), 'hell', 'damn', 'Gawd', and every other profane and vulgar expression however it may be spelt;
- Any licentious or suggestive nudity – in fact or in silhouette; and any lecherous or licentious notice thereof by other characters in the picture;
- The illegal traffic in drugs;
- Any inference of sex perversion;
- White slavery;
- Miscegenation (sex relationships between the white and black races);
- Sex hygiene and venereal diseases;
- Scenes of actual childbirth – in fact or in silhouette;
- Children's sex organs;
- Ridicule of the clergy;
- Wilful offense to any nation, race or creed;

And be it further resolved, that special care be exercised in the manner in which the following subjects are treated, to the end that vulgarity and suggestiveness may be eliminated and that good taste may be emphasized:

- The use of the flag;

- International relations (avoiding picturizing in an unfavourable light another country's religion, history, institutions, prominent people, and citizenry);
- Arson;
- The use of firearms;
- Theft, robbery, safe-cracking, and dynamiting of trains, mines, buildings, etc. (having in mind the effect which a too-detailed description of these may have upon the moron);
- Brutality and possible gruesomeness;
- Technique of committing murder by whatever method;
- Methods of smuggling;
- Third-degree methods;
- Actual hangings or electrocutions as legal punishment for crime;
- Sympathy for criminals;
- Attitude toward public characters and institutions;
- Sedition;
- Apparent cruelty to children and animals;
- Branding of people or animals;
- The sale of women, or of a woman selling her virtue;
- Rape or attempted rape;
- First-night scenes;
- Man and woman in bed together;
- Deliberate seduction of girls;
- The institution of marriage;
- Surgical operations;
- The use of drugs;
- Titles or scenes having to do with law enforcement or law-enforcing officers;
- Excessive or lustful kissing, particularly when one character or the other is a 'heavy'.

Appendix Two

Specific reference to *cartoon physics* extends back at least to June 1980, when an article 'O'Donnell's Laws of Cartoon Motion' appeared in *Esquire*. A version printed in V.18 No. 7 p.12, 1994 by the IEEE in a journal for engineers helped spread the word among the technical crowd, which has expanded and refined the idea. These laws are outlined on dozens of websites.[5] O'Donnell's examples include:

- Any body suspended in space will remain in space until made aware of its situation. Then the regular laws of gravity take over. This is why babies can defy gravity for elongated amounts of time. (The character walks off the edge of a cliff, remains suspended in midair, and doesn't fall until he looks down.) If this is referenced by a character in the cartoon as 'Defying the law of gravity', it is often explained that the character(s) involved have 'never studied law'.

- Any body passing through solid matter (usually at high velocities) will leave a perforation conforming to its perimeter (the 'silhouette of passage').

- Certain bodies can pass through solid walls painted to resemble tunnel entrances; others cannot. Corollary: portable holes work.

- All principles of gravity are negated by fear (i.e. scaring someone causes him to jump impossibly high in the air).

- Any violent rearrangement of feline matter is impermanent. (In other words, cats heal fast and/or have an infinite number of lives.) Corollary: cats can fit into unusually small spaces.

- Everything falls faster than an anvil. (A falling anvil will always land directly upon the character's head, regardless of the time gap between the body's and the anvil's respective drops.)

---

[5]See also http://funnies.paco.to/cartoon.html

- Any vehicle on a path of travel is at a state of indeterminacy until an object enters a location in the path of travel. (Wolf looks both ways down the road, sees nothing, but gets run over by a bus as soon as he tries to cross.)

Filmography

8 Heads in a Duffel Bag (1997), [Film] Dir. T. Schulman, USA: Orion.
12 Years a Slave (2013), [Film] Dir. S. MacQueen, USA: Twentieth Century Fox.
18 Again (1988), [Film] Dir. P. Flaherty, USA: New World Entertainment.
21 Jump Street (2012), [Film] Dir. C. M. Phil Lord, USA: Columbia Pictures.
48 Hrs (1982), [Film] Dir. W. Hill, USA: Paramount.
500 Days of Summer (2009), [Film] Dir. M. Webb, USA: Fox Searchlight Pictures.
A Clockwork Orange (1971), [Film] Dir. S. Kubrick, USA: Warner Bros.
A Fish Called Wanda (1988), [Film] Dir. C. Crichton, USA: Metro-Goldwyn-Mayer.
A Hard Day's Night (1964), [Film] Dir. R. Lester, UK: Proscenium Films.
A Million Ways to Die in the West (2014), [Film] Dir. S. MacFarlane, USA: Bluegrass
    Films.
A Night at the Museum (2006), [Film] Dir. S. Levy, USA: Twentieth Century Fox.
Adam's Rib (1949), [Film] Dir. G. Cukor, USA: Metro-Goldwyn-Mayer.
Airbag (1997), [Film] Dir. J. B. Ulloa, Germany: Asecarce Zinema.
Airplane! (1980), [Film] Dir. Z. A. Abrahams, USA: Paramount Pictures.
Alfie (1966), [Film] Dir. L. Gilbert, UK: Sheldrake Films.
Ali G Indahouse (2002), [Film] Dir. M. Mylod, UK: FilmFour.
Alias Smith and Jones (1971–3), [TV series] Prod. G. A. Larson and Dir. Various, USA:
    Universal Television.
All about Eve (1950), [Film] Dir. J. Mankiewicz, USA: Twentieth Century Fox.
All of Me (1984), [Film] Dir. C. Reiner, USA: Kings Road Entertainment.
All You Need is Cash (1978), [Film] Dir. W. Idle, UK/USA: Above Average Productions
    Inc.
American Pie (1999), [Film] Dir. P. C. Weisz, USA: Universal Pictures.
American Psycho (2000), [Film] Dir. M. Harron, USA: Am Psycho Productions.
An American Werewolf in London (1981), [Film] Dir. J Landis, USA: Polygram Filmed
    Entertainment.
Analyze That (2003), [Film] Dir. H. Ramis, USA: Warner Bros.
Analyze This (1999), [Film] Dir. H. Ramis, USA: Village Roadshow Pictures.
Anchorman (2004), [Film] Dir. A. McKay, USA: Dreamworks.
Animal Farm (1954), [Film] Dir. Dir. B. Halas, UK: Halas & Batchelor.
As Good as it Gets (1997), [Film] Dir. J. L. Brooks, USA: TriStar Pictures.
Ate que a Sorte nos Separe (2013), [Film] Dir. R. Santucci, Brazil: Gullane Films.
Austin Powers International Man of Mystery (1997), [Film] Dir. J. Roach, USA: Capella
    International.
Bachelorette (2012), [Film] Dir. L. Headland, USA: Gary Sanchez Productions.

Back to the Future (1985), [Film] Dir. R. Zemeckis, USA: Universal Pictures.
Bad Santa (2003), [Film] Dir. T. Zwigoff, USA: Columbia Pictures Corporation.
Bad Teacher (2012), [Film] Dir. J. Kasdan, USA: Columbia Pictures Corporation.
Beau Hunks (1931), [Film] Dir. J. W. Home, USA: Hal Roach Studios.
Bedazzled (1968), [Film] Dir. S. Donen, UK: Stanley Donlen Films.
Behind the Mask: The Rise of Leslie Vernon (2006), [Film] Dir. S. Glossermann, USA: Glen Echo Entertainment.
Being John Malcovitch (1999), [Film] Dir. S. Jonze, USA: Astralwerks.
Being There (1979), [Film] Dir. H. Ashby, USA: BSB.
Bend it Like Beckham (2002), [Film] Dir. G. Chadha, UK: Kintop Pictures.
Beverly Hills Cop (1984), [Film] Dir, M. Brest, USA: Paramount Pictures.
Black Sheep (2006), [Film] Dir. J. King, New Zealand: New Zealand Film Commission.
Blazing Saddles (1974), [Film] Dir. M. Brooks, USA: Warner Bros.
Big (1988), [Film] Dir. P. Marshall, USA: American Entertainment Partners.
Borat (2006), [Film] Dir. L. Charles, UK/USA: Four by Two.
Bob & Ted & Carol & Alice (1969), [Film] Dir. P. Mazursky, USA: Columbia Pictures Corporation.
Born Yesterday (1950), [Film] Dir. G. Cukor, USA: Columbia Pictures Corporation.
Boys' Night Out (1962), [Film] Dir. M. Gordon, USA: Joseph E. Levine Productions.
Brain Dead (1990), [Film] Dir. P. Jackson, USA: Concorde Pictures.
Brazil (1985), [Film] Dir. T. Gillam, UK: Embassy International Pictures.
Bridesmaids (2011), [Film] Dir. P. Feig, USA: Universal Pictures.
Bringing Up Baby (1938), [Film] Dir. H. Hawks, USA: RKO Radio Pictures.
Brüno (2009), [Film] Dir. L. Charles, USA: Universal Pictures.
Buddy, Buddy (1981), [Film] Dir. B. Wilder, USA: Metro-Goldwyn-Mayer.
Bullets over Broadway (1994), [Film] Dir. W. Allen, USA: Miramax.
Butch Cassidy and the Sundance Kid (1969), [Film] Dir G. R. Hill, USA: Twentieth Century Fox.
Cabin in the Woods (2012), [Film] Dir. D. Goddard, USA: Twentieth Century Fox.
Carry on Screaming (1966), [Film] Dir. G. Thomas, UK: Peter Rogers Productions.
Casino Royale (1967), [Film] Dir. Various, UK/USA: Columbia Pictures Corporations.
Catch-22 (1970), [Film] Dir. M. Nichols, USA: Paramount Pictures.
Charlie's Angels (2000), [Film] Dir. J. McGinty, USA: Columbia Pictures Corporation.
City Lights (1931), [Film] Dir. C. Chaplin, USA: Charles Chaplin Productions.
City Slickers (1991), [Film] Dir. R. Underwood, USA: Castle Rock Entertainment.
Clockwise (1986), [Film] Dir. C. Morahan, UK: Thorn EMI Entertainment.
Cowboys & Aliens (2011), [Film] Dir. J. Favreau, USA: Universal Pictures.
Crazy People (1990), [Film] Dir. T. Bill, USA: Paramount Pictures.
Dallas Buyer's Club (2013), [Film] Dir. J. M. Vallee, USA: Truth Entertainment.
Day of the Jackal (1973), [Film] Dir. F. Zinnerman, UK/France: Warwick Film Productions.
Dirty Rotten Scoundrels (1988), [Film] Dir. F. Oz, USA: Orion Pictures.
Django Unchained (2012), [Film] Dir. Q. Tarantino, USA: Western Company.
Dog Day Afternoon (1975), [Film] Dir. S. Lumet, USA: Warner Bros.
Down Periscope (1996), [Film] Dir. D. S. Ward, USA: Twentieth Century Fox.
Down with Love (2003), [Film] Dir. P. Red, USA: Hollywood Centre Studies.
Dr. Strangelove (1964), [Film] Dir. S. Kubrick, USA: Columbia Pictures Corporation.
Duck Soup (1933), [Film] Dir. L. MacCarey, USA: Paramount Pictures.
Ed Wood (1994), [Film] Dir. T. Burton, USA: Touchstone Pictures.

Euro Trip (2004), [Film] Dir. J. Scahffe, A. Berg and D. Mandel, USA: Dreamworks.

Every Which Way but Loose (1978), [Film] Dir. J. Fargo, USA: Warner Bros.

*Everything You Always wanted to Know About Sex *But Were Afraid to Ask* (1972), [Film] Dir. W. Allen, USA: Rollins-Joffe Productions.

Fatal Instinct (1993), [Film] Dir. C. Reiner, USA: Metro-Goldwyn-Mayer.

Fever Pitch (1997), [Film] Dir. D. Evans, UK: Channel Four Films.

Fight Club (1999), [Film] Dir. D. Fincher, USA: Fox 2000 Pictures.

Flawless (1999), [Film] Dir. J, Schumaker, USA: Tribeca Productions.

Forget Paris (1995), [Film] Dir. B. Crystal, USA: Castle Rock Entertainment.

Four Weddings and a Funeral (1994), [Film] Dir. M. Newell, UK: Polygram/Channel Four Films.

Forgetting Sara Marshall (2008), [Film] Dir, N. Stoller, USA: Universal Pictures.

Freaky Friday (1976), [Film] Dir. G. Nelson, USA: Walt Disney Productions.

Freaky Friday (2003), [Film] Dir. M. Waters, USA: Walt Disney Productions.

Friends with Benefits (2011), [Film] Dir. W. Gluck, USA: Castle Rock Entertainment.

Fritz the Cat (1972), [Film] Dir. R. Bakshi, USA: Aurica Finance Company.

Galaxy Quest (1999), [Film] Dir. D. Parisot, USA: Dreamworks.

Gambit (1966), [Film] Dir. R. Neame, USA: Universal Pictures.

Genevieve (1953), [Film] Dir. H. Cornelius, UK: J. Arthur Rank Organisation.

Get Shorty (1995), [Film] Dir. B. Sonnenfeld, USA: Metro-Goldwyn-Mayer.

Good Morning Vietnam (1987), [Film] Dir. B. Levinson, USA: Touchstone Productions.

Goodfellas (1990), [Film] Dir. M. Scorsese, USA: Warner Bros.

Gregory's Girl (1981), [Film] Dir. B. Forsyth, UK: Lake Films.

Gremlins (1984), [Film] Dir. J. Dante, USA: Warner Bros.

Groundhog Day (1993), [Film] Dir. H. Ramis, USA: Columbia Pictures Corporation.

Grumpy Old Men (1993), [Film] Dir. D. Petrie, USA: Warner Bros.

Gunless (2010), [Film] Dir. W. Phillips, Canada: Alliance Films.

Harold & Kumar Go to White Castle (2004), [Film] Dir. D. Leiner, USA: Endgame Entertainment.

Harold and Maude (1971), [Film] Dir. H. Ashby, USA: Paramount Pictures.

Heathers (1988), [Film] Dir. M. Lehmann, USA: New World Pictures.

He's Just Not That Into You (2009), [Film] Dir. S. Kubrick, USA: New Line Cinema.

Home Alone (1990), [Film] Dir. C. Columbus, USA: Twentieth Century Fox.

Horrible Bosses (2011), [Film] Dir. S. Gordon, USA: New Line Cinema.

How to Lose a Guy in 10 Days (2003), [Film] Dir. D. Petrie, USA: Lynda Obst Productions.

How to Murder Your Wife (1965), [Film] Dir. R. Quine, USA: Murder Inc.

I Give it a Year (2013), [Film] Dir. D. Mazer, UK: StudioCanal.

I Love You, Man (2009), [Film] Dir. J. Hamberg, USA: Dreamworks.

I'm No Angel (1933), [Film] Dir. W. Ruggles, USA: Paramount Pictures.

In Bruges (2008), [Film] Dir. J. M. Donagh, UK/USA: Blueprint Pictures.

It's Complicated (2009), [Film] Dir. N. Meyers, USA: Universal Pictures.

It's a Mad, Mad, Mad, Mad World (1963), [Film] Dir. S. Kramer, USA: Casey Productions.

It's A Wonderful Life (1946), [Film] Dir. F. Capra, USA: Liberty Films (II).

Jumanji (1995), [Film] Dir. J. Johnston, USA: TriStar Pictures.

Juno (2007), [Film] Dir. J. Reitman, USA: Fox Searchlight Pictures.

Kelly's Heroes (1970), [Film] Dir. B. G. Hutton, USA: Metro-Goldwyn-Mayer.

Kind Hearts and Coronets (1949), [Film] Dir. R. Hamer, UK: Ealing Studios.

Knight and Day (2010), [Film] Dir. J. Mangold, USA: Twentieth Century Fox.

Knocked Up (2007), [Film] Dir. J. Apatow, USA: Universal Pictures.

Kung Fu Hustle (2004), [Film] Dir. S. Chow, Hong Kong/China: Columbia Pictures Corporation.

La Cage aux Folles (1973), [Film] Dir. E. Molinaro, France: Da Ma Produzione.

Lambchops (1929), [Film] Dir. M. Roth, USA: Warner Bros.

Laughing Times (1981), [Film] Dir. J. Woo, Hong Kong: Cinema City & Films Co.

Le Placard (2000), [Film] Dir. F. Veber, France: Gaumont.

Left Right and Centre (1959), [Film] Dir. S. Gilliat, UK: Vale Film Productions.

Leon (1984), [Film] Dir. L. Besson, France: Gaumont.

Les Infidéles (The Players) (2012), [Film] Dir. M. Hazanavicius, France: JD Prod.

Liar, Liar (1997), [Film] Dir. T. Shadyac, USA: Universal Pictures.

Life is Beautiful (1997), [Film] Dir. R. Begnini, Italy: Melampo Cinematografica.

Life of Brian (1979), [Film] Dir. T. Jones, UK: Handmade Films.

Like Father Like Son (1987), [Film] Dir. R. Daniel, USA: Image Films Entertainment.

Mafia! (1988), [Film] Dir. J. Abrahams, USA: Tapestry Films.

Man Bites Dog (1992), [Film] Dir. R. Belvaux, Belguim: Les Artistes Anonymes.

Man on the Moon (1999), [Film] Dir. M. Forman, USA: Universal Pictures.

Manhattan (1979), [Film] Dir. W Allen, USA: Rollins-Joffe Productions.

Mars Attacks (1996), [Film] Dir. T. Burton, USA: Tim Burton Productions.

Mato Sem Cachorro (2013), [Film] Dir. P. Amorim, Brazil: Lupa Filmes.

Maverick (1957–62), [TV series] Prod. R. Huggins, USA: Warner Bros.

Meet the Fockers (2004), [Film] Dir. J. Roach, USA: Universal Pictures.

Meet the Parents (2000), [Film] Dir. J. Roach, USA: Universal Pictures.

Mickey Blue Eyes (1999), [Film] Dir. K. Makin, USA: Castle Rock Entertainment.

Midnight Run (1988), [Film] Dir. M. Brest, USA: Universal Pictures.

Mike Bassett: England Manager (2001), [Film] Dir. S. Barron, UK: Artists Independent Productions.

Minha Mae e uma Peca (2013), [Film] Dir. A. Pellenz, Brazil: Cenoura Filmes.

Miss Congeniality (2000), [Film] Dir. D. Petrie, USA: Castle Rock Entertainment.

Monty Python and the Holy Grail (1975), [Film] Dir. J. Gillam, UK: Michael White Productions.

Monty Python's Life of Brian (1979), [Film] Dir. T. Jones, UK: Handmade Films.

Monty Python's The Meaning of Life (1983), [Film] Dir. T. Jones, UK: Celadine Films.

Mr. and Mrs. Smith (2007), [Film] Dir. D. Liman, USA: Fox Television Studios.

Mrs Brown's Boys D'Movie (2014), [Film] Dir. B. Kellet, UK/Ireland: BBC Films.

Mrs. Doubtfire (1993), [Film] Dir. C. Columbus, USA: Twentieth Century Fox.

Muriel's Wedding (1994), [Film] Dir. P. J. Hogan, Australia: CiBy 2000.

My Best Friend's Wedding (1997), [Film] Dir. P. J. Hogan, USA: TriStar Pictures.

My Blue Heaven (1990), [Film] Dir. H. Ross, USA: Hawn/Sylbert Movie Company.

My Cousin Vinny (1992), [Film] Dir. J. Lynn, USA: Palo Vista Productions.

National Lampoon's Animal House (1978), [Film] Dir. J. Landis, USA: Universal Pictures.

Natural Born Killers (1994), [Film] Dir. O. Stone, USA: Warner Bros.

Network (1976), [Film] Dir. S. Lumet, USA: Metro-Goldwyn-Mayer.

Nine to Five (1980), [Film] Dir. C. Higgins, USA: Twentieth Century Fox.

Noises Off! (1992), [Film] Dir. P. Bogdanovich, USA: Touchstone Pictures.

Nosotros los Nobles (2013), [Film] Dir. G. Alazraki, Mexico: Alazaki Films.

Not Another Teen Movie (2001), [Film] Dir. J. Gallen, USA: Columbia Pictures Corporation.

Now You See Me (2013), [Film] Dir. L. LeTerrier, France/USA: Summit Entertainment.

O Concurso (2013), [Film] Dir. P. Vasconcelos, Brazil: Filmland International.

Obvious Child (2014), [Film] Dir. G. Robespierre, USA: Rooks Nest Entertainment.

Ocean's Eleven (2001), [Film] Dir. S. Soderberg, USA: Warner Bros.

Office Space (1999), [Film] Dir. M. Judge, USA: Twentieth Century Fox.

Old School (2003), [Film] Dir. T. Phillips, USA: Dreamworks.

One Week (2008), [Film] Dir. M. McGowan, Canada: Mongrel Media.

Out of Sight (1998), [Film] Dir. S. Soderburgh, USA: Universal Pictures.

Outrageous Fortune (1987), [Film] Dir. A. Hiller, USA: Touchstone Pictures.

Pepi, Luci, Bom y otras chicas del montón (1980), [Film] Dir. Dir. P. Almodovar, Spain: Figaro Films.

Piranha 3D (2010), [Film] Dir. A. Aja, USA: Dimension Films.

Planes, Trains and Automobiles (1987), [Film] Dir. J. Hughes, USA: Paramount Pictures.

Porky's (1982), [Film] Dir. B. Clark, Canada/USA: Melvin Simon Productions.

Purely Belter (2000), [Film] Dir. M. Herman, UK: FilmFour.

Raiders of the Lost Ark (1981), [Film] Dir. S. Spielberg, USA: Paramount.

RED (2010), [Film] Dir. R. Schwentke, USA: Summit Entertainment.

Repossessed (1990), [Film] Dir. B. Logan, USA: Carolco Pictures.

Revenge of the Nerds (1984), [Film] Dir. J. Kenew, USA: Twentieth Century Fox.

Road Trip (2000), [Film] Dir. T. Phillips, USA: Dreamworks.

Rocky (1976), [Film] Dir. J. G. Avilsden, USA: United Artists.

Romauld et Juliet (1989), [Film] Dir. C. Serreau, France: Cinéa.

Rosalie Goes Shopping (1989), [Film] Dir. P. Adlon, USA/Germany: Bayerischer Rundfuk (BR).

Ruthless People (1986), [Film] Dir. D. Zucker, J. Abrahams and J. Zucker, USA: Touchstone Pictures.

Salo, or the 120 days of Sodom (1975), [Film] Dir. P. P. Pasolini, Italy: Pruduzioni Europe Associati.

Save the Green Planet! (2003), [Film] Dir. J.-H. Jang, South Korea: CJ Entertainment.

School for Scoundrels (1960), [Film] Dir. R. Hamer, USA: Dimension Films.

Shallow Grave (1994), [Film] Dir. D. Boyle, UK: Channel Four Films.

Shampoo (1975), [Film] Dir. H. Ashby, USA: Columbia Pictures Corporation.

She Done Him Wrong (1933), [Film] Dir. L. Sherman, USA: Paramount Pictures.

Sideways (2004), [Film] Dir. A. Payne, USA: Fox Searchlight Pictures.

Silence of the Hams (1994), [Film] Dir. E. Greggio, Italy/USA: Silvio Berlusconi Communications/Thirtieth Century Wolf.

Slither (2006), [Film] Dir. J. Gunn, Canada/USA: Gold Circle Films.

Soft Beds, Hard Battles (1974), [Film] Dir. R. Boulting, UK: Charter Film Productions.

Some Like it Hot (1960), [Film] Dir. B. Wilder, USA: Ashton Productions.

South Park: Bigger, Longer & Uncut (1999), [Film] Dir. T. Parker, USA: Comedy Central Films.

Spring Breakers (2012), [Film] Dir. H. Korine, USA: Muse Productions.

Spy Kids (2001), [Film] Dir. R. Rodriguez, USA: Dimension Films.

Stan Helsing (2009), [Film] Dir. B. Zenga, Canada/USA: Boz Productions.

Starbuck (2011), [Film] Dir. K. Scott, Canada: Caramel Film.

Stardust (2007), [Film] Dir. M. Vaughn, UK/USA: Paramount Pictures.

Starsky & Hutch (2004), [Film] Dir. T. Phillips, USA: Dimension Films.

Superbad (2007), [Film] Dir. G. Mottola, USA: Columbia Pictures Corporation.

Swimming With Sharks (1994), [Film] Dir. G. Huang, USA: Cineville.

Team America: World Police (2004), [Film] Dir. T. Parker, USA: Paramount Pictures.

Ted (2012), [Film] Dir. S. MacFarlane, USA: Universal Pictures.

Thank You for Smoking (2005), [Film] Dir. J. Reitman, USA: Room 9 Entertainment.

The 40-Year-Old Virgin (2005), [Film] Dir. J. Apatow, USA: Universal Pictures.

The Adventures of Barry Mackenzie (1972), [Film] Dir. B. Beresford, Australia: Longford Productions.

The Adventures of Priscilla Queen of the Desert (1994), [Film] Dir. S. Elliott, Australia: Polygram.

The Apartment (1960), [Film] Dir. B. Wilder, USA: Mirisch Corporations Productions.

The Artist (2011), [Film] Dir. M. Hazanavicius, France: Studio 37.

The Aristocrats (2005), [Film] Dir. P. P. Penn Jillette, USA: Mighty Cheese Productions.

The Associate (1996), [Film] Dir. D. Petrie, USA: Hollywood Pictures.

The Belles of St Trinian's (1954), [Film] Dir. F. Launder, UK: London Film Productions.

The Blues Brothers (1980), [Film] Dir. J. Landis, USA: Universal Pictures.

The Commitments (1991), [Film] Dir. A. Parker, Ireland/UK: Beacon Communications.

The Day the Clown Cried (1972), [Film] Dir. J. Lewis, USA: [unreleased].

The Dictator (2012), [Film] Dir. L. Charles, USA: Paramount Productions.

The Discreet Charm of the Bourgeoisie (1972), [Film] Dir. L Bunuel, France: Greenwich Film Productions.

The Football Factory (2004), [Film] Dir. N. Love, UK: Vertigo Films.

The Full Monty (1997), [Film] Dir. P. Cattaneo, UK/USA: Channel Four Films/Twentieth Century Fox.

The Godfather (1972), [Film] Dir. F. F. Coppola, USA: Paramount Pictures.

The Gods Must Be Crazy (1980), [Film] Dir. J. Uys, South Africa: CAT Films.

The Good Girl (2002), [Film] Dir. M. Arteta, USA: Fox Searchlight Pictures.

The Great Dictator (1940), [Film] Dir. C. Chaplin, USA: Charles Chaplin Productions.

The Great Train Robbery (1903), [Film] Dir. E. S. Porter, USA: Edison Manufacturing Company.

The Guard (2011), [Film] Dir. J. M. Donagh, Ireland: Reprisal Films.

The Happiest Days of Your Life (1950), [Film] Dir. F. Launder, UK: London Film Productions.

The Heat (2013), [Film] Dir. P. Feig, USA: Twentieth Century Fox.

The Hooligan Factory (2013), [Film] Dir. N. Nevern, UK: Think Big Productions.

The Hungover Games (2014), [Film] Dir. J. Stolberg, USA: Sense and Sensibility Ventures.

The Inbetweeners 2 (2014), [Film] Dir. D. B. Morris, UK: Bwark Productions.

The Inbetweeners Movie (2011), [Film] Dir. B. Palmer, UK: Film4.

The Internship (2013), [Film] Dir. S. Levy, USA: Twentieth Century Fox.

The Italian Job (1969), [Film] Dir. P. Collinson, UK: Oakhurst Productions.

The Kentucky Fried Movie (1977), [Film] Dir. J. Landis, USA: KFM Films.

The Killing (1956), [Film] Dir. S. Kubrick, USA: Harris-Kubrick Productions.

The Little Shop of Horrors (1986), [Film] Dir. F. Oz, USA: Santa Clara Productions.

The Man in the White Suit (1951), [Film].] Dir. A. Mackendrick, UK: J. Arthur Rank Organisation.

The Meaning of Life (1983), [Film] Dir. T. Jones, UK: Celadine Films.

The Mouse that Roared (1959), [Film] Dir. J. Arnold, UK: Columbia Pictures Corporation.

The Odd Couple (1968), [Film] Dir. G. Saks, USA: Paramount Pictures.

The Odd Job (1978), [Film] Dir. P. Medak, UK: Charisma Films.
The Opposite of Sex (1998), [Film] Dir. D. Roos, USA: Rysher Entertainment.
The Player (1992), [Film] Dir. R. Altman, USA: Avenue Picture Productions.
The Ref (1994), [Film] Dir. T. Demme, USA: Touchstone Pictures.
The Rise and Rise of Michael Rimmer (1970), [Film] Dir. K. Billington, UK: Warner Bros./ Seven Arts.
The Runaway Bride (1999), [Film] Dir. G. Marshall, USA: Paramount Pictures.
The Skin I Live In (2011), [Film] Dir. P. Almodovar, Spain: Blue Haze Entertainment.
The Sopranos (1999–2007), [TV programme] Writer D. Chase, USA: HBO.
The Van (1996), [Film] Dir. S. Frears, UK: Beacon Communications.
The War of the Roses (1989), [Film] Dir. D. DeVito, USA: Twentieth Century Fox.
Theater of Blood (1973), [Film] Dir. D. Hickox, UK: Harbour Productions Limited.
Thelma & Louise (1991), [Film] Dir. R. Scott, USA: Pathé Entertainment.
There's Only One Jimmy Grimble (1999), [Film] Dir. J. Hay, UK: Impact Films & TV.
There's Something about Mary (1998), [Film] Dir. P. Farrelly and B. Farrelly, USA: Twentieth Century Fox.
This is Spinal Tap (1984), [Film] Dir. R. Reiner, USA: Spinal Tap Productions.
Three Kings (1999), [Film] Dir. D. O. Russell, USA: Warner Bros.
Throw Momma from the Train (1987), [Film] Dir. D. DeVito, USA: Orion Pictures.
Those Magnificent Men in Their Flying Machines (1965), [Film] Dir. K. Annakin, UK: Twentieth Century Fox.
To Wong Foo Thanks for Everything, Julie Newmar (1995), [Film] Dir. B. Kidron, USA: Universal Pictures.
Tokyo Gore Police (2008), [Film] Dir. Y. Nishimura, USA/Japan: Fever Dreams.
Tootsie (1982), [Film] Dir. S. Pollack, USA: Columbia Pictures Corporation.
Top Secret! (1984), [Film] Dir. D. Zucker, J. Abrahams and J. Zucker, USA: Kingsmere Properties.
Toy Story (1995), [Film] Dir. J. Lasseter, USA: Pixar Animation Studios.
Trouble in Store (1953), [Film] Dir. J. P. Carstairs, UK: Maurice Cowan Productions.
True Lies (1994), [Film] Dir. J. Cameron, USA: Twentieth Century Fox.
Tucker and Dale vs. Evil (2010), [Film] Dir. E. Craig, Canada: Reliance Big Pictures.
Twins (1988), [Film] Dir. I. Reitman, USA: Universal Pictures.
Unforgiven (1992), [Film] Dir. C. Eastwood, USA: Warner Bros.
Vai Que Dar Certo (2013), [Film] Dir. M. Farias, Brazil: Imagem Filmes.
Vice Versa (1948), [Film] Dir. P. Ustinov, UK: George H. Brown Productions.
Vice Versa (1988), [Film] Dir. B. Gilbert, USA: Columbia Pictures Corporation.
Wag the Dog [Film] (1997), Dir. B. Levinson, USA: Baltimore Pictures.
Wall Street (1987), [Film] Dir. O. Stone, USA: Twentieth Century Fox.
Wedding Crashers (2005), [Film] Dir. D. Dubkin, USA: New Line Cinema.
Weekend at Bernie's (1989), [Film] Dir. T. Kotcheff, USA: Gladden Entertainment.
We're the Millers (2013), [Film] Dir. R. M. Thurber, USA: New Line Cinema.
What We Do in the Shadows (2014), [Film] Dir. W. Clement, New Zealand: Unison Films.
When Harry Met Sally (1989), [Film] Dir. R. Reiner, USA: Castle Rock Entertainment.
When Saturday Comes (1996), [Film] Dir. M. Giese, UK: Guild.
Wild Wild West (1999), [Film] Dir. B. Sonnenfeld, USA: Peters Entertainment.
Working Girl (1988), [Film] Dir. M. Nichols, USA: Twentieth Century Fox.
Y Tu Mamá También (2001), [Film] Dir. A. Cuaron, Mexico: Anhelo Producciones.
Zack and Miri Make a Porno (2008), [Film] Dir. K. Smith, USA: Blue Askew.

Works Cited

Babuscio, J. (1993), 'Camp and the Gay Sensibility', in D. Bergman (ed.), *Camp Grounds: Style and Homosexuality*, 19–38, Amherst: University of Massachusetts Press.

Bartlett, R. (2014), 'Noboru Iguchi: Master of Movie Mayhem,' *Twitch*, 3 July. Available online: http://www.tofugu.com/2014/07/03/noboru-iguchi-master-of-movie-mayhem/

Bergson, H. (1900), 'Laughter: An Essay on the Meaning of the Comic', trans. C. Brereton and F. Rothwell. Available online: http://www.gutenberg.org/files/4352/4352-h/4352-h.htm

Capra, F. ([1927] 2001). *The Film Comedy Reader*, ed. G. Rickman, New York: Limelight Editions.

Carroll, N. (1996), *Theorizing the Moving Image*, Cambridge: Cambridge University Press.

Dessau, B. (2011), *Beyond a Joke*, London: Preface.

Elliott, T. (2007), 'A grand bromance', *The Age*, 23 August. Available online: http://www.theage.com.au/news/relationships/a-grand-bromance/2007/08/23/1187462423868.html

Errigo, A. (2004), 'Empire Essay: *Some Like It Hot*', *Empire Online*, July. Available online: http://www.empireonline.com/reviews/reviewcomplete.asp?FID=132873

Giglio, K. (2012), *Writing the Comedy Blockbuster: The Inappropriate Goal*, Studio City: Michael Weise Productions.

Harries, D. (2000), *Film Parody*, London: British Film Institute.

King, G. (2002). *Film Comedy*, London: Wallflower Press.

Lubitsch, E. (1942). 'Mr. Lubitsch Takes the Floor for Rebuttal', *The New York Times*, 29 March: X3.

McCabe, B. (2005), *The Rough Guide to Comedy Movies*, London: Rough Guides.

McCann, G. (1998), *Cary Grant: A Class Apart*, New York: Columbia University Press.

Nathan, I. (2005), 'The Belles of St. Trinian's (1954)', *Empire Online*. Available online: http://www.empireonline.com/reviews/reviewcomplete.asp?FID=132827

Paulson, R. (1967), *The Fictions of Satire*, Baltimore: The Johns Hopkins University Press.

Petri, S. V. (2003), *Writing the Comedy Film*, Studio City: Michael Wiese Productions.

Richards, J. (1997), *Films and British National Identity: From Dickens to Dad's Army*, Manchester: Manchester University Press.

Sarris, A. (1996), *The American Cinema: Directors and Directions 1929–1968*, Boston: Da Capo Press.

Schopenhauer, A. ([1818] 1909). *The World as Will and Idea*, trans. R. B. Haldane and
   J. Kemp, 7th edn, London: Kegal Paul, Trench, Trübner & Co.
Snodgrass, M. (1996), *Encyclopedia of Satirical Literature*, Santa Barbera, CA: ABC
   CLIO.
Stuart Voytilla, S. P. (2003), *Writing the Comedy Film*, Studio City: Michael Wiese
   Productions.
West, M. and Schlissel, L. (1997), *Three Plays by Mae West: Sex, the Drag, the
   Pleasure Man*, New York and London: Routledge.
Willmore, A. (2014). '"The Other Woman", "Walk of Shame", And the Fake Feminist
   Comedy', *Buzzfeed*, 3 May. Available online: http://www.buzzfeed.com/alisonwillmore/
   the-other-woman-walk-of-shame-and-the-fake-feminist-comedy#1evngky
Yapp, C. (2009). 'Python stars for special showing', *BBC News*, 27 February. Available
   online: http://news.bbc.co.uk/1/hi/wales/mid/7915623.stm

Index

Strand Book Store $14.00
03/04/16 / P   List Price $27.95
Blake/Writing the Comedy Movie
FILM & DRAMA

9 789930 016213